VOLUME ONE

WHISKEY LORE

BOURBON + SCOTCH + IRISH WHISKEY

THE REAL STORIES BEHIND
THE BIGGEST MYTHS AND LEGENDS

BEST-SELLING AUTHOR AND HOST OF THE
WHISKEY LORE® PODCAST

DREW HANNUSH

Copyright © 2025 by Drew Hannush

Whiskey Lore: Volume One

All rights reserved. No part of this publication may be reproduced, distributed or transmitted in any form or by any means, including photocopying, recording, or other electronic or mechanical methods, without the prior written permission of the publisher, except in the case of brief quotations embodied in critical reviews and certain other noncommercial uses permitted by copyright law.

Neither the author nor the publisher assume any responsibility or liability whatsoever on behalf of the consumer or reader of this material.

The content in this book is intended for educational purposes.

First Edition 2025, Published by Travel Fuels Life, LLC (dba Whiskey Lore)

ISBN: 978-1-7348651-9-6
Kindle ISBN: 978-1-7348651-5-8

Audiobook available at whiskey-lore.com/audio

Whiskey Lore

"Unlocking the Real Stories Behind Whiskey's Greatest Myths and Legends"

"You know a well-blended whisky is exceptional when the flavours tell a story with the senses. Drew's storytelling ability is like that exceptional dram of whisky."
—Dr. Don Livermore (Master Blender at Hiram Walker Distillery)

"Whiskey has embraced myth since the magic of distillation was first discovered; it's part of the spirit's DNA. Drew Hannush aims to set the record straight while respecting this tradition. It's part exposé, part history lesson, and part fast-paced romp through time. I can't wait to see what Volume Two digs up!"
—Brian Haara, author of *Bourbon Justice: How Whiskey Law Shaped America*

"Prepare to have everything you thought you knew about whisky turned upside down. Whiskey's own myth-buster searches out the facts behind the marketing myths."
—Mark Gillespie (WhiskyCast Podcast)

"This is hands-down the most comprehensive collection of whisky myths, legends, and the history behind them I've ever read. An absolute must-read for any historian or whisky drinker."
—Amanda Young (Duchess of Islay on Instagram)

"Drew brings the fascinating cadence and storytelling of his Whiskey Lore podcast to life in the pages of this first volume. Dismissing whiskey myths and adding textural intrigue to mystery, marketing, and facts."
—Alan Bishop (Head Alchemist of Old Homestead Distillery)

CONTENTS

Dedication

To the die-hard whiskey fans, tour guides, distillers, and historians that crave the real stories behind the lore.

Here's to you. *Cheers and slàinte mhath!*

Introduction to Whiskey Lore

Picture a young man, riding in the passenger seat of his father's automobile, traveling for miles and miles across the flat terrain of Ohio—an endless supply of farms and fence posts stretching far into the horizon.

On a family trip, these monotonous miles would have been tracked by the sounds of instrumental music coming from the car radio, the father driving, the mother knitting in the front seat, and his sister dozing while the boy kept count of the cars his father passed, inventing a race-car competition in his mind to pass the time.

But this trip was different—it was father and son time. Taking advantage of his position in the front seat, the young man peppered his father with questions, feeding his natural curiosity about things. Most of his questions centered on the place they were heading to.

There was a certain spark in his father's eyes as he spoke—for they were heading place of his birth, of his formative years, his work life, and his family roots. For fifty years, there was no other place on earth he could see his family. The stories he shared with the boy were filled with happy memories, but there was always a hint of disappointment, knowing the city he loved was a shell of its former self.

For the young man, even though he hadn't had the same time investment with the city, this place was thick with memories; of childhood play, the best friends he'd left behind, the times he went to ball games with his dad, and hours sitting in his grandmother's high-rise apartment near the center of the city—listening to the adults talk while he looked out the window, daydreaming about the freedom of exploring that greater world outside.

With a longing to feed his nostalgia, the father reached for the radio, flipped the knob to the AM frequencies and pulled in the crackling sounds of their old hometown radio station. The traffic report alone brought waves of familiarity—Gratiot, Woodward, Telegraph. The boy sensed his father soaking it all in. As the report concluded, up popped the familiar voice of the venerable morning talk show host J.P. McCarthy. As they crossed the state-line—just 50 miles from their destination—J.P. introduced the mid-morning host David Newman and the man he was about to interview.

The guest was Harrison Edward Livingstone, an author who was promoting his new book about the John F. Kennedy assassination. For 30 minutes, the young man and his father listened intently to stories of the Warren Commission and the inconsistencies in their findings. Knowing his father's passion for presidential history, the young man asked for his perspective on the subject. When the answers came, he absorbed every detail, marveling at the breadth of knowledge his father brought to the subject.

It was at this moment that the young man realized how much he loved history. While others his age might have been fidgeting over such a long car ride or wishing they were at the beach or an amusement park, he was relishing his father's stories.

And what always amazed this young man was the wealth of historical information that flowed from his father like water. Powerful stories just waiting to be explored, and all available for the price of a road trip, family vacation, or a visit to his father's den.

In the years that followed that trip, the young man grew into his own skin and challenged some of his father's stories, letting his own developing biases into the mix. Occasionally, it built a wall between him and his father as certain stories no longer resonated.

Yet he always came back.

And whether or not his father knew it, through sharing his own love and passion for travel and history, he had instilled those same loves and passions in his son.

Dreams Deferred

By now, you've probably guessed that the young man in the story is me.

As I think back, it's hard to understate the impact my father had on my life. His passions for travel and history imbedded into my soul from an early age.

From my earliest recollections, we were always packing up the car and heading somewhere of interest. By the time I was 18, I had been to every state east of the Mississippi, except for Maine.

At home, I'd sit for hours and hours with a Rand McNally atlas learning all the capitals, analyzing the numbering system of U.S. highways, and artistically drawing in new highways that I thought would be more efficient. I got so good at it, my father actually planned a trip where he mistakenly picked one of my imaginary roads. You can imagine his frustration when he couldn't find the exit for it. For me, maps were a way to travel in my imagination while I waited until I was old enough to travel on my own.

When I got my own wheels, I was unstoppable. A documentary on the Vikings inspired my first major solo trip. I decided I needed to go to Newfoundland to see where they landed. I flew to Boston, drove through Atlantic Canada, and took a ferry across to Newfoundland. Any fears I had about traveling on my own disappeared instantly. I began to crave this kind of adventure.

The other gift my father gave me was his passion for history and research. Not only research, but getting to the heart of things—the harder-to-find truth bubbling beneath the surface. I saw this desire in him through his dedication to researching our family tree. Not satisfied with what was easily accessible, he learned German, French, and a little Czech, then headed off to the old country to walk through graveyards and dig through church records. There had to be firm evidence before he would consider any new branch to the family tree.

It seems like my developing love for travel and history might have sent me down the path of being a travel writer, cartographer, or historian. But the one passion I had that didn't come from my father was a love of music. It didn't matter the style of music. I could sit for hours and hours listening to records, humming along. When, at seven years of age, I sat in a radio station with my brother-in-law, watching him playing records and talking, it looked like the perfect life for me. I saw it as my life path and practiced talking up record intros with my own records until I got my first DJ job at age 16. As I grew older, to survive on the pennies they paid disc jockeys, I worked a variety of other jobs. It wasn't long before the need for money pushed me out of radio and into retail management. I remember my father asking me why I jumped from career to career. I couldn't answer him.

Then, in 1998, exasperated with working just to work, I shifted into web design. It was a marvelous outlet for my creative energy and it wasn't long before I went from corporate work to having my own web design business. I loved helping small businesses get exposure to the web, and I finally felt like all of those skills I learned through a variety of dispirit careers finally had meaning. They served as a foundation, so I could become an entrepreneur. I slowly built up my staff and was running a thriving small business. But by 2015, the business was changing. To support a larger business, I had to charge more and my small business clients started falling by the wayside—replaced by corporate clients. I no longer felt like I was helping people build their dreams, and I felt like I was going through the motions.

It was at this point that I discovered the book *The 4-Hour Work Week* by Tim Ferriss. It was an incredible wake-up call. I realized I was spending day after day filling each hour with soulless, busy work. I had a staff developing the sites while I was sitting around shuffling emails and taking calls with clients from time to time. Lessons from the book showed me how to optimize my workflow so I could take up a passion project to fill the void. But what would that project be?

The answer was simple—become a travel writer. And I had the perfect job for it. All I needed was a lightweight laptop and packing skills that would allow me to avoid baggage fees. To test the waters, I stayed close to home for my first adventure. Inspired by the TV show *Turn: Washington's Spies*, I planned a trip to one of its filming locations—Colonial Williamsburg. After an amazing time I returned home, I posted pictures and stories on Facebook. I realized I needed to start a blog. Needing a name for it, I brainstormed a list of words and pieced together the best of them to arrive at *Travel Fuels Life*. I decided it was time to go all in on exploring a travel lifestyle, with the goal of sharing the tips and stories in a blog.

One of the lifestyle concepts I explored was the use of airline miles to cut down on travel costs. I signed up for an American Express business card that offered 70,000 miles for spending over $10,000 in three months. I had an office I was building out, so I knew I would exceed that amount. I signed up and collected my miles.

I decided the best place to travel was to Paris. I'd learned French in high school and thought this was an excellent opportunity to learn the culture firsthand and immerse myself in the language. For some reason, I planned 16 days there, but I knew my wandering heart would not be satisfied with just visiting one city on my first solo trip to Europe. Instead, I hired a rental car and went all in on a hunt for James Bond locations across Europe.

During 16 days, I covered 12 countries and saw some of the most incredible scenery I could imagine. When I returned home, I wrote up all the places I visited in my blog, so others could plan out a similar journey. People loved the stories I shared, but the same question kept coming up from readers—how were you able to travel like that? With some urging from my friends, I resurrected my radio skills and started the *Travel Fuels Life* podcast. By interviewing other travelers, I could learn tips and tricks along with the audience. It seemed like the perfect marriage of broadcasting, travel, and my desire to help others learn and build something special for themselves.

Then something unexpected occurred that changed my life forever.

Discovering Whiskey

The seminal event that struck me is something philosopher Thomas Kuhn's book *The Structure of Scientific Revolutions* (1962) describes the as a paradigm shift. As his book describes, it wasn't something that happens in an instant—it only seems that way. Things build to a climax as changes in personal attitudes grow below the surface. When the shift occurs, it's like opening a box that has been sitting for months under a Christmas tree. What was hidden immediately becomes clear. The new direction seems fresh, energizing, and logical, like it was always meant to be. The old direction seems tired and pointless.

The seeds of my shift were planted innocently enough.

For years, I'd been a faithful beer drinker—exploring bottles from around the world. But in 2017, I watched a movie that suddenly made beer seem boring. It was a film called *Sideways* (2004). The story involves two friends on a bachelor road trip to Napa Valley. Along the way, the character played by Paul Giamatti exudes his passion for wine by talking about the flavors, history, and origins of the bottles he prizes. It made me think how boring beer had become for me.

Then a friend invited me to a whiskey tasting at his home. I told him it probably wasn't a good idea, because I still hadn't gotten over a terrible experience as a youth with a bottle of Tennessee whiskey. Just the smell of whiskey set off my gag reflex. He convinced me to at least try. His suggestion was to start with Scotch, which he said wouldn't have the same odors as American whiskey. It was an inspired idea and by our third tasting event I found I could start sampling Bourbons without issue.

After sampling my second Bourbon, I started throwing out questions about what made a Bourbon a Bourbon. We talked about things like limestone-filtered water and how Bourbon only comes from Kentucky. To an outside observer, it might have sounded like we knew what we were talking about, but to me, it felt like we were spinning false tales. I quickly found myself missing that authority voice that my father always used to bring to discussions. I needed someone to set me straight on the facts about this intriguing yet oddly named drink.

Then it hit me—*Travel Fuels Life*. I could head off to Kentucky and do another theme trip, like I did with James Bond. It would give me a chance to learn all about the spirit from the people who make it. I decided to video blog my experience so people could learn along with me and see my transformation from novice to becoming Bourbon literate. Like my James Bond trip, this was going to be an extensive trip, seeing the widest variety of distilleries I could find. I put 19 distilleries on an eight-day agenda. It was aggressive, but I was determined to discover the secrets of Bourbon.

The Journey to Lore

For someone not acclimated to traveling whiskey trails, day one was extreme. I started out at the historic Makers Mark Distillery at Star Hill Farms, then made my way to the scientifically focused Wilderness Trail Distillery in Danville, and ended the day at Town Branch in Lexington, which gave me a combined view of a brewery and Scottish pot stills. Talk about a diverse day of discovery. I found myself absorbed in the different processes and soaked in history. Over the next day and the day after that, I learned about how Bourbon is made and learned of distilling legends and the people who made the industry tick. All of this information filled my imagination and gave spirit and character to each distillery.

Best of all, by the end of my trip, I felt like I could teach fellow whiskey fans about the spirit and how to explore the trail.

While I enjoyed the trip, something gnawed at me about the experience. As I traveled from distillery to distillery, I noticed there were a lot of contradictions in the stories I was hearing about Bourbon history. It didn't sound like everyone agreed. For someone looking for clarity, these contrasting stories made me question whether these stories were real or made up. But I didn't give it a second thought and moved onto my next *Travel Fuels Life* adventure.

Over the following six months, I recorded 20 podcasts and explored Pennsylvania, New York, Hawaii, Las Vegas, and my 50th state, North Dakota. Then I discovered a whiskey-focused Instagrammer, Leslie McBride (*Whiskey Is My Yoga*). I invited her on my show to talk about her trip to distilleries in Scotland. Suddenly, my interest in exploring distilleries was rekindled. After our talk, I planned out a three-week trip to Scotland and called it my "Castles and Drams Tour." I split the adventure evenly between distilleries and castles—and sliced off four days to explore Ireland. It was an incredible trip. The distillery stories were fantastic as were their spirits. But again, there were stories that didn't gel with other whisky stories I'd heard.

Still, I went on with my travel blogging and podcasting. I was determined to fill my Instagram and blog with as many inspiring pictures as possible. Meanwhile, having covered whiskey extensively, I decided it was time to head to Germany to learn the stories surrounding beer. But for the first time in my life, I just couldn't bring myself to put together an itinerary. Indecision turned to frustration. I questioned whether I was burning out on travel. When I took stock of what I was doing, I had to ask myself, "what was all this travel accomplishing?" It was great seeing these places, but I felt like I was just posting the same photos other Instagrammers were posting.

Then the moment arrived. The paradigm shift that changed my world. I was chatting about my struggles with planning out my German brewery adventure with a friend, when they asked me what seemed to be an innocent sounding inquiry. "Why don't you just go back to Scotland and visit more distilleries?"

If there was ever a spiritual palm to the forehead moment, this was it. How had I missed something so obvious? No disrespect to Germany, but there was something about the endless mysteries surrounding Scottish and American distilleries that stirred my love of history. I wanted to learn more. I wanted to break through those contradictions. And I wanted to share my passion for the spirit and its history with others. Completely inspired, I sat down and sketched out a Scottish whisky adventure within hours.

When I looked at my final itinerary, there wasn't a single castle on the agenda. I had decided: I was going full force into whiskey travel. But what of my *Travel Fuels Life* audience? A second podcast would be needed. There I could incorporate my love for historical research—the gift my father had given me. I could travel to Kentucky, Scotland, and beyond—learning about, researching, and dispelling myths about whiskey.

The Podcast That Brought It All Together

Whether it is a book, song, or podcast, nothing sets the tone and focuses the work better than a well-defined title. Just as *Travel Fuels Life* defined my podcast as one delving into a travel lifestyle, my whiskey history podcast needed a name that would inspire my storytelling. Again, I began brainstorming words on a sheet of paper. I came up with a handful of names, but within minutes *Whiskey Lore* jumped off the page. My business brain questioned whether I'd looked hard enough. But my heart knew exactly what it wanted. I bought domain names, set up social media accounts, and prepared for the new podcast—knowing my mission was to share the stories I'd heard on the whiskey trail, but only after researching and finding consensus between online resources.

As I started plotting out my first season, the structure of the episodes became the first hurdle. For anyone that has ever tried to write a book, that first sentence is the hardest to write. Then I thought back to the previous summer. While trying to conquer my 50th state and 10th Canadian province, I heard a podcast called *Under the Influence*. You might think it was a whiskey podcast, but instead it was about the history of marketing. What I loved about the show was how it seemed to begin off subject, but within minutes the connection to the topic became apparent. I loved how it showed the power of storytelling and how history repeats in ways we could never fathom. In illustrating the impact of a whiskey story, I could draw a correlation to something that happened elsewhere in history. It is a great way to analyze history and bring people along for the ride. It also opens them up to seeing how history does truly repeat. Everything is built on human nature, after all.

When I got my first season's subjects all sorted, I reached out to industry people in both Scotland and Kentucky. I wanted to know more about the Four Roses story, so I reached out to Al Young, a onetime distillery manager who, along with Jim Rutledge, brought the brand back to the States after decades of banishment overseas. I contacted Richard Paterson, a 50-year master blender who created the Shackleton blended whisky after nosing and tasting a 100-year-old whisky trapped under explorer Sir Ernest Shackleton's hut in Antarctica. I was surprised at how eager people were to meet with me after telling them what I was trying to accomplish.

But one story I was chasing threw me an emotional twist I didn't see coming.

In my very first episode, I wanted to pay homage to the marketing genius of Tommy Dewar of Dewar's whisky fame. The goal was to start the episode with a quirky marketing story centered on James Allardice, the founder of the Glendronach Distillery. While touring the distillery, I heard bits of an entertaining story about how he enlisted the help of ladies of the evening in Edinburgh to promote his whisky. After this lighthearted opener, the plan was to dive into the story of Tommy Dewar and the techniques he used to promote his family's whisky.

While digging into Tommy's life, I learned about an incredible two-year marketing trip he took in 1892, to introduce the world to his family's whisky. He used the best transportation of the day: steamships, streetcars, and trains. His travels took him through the United States and Canada, then down to Australia, Indonesia, Japan and back through the Middle East. It was the perfect kickoff, as the story would contain all three of my passions, travel, history, and now my new love—whisky.

When I found out he'd written a personal journal about the trip, later releasing it as a book called *A Ramble Round The Globe* (1894), I jumped on Google and started searching to see if there was an online version I could read. To my amazement, there was another book called *A Ramble Round the Globe Revisited: In the Footsteps of Tommy Dewar* (1999) by Malcolm Greenwood. I read over the synopsis. Apparently, this modern-day whisky sales manager followed the same path that Tommy Dewar took over 100 years before, comparing and contrasting his 20th-century experiences with Tommy's in the 19th. It took me all of two seconds to hit the purchase button.

When the book arrived, I plowed right through it, enjoying Malcolm's humorous look at his own travel style. You could feel his yearning for the slower pace of the 19th century and glorious hotels of the Gilded Age.

Adding his voice to the first episode of *Whiskey Lore* was a must. I knew his stories of his travels would make the episode come alive. Even if he didn't agree to the interview, at the very least I wanted to sit down with him and share a dram while discussing his adventures.

However, finding him was turning out to be a challenge. He wasn't on LinkedIn and his name didn't appear in any Google searches. I decided to dig through the book to see if I could find some clues, but I didn't hold out much hope, since it was almost 20 years old. But I found out which distillery he worked for, so I went to their website and filled out a contact form. Hopefully, someone would know his whereabouts.

The next morning, as I sat in my office chair, I felt a rush of adrenaline as I saw the distillery's reply appear in my inbox. But when I read the reply, my heart sank. They said they weren't familiar with Mr. Greenwood. But they'd ask around. I thanked them and hoped for the best.

The next morning, I sat down with my morning coffee and dug through the messages that came in overnight. I saw that the previous reply from the distillery was still grayed out. Then suddenly the text bolded, alerting me of a new message in the thread. I smiled as I started wondering if this is how a journalist feels when they get a scoop. I already knew some of the first questions I wanted to ask Malcolm. I figured we'd probably need to plan out a couple hours for our visit.

And then came one of the most profound moments in my life—out of the blue.

For a moment, the world fell away, and I forgot I was in my office. I let out an emotional "Oh no!"

I slumped back in my seat.

The message read that sadly Mr. Greenwood had passed away a few years ago and unfortunately, they couldn't offer any other details. I sat in stunned silence.

For the rest of the day, I was in a fog. And it wasn't until later that night, at home alone with my thoughts, that I finally had a chance to process not only the news, but my sudden and startling reaction to it.

Malcolm Greenwood left this world with a story to tell. In an instant, all of his memories, all of his knowledge, all of his humanity was gone. The only things that remained were the memories his family and friends shared—and this one little book that was sitting on my desk.

Then I realized this wasn't the first time I'd had these thoughts.

On the day my father passed away, emotions hit me like a hammer. I remembered heading home from hospice, not knowing how to process what had just happened. I did some cathartic writing to help me get through those painful moments. An amateur songwriter, I channeled all of my emotions into writing song lyrics. It was truly a healing moment.

After I cleared the clouds from my heart and my mind, I suddenly recognized how lucky my dad was. After retiring on a disability pension from the police force, he spent his remaining 30 years traveling, studying history, and exploring his passions. If only we all could be so lucky.

But what of all his stories? In a moment, all that history, all those life experiences, were gone in his final heartbeat.

Suddenly, my efforts in collecting these stories found a more profound purpose. Through my podcast, not only could I preserve the stories locked away in my skull, I could help others in the industry share their stories before human frailty stole them away.

After an amazing trip to Scotland and traveling to Kentucky in November 2019 to meet Al Young at Four Roses, I returned home to produce my first five episodes. I was excited to piece together Al's information and the details he uncovered in his book *Four Roses: The Return of a Whiskey Legend* (2010). I couldn't wait to share his story, as he had been way too modest to reveal his own impact on the brand in his book. I knew he'd be proud of the episode when I completed it. But days before I began writing the script, I opened my Instagram account and saw a devastating message—Al had passed away. I could only shake my head. I felt a divine hand in falling into this interview just weeks before he died. Even so, there were so many other questions I could have asked him.

Then, getting my mind back into production, I began contemplating how I was going to open and close the show. I needed a theme song and thought about writing one from scratch. Then suddenly, I remembered the song I wrote back in 2013, the night my father died. The lyric told of a man looking for any way to ease the pain in his soul. In his mind, he pictures a river of whiskey carrying him away from troubles. I have no idea where that idea came from—I was not a whiskey drinker at the time and neither was my dad. But what better song to use for a whiskey podcast than one called *River Whiskey*? I took the musical hook out of the pre-chorus and played it on the piano. It was the symbolically perfect final touch—serendipity at work.

The world is truly a strange and marvelous place.

From Marketing Myths to Real History

As of this writing, I've recorded seven seasons of stories for the *Whiskey Lore®* podcast. I have chased many of my favorite whiskey stories, myths, and legends—applying the art of storytelling I inherited from my father. I interviewed over 100 distillers, founders, and historians, providing my audience with the same education I've been receiving. And I've used my travel to over 300 distilleries around the globe to write two whiskey travel books that are now becoming the foundation of what is planned to be the largest online distillery travel guide in the world (whiskey-lore.com/travel).

I felt I was doing everything right. I felt confident all the stories I was telling on the podcast were extremely well researched and as close to the truth as I could get them. No piece of marketing lore was safe. As my friend Pete says jokingly, I'm the whiskey butcher, "taking out whiskey's sacred cows right and left." But I still had another major lesson to learn in how I was researching my stories.

It all started when I received an email from a whiskey company that was looking to clarify their brand's history, hoping to find some historic marketing angles they could use. It was a brand that caught my attention when I traveled to the Oscar Getz Whiskey History Museum in Bardstown.

The brand was Chicken Cock and yes; it is a bizarre name that conjures up several questions. Doing some quick research, I found the brand's history was pretty straightforward. Multiple books and websites talked about a Mr. Foley who built a distillery in Paris, Kentucky, in 1856. For some reason Foley sold the distillery almost instantly to a distiller named James A. Miller. Miller would pass away four years later and the distillery and the Chicken Cock brand passed on to his bookkeeper, George G. White.

But, the researcher in me was confused by one fact surrounding this distiller that didn't ring true. James A. Miller was considered a legend and his name clung to the brand throughout the 19th century. How could a man who only owned a distillery for four years earn such a reputation?

Then I found an article in the 1859 *Louisville Courier-Journal* that mentioned James A. Miller returning from his 19th annual sales trip selling his whisky in New Orleans.[1] It confirmed that Miller was making whiskey all the way back to at least 1838. This would make him a distilling contemporary of the legendary James C. Crow of Old Crow fame. Crow has long been touted as the man who brought Kentucky whiskey into the modern age.

I decided to dig deeper. Newspaper research painted a partial picture, but I needed to find out more about what property James A. Miller owned, who his family was, and if there were any other public records related to him. I traveled to Bourbon County and spent a couple of days at the courthouse, combing through title deeds. When I turned the research over to Grain & Barrel, the owners of the Chicken Cock brand, the story I revealed differed completely from the ones covered in history books. It appears the historians of the past had relied too heavily on oral tradition. What I found was concrete evidence through government records that ran contrary to what turned out to be lore. I couldn't believe how far off the mark those storytellers of old had been.

With that research completed, I started working on a third travel guide—this time focusing on Tennessee whiskey. But having traveled to most of the distilleries in the state, I was a little frustrated that no one seemed to know anything about the state's distilling history beyond moonshine, Jack Daniel, and George Dickel. I bumped into a couple of additional 19th-century stories around Charles Nelson of Nelson's Greenbrier Distillery and Nearest Green thanks to Nelson Eddy of Jack Daniel's and Fawn Weaver of Uncle Nearest, but beyond that, Tennessee's whiskey history seemed empty.

But it was another story Nelson Eddy told me that made me curious as to how much deeper the Tennessee story might go. It seems that a great shootout in the City of Nashville between two newspaper men led to the state going into Prohibition ten years before the rest of the country. Using my research techniques adopted during my Chicken Cock search, I began scouring 19th-century newspapers. I realized a greater story was buried in the sands of time. But writing a history book would be a grand undertaking. I honestly didn't think I had it in me. So I went back to researching my travel guide.

Then one day I was at Thompson Station in Tennessee chatting with one of the state's early craft distillers, Heath Clark. I mentioned that I had contemplated writing and researching a book on Tennessee whiskey history, but that I was setting it aside to work on a distillery travel guide. After telling him a few things I had uncovered, he urged me to write the history book. "We need that!"

He didn't have to ask me twice. I dug right in. Gone were my distillery travel plans, replaced by trips to archives and courthouses across the state of Tennessee. Then I traveled down to the National Archives in Atlanta to get distillery records. I was taking my research to the deepest levels, getting in the weeds, the way my father would.

The problem was, the deeper I went, the more I started finding flaws in some of the *Whiskey Lore* episodes I was so proud of. I was at a loss. Through this entire journey, my number-one goal was building trust in my stories. Now suddenly, stories were crumbling under the super hot spotlight. I thought about fixing them as quickly as possible. The first episode I approached was my Bottled-in-Bond episode from Season 1, but fixing that story seemed nearly impossible. My lead story and my conclusion were all built around a character I found out had little to do with the story. Sadly I had fallen into the trap of marketing lore.

I rewrote a good portion of that episode and let the listeners know why the old story had to be tossed away. Still, it was embarrassing, and I realized I had to change my strategy. I needed firmer research and more trusted documentation. It led me to go overboard in footnoting my book *The Lost History of Tennessee Whiskey* (2023) and it gave me pause about doing any more *Whiskey Lore* podcast episodes. I still wanted to tell the stories, but I needed more time for research and this required money. But from the beginning, I refused to put advertising on Whiskey Lore's story episodes. I didn't want anyone assuming the stories were influenced by marketing departments. I desperately needed a solution.

From Podcast to Book Series

Introducing the *Whiskey Lore* book series. Just like my podcast seasons, each book will explore whiskey myths, some false, some complex, and others with a level of subjectivity. Most are stories you've heard and sometimes they are myths that are passed around without a second thought for their accuracy. Within each chapter, I will continue my trademark storytelling style to get to the heart of the myth, while providing footnotes to the research that built my conclusion. The goal is to entertain, inform, and leave breadcrumbs for further research into each subject.

To add a unique twist to the books, I will start my research by asking Artificial Intelligence (AI) whether it believes the myth is true, false, complicated, or subjective. This serves two purposes. First, since AI is based on articles and information from books and Internet sources, it will be an unbiased source for what the world collectively thinks the truth is. Second, it will show us how groupthink and marketing permeate the web. This is an effort to disprove the theory that you can find the truth by locating two or more sources. Sadly, syndication, lack of documentation, lazy research, marketing, and oral tradition have been some of the greatest barriers to the truth and for now, AI is just a representation of how far we can be led astray.

The good researcher questions everything, and documentation should be scrutinized. By showing the results of AI, I hope to encourage future whiskey writers to bring skepticism with them into everything they read. Just putting an attribution or bibliography in the back of a book is not quality documentation. Footnotes are a must to earn trust as future authors and historians need to be able to follow up on the quality of your sources to avoid perpetuating lore.

As for the myths I cover, some will be based on legends and marketing. Others will focus on tasting, business subjects, and what they call old wives' tales. As with the podcast, this will cover not only Bourbon but also Scotch, Irish whiskey, and a world of other whiskies.

To readers unfamiliar with my *Whiskey Lore* storytelling style, don't be surprised if a chapter starts off with something completely unrelated to the myth or whiskey in general. Stick with me. As the chapter unfolds, these stories that originate from many sources will help create in you a sense of how myths develop while we search for the ultimate answer to that myth.

By the end of each chapter, not only will you know the story behind some of whiskey's great myths, you'll also learn a bit of history that will help you connect the dots to how the lore came into being or how it is simply the result of human nature. It won't be long before you're amazing your friends with your breadth of knowledge about simple things like why whiskey has two different spellings and why claiming firsts in the history of distilling is a fool's errand.

Know That Whiskey History Is Rarely 100% Accurate

You're almost ready to jump into the first story. But before we get there, just one piece of advice. Be humble. This book and the books that follow are sure to create some interesting conversations between whiskey fans. But be careful about being too passionate or matter-of-fact with whiskey history.

While legends like George Washington, Winston Churchill, and Mahatma Gandhi are well documented, to the whiskey distillers of the past, the idea of documenting them would be like documenting someone cutting hay or planting a crop. It was a hearth skill that developed into an industry. Once it became an industry, unless they owned the distillery, 18th- and 19th-century distillers were mostly seen as average workers. The distillery owners did not know we would be so fascinated with what their employees did day to day.

With just fragments of information available, whiskey storytellers have been left to fill in the gaps with speculation and oral tradition. Unfortunately, this leads to a lot of mistakes and misdirection. And sometimes stories edge from accurate history into historical fiction, further muddying the waters.

As an example, in Ben Green's landmark 1967 book *Jack Daniel: Legacy*, he goes in depth on the history of the legendary distiller. The book is based heavily on oral tradition gathered through family bibles and interviews with friends and family members. It's an epic story, but it loses credibility in its establishment of false timelines. These inaccuracies are to be expected when considering how memories shift and tales grow taller over the years. To fill in the holes, Green took liberties in creating an exciting story, but in using the book for my *Whiskey Lore* episode, it caused me to perpetuate many of the false narratives written in the book. What I interpreted as a book of facts turned out to be facts mixed with creative embellishments. Yet, in the world of whiskey, this kind of historical myth telling has long been acceptable.

But even great scholarship can fall victim to falsehoods through simple speculation. Author Henry Crowgey's landmark book *Kentucky Bourbon: The Early Years of Whiskeymaking* (1971), a book I highly praise for its intensely footnoted content, fell victim to the dangers of speculation. His thesis was that the term "Old Bourbon" was used in the 1820s, not to denote longer aged whiskeys from Bourbon County, but to suggest it referred to whiskey from a county that used to be part of a larger historic Bourbon County, before it split up into smaller counties. Any historian worth their salt wants to find something that goes against conventional wisdom, creating an "Aha!" moment. But he let his desire to find that answer cloud his research. While his narrative seems to work, so does the theory that it meant old whiskey from a much smaller Bourbon County. Taken at face value from a trusted resource, this leads anyone looking at their research to make the same false conclusion. Because of his speculation, generations of historians have used his logic to the detriment of the genuine history of Bourbon County, in its modern dimensions, and its impact on the name of the spirit. It wasn't his intention, but it shows how delicately historians need to tread when it comes to overselling their own theories.

I too have fallen into the trap of speculation, only to have been proven wrong. My *Whiskey Lore* episode about New Orleans and its connection to the name Bourbon made the assumption flatboats didn't have access to the Mississippi River in the 1780s because Spain refused Americans access. However, a year after releasing the episode, I ran into an American-Spanish treaty that debunked my speculation. It was the moment I learned I should never get cocky about things I think I've discovered—and I don't want you to fall into the same trap.

Then there are all the other landmines, like newspapers that slant stories in a particular direction. History books with a bibliography but no firm footnotes. And excitement over hearing a great piece of information based on oral tradition, and then running with it, only to discover it has little basis in reality.

Be humble or you will be humbled. History continues to evolve as we get past the commonly held myths, and as historic documents are uncovered that further the story.

My intention with this and future books is to reduce speculation and push forward as many facts as possible. But nothing is 100% accurate, so don't stick your foot in your mouth by being too "matter of fact" about any story contained within these pages. I will make them as accurate as I can with the information available to me. And if the myth I'm dispelling stands on shaky evidence, I won't include it in a book until I've firmed things up a bit more. This is a series, after all.

Also know that I will upset a few apple carts with this series and it gives me no great pleasure to do so. I'm here for the truth, not the marketing. But I know some of these stories are beloved. It's not my intention to remove them from our minds forever. Stories, true or not, say something about who we are now, what we value, and who we were in the past. And while it will seem like I'm giving tour guides a little grief in this book, I know most of them want to tell the true stories. In reality, this series of books should be of great value to them. Some are master storytellers in their own right and I know they'll do this information justice.

Now that you know me, my passions, and my focus, prepare to be amazed as we dive into some of the greatest myths from the worlds of Scotch, Bourbon, Irish, and a world of whiskey experiences. I hope you have as much fun with the jaw-dropping moments in this book as I had when I discovered these truths behind the lore.

And to my dad, thank you for the gift of storytelling you passed on to me. I hope I'm making you proud.

America's Native Spirit

Myth: Congress designated Bourbon as "America's Native Spirit."

AI: False

When it comes to baseball's pitching achievements, the perfect game is one of the rarest and most remarkable accomplishments for a pitcher to complete. It requires tossing nine innings of baseball, facing 27 batters and not allowing a single one to reach base. No errors, hit-by-pitches, and no walks.

In nearly a century of professional baseball, perfection had only been achieved six times by the time Philadelphia Phillies' right-handed pitcher Jim Bunning found himself one out away from this incredible feat. It was Father's Day 1964 and 32,026 people had come out to Shea Stadium in New York to watch the Mets battle a division rival. And oh, what a game they saw.

Bunning's pinpoint control and mastery of the strike zone were on full display. Inning by inning, hitter after hitter fell by the wayside.

This wasn't the first time Bunning attempted to reach baseball immortality. Back in 1958, the then 26-year-old side-winding pitcher from Southgate, Kentucky, tossed a no-hitter for the Detroit Tigers against the Boston Red Sox. The final out came after getting the best hitter in baseball, Ted Williams, to fly out to right field. But while he didn't give up a hit in that game and had twelve strikeouts, the two walks he issued left him just shy of perfection.

This Father's Day crowd watched Jim mow down nine batters with strikeouts and he was three strikes away from perfection when left-handed pinch-hitter Johnny Stephenson stepped into the batter's box. This wasn't a favorable matchup for a right-handed pitcher. His devastating curveball was easy pickin's for batters standing to the left of the plate.

When the first pitch crossed the plate, Stephenson swung harmlessly over the ball. A cheer rose from the crowd. To the uninitiated, it may have seemed strange to see the hometown fans actively supporting a rival pitcher, but this was baseball history—a chance to see something few people had seen. Team loyalty would have to wait. Bunning wound up and tossed his second pitch. Stephenson stood there and watched it fly by.

"Strike two!" yelled the umpire.

The crowd came to their feet, cheering loudly for an anticipated third strike. Yet, the next two pitches disappointed as they slid outside the strike zone, with Stephenson watching them float harmlessly by. He must have been taken aback when the crowd booed in frustration after the umpire called out "ball."

Bunning picked up the rosin bag to dry his sweaty palms, dropped it in a cloud of dust at his feet and rubbed up the baseball. He knew right where he wanted to place it and what pitch to throw. It would be his curveball. If he placed it close to the batter's feet, it would look like a juicy pitch heading for the heart of the plate, too tempting to resist. But then, it would break suddenly down toward the batter's feet. Bunning wound up, kicked his leg, and brought the pitch forward to the plate. The batter's eyes grew wide. He pulled the bat back, cranked it through the air, and swung harmlessly over the pitch.

"Strike three!"

The crowd erupted. A smile covered the Kentuckian's face and he slapped his glove in celebration. In an instant, his teammates swarmed him from all directions.

For those that saw it, it was a day they wouldn't soon forget.

A Wild Pitch

When it came to throwing the perfect pitch at the right time, Jim Bunning was a man you could depend on. He wasn't there to dazzle hitters with his fastball; during his 19 major league seasons, it was the right-hander's pinpoint control that made him so effective. He used his curveball, slider, and changeup to keep batters off balance.

When he left the game, Bunning made a dash for politics, entering the Kentucky State House in 1980. Over the next twenty years, he was a champion of fiscal responsibility, taking his message all the way to the U.S. Senate in 1999.

For a man so focused on achieving goals and being precise, it seems strange to think his error led to the development of one of Kentucky's often-touted pieces of whiskey lore.

His misstep occurred in August 2007 as Bardstown was preparing to host their 16th Annual Kentucky Bourbon Festival. Primed for the celebration, Senator Bunning put forth Senate Resolution 294, designating the month of September as National Bourbon Heritage Month. But in the document, he made a factual error. He concluded that in a joint act, "Congress declared bourbon as America's Native Spirit in 1964, making it the only spirit distinctive to the United States."[2]

Unfortunately, this statement misrepresents two critical facts. While the original 1964 bill, authored by Kentucky Senator Thurston Morton and Representative John C. Watts designated Bourbon as a "distinctive product of the United States,"[3] it didn't declare it as the "only spirit distinctive to the United States" and nowhere in the language did it call Bourbon "America's Native Spirit."

Was Senator Bunning just getting carried away with his love for his home state's contribution to American whiskey and exaggerating to make things bigger than they really were? Or was he a casualty of Bluegrass State marketing?

Bourbon Braggadocio

To discover the answers, let's turn back the clock back to 1999. The Bourbon industry was rising again after a downturn over the previous two decades. Throughout that drought, consumer preferences steered toward clear spirits like vodka, rum, and gin. It took a series of premium releases like Booker's, Blanton's, and Pappy Van Winkle's and good press for brands like Maker's Mark and Woodford Reserve to make the market move again.

As sales and interest grew, the Kentucky Distillers' Association reacted by creating the Kentucky Bourbon Trail. It wasn't long before brown highway signs appeared along I-64 between Lexington and Louisville, promoting distilleries as tourist stops. In turn, the distilleries offered free tours and introduced themselves to a new generation of whiskey drinkers.

Several distilleries launched advertising campaigns to build awareness, with Labrot & Graham Distillery (who later changed their name to Woodford Reserve to match their whiskey brand) among the most assertive. Their ads showcased the beauty of Kentucky horse farms, the distillery's legacy dating back to 1812, and the Bourbon they proudly touted as "Kentucky's native spirit."[4] And rightly so, given Bourbon's roots in the state and its enduring cultural importance. For Labrot & Graham, it was a statement of pride in a spirit that had become inseparable from the region's identity.

With the repetition of this advertisement over a couple of years, it's hard not to see how Senator Bunning was introduced to the "native spirit" concept. So who elevated it from Kentucky to America?

It wasn't Bunning, nor was it a Kentuckian. Instead, the first references pre-date the Labrot & Graham advertisements. The first appearance is in the May 12, 1972 edition of the *Miami Herald*. Beneath an accounting of oil import numbers and government lawsuits, there is a note about American exports to West Germany. The paragraph points to that European country as an early top market for Bourbon "as the popularity of America's native spirit keeps growing."[5] While this was an isolated mention, the words reappeared eight years later in the *Atlanta Journal and Constitution*'s weekend edition[6] and a year after that in *The New York Daily News*.[7] So it wasn't Senator Bunning's invention. The lore was already in the wild. Although none of the references indicate the 1964 act was the reason for their assertion.

What Makes a Spirit Native?

While the 1964 act didn't formally declare Bourbon as America's Native Spirit, is it a title it could rightfully hold?

That requires an examination of the words "native spirit." What makes a spirit native?

With Scotch, it seems to be obvious. The law states that the spirit can only be made in Scotland—and the spirit's very name comes from the Scottish people. Irish whiskey is also a no-brainer from a name standpoint. The spirit can only be produced in countries with Ireland in their names—the Republic of Ireland and Northern Ireland.

Bourbon isn't even an English word. It originates from the royal French House of Bourbon. Since Bourbon is only the name of two counties (Kentucky and Kansas) in the United States, does it legitimately earn the right to be claimed by the whole country?

Let's look at some of the reasons it is difficult to term Bourbon as America's Native Spirit:

- It doesn't require the use of native ingredients.
- It wasn't the first spirit born in America. AppleJack, a uniquely American style of brandy, predates Bourbon by several decades. This also dispels Senator Bunning's statement that Bourbon was the "only spirit distinctive to the United States."
- Rum, brandy, and rye whiskey were America's first choice before Bourbon came on the scene.
- Bourbon isn't 100% uniquely American. At its heart, it is corn whiskey, which may be more synonymous with America, but it was made using techniques that originated in the Old World. This reasoning disqualifies AppleJack as well.

But some of these could be turned on their head to support the idea of Bourbon being America's Native Spirit. Here are some of those reasons, with a couple of others:

- Bourbon is a "distinctive product" of the United States, thanks to the 1964 resolution. It can be mimicked, but it can't be sold as Bourbon anywhere else in the world.
- The concept of Bourbon whiskey originated in the United States.
- America is a melting pot and this influence is felt in many forms. Like jazz, Bourbon draws influences from around the world, but is a distinctly American expression.
- Bourbon production tops that of all other American spirits, showing its importance to the success of American distillers.
- Mexico has a *Denominación de Origen* (Designation of Origin) for Tequila, which was named after a town. Champagne and Cognac are designations named for regions in France. So why not Bourbon based

on a county?

It is no wonder the 1964 joint resolution went with "distinctive product" rather than overreaching with "native spirit."

America's Right to Bourbon

The next question is: did Kentucky want the United States to co-opt something that was born within their borders?

The earliest answer to this question came in 1993, when Jim Beam became an early entrant into the whiskey tourism scene. When they opened the doors of the Clermont, Kentucky distillery to visitors, they touted the facility as the "home of the world's finest bourbon," and wholeheartedly embraced it as "America's native spirit!"[8] Soon Maker's Mark, Heaven Hill, and various authors and critics incorporated it into their advertisements and articles. It's no wonder Senator Bunning used the term—it was everywhere.

So what harm has this marketing lore caused?

Well, it obviously led a U.S. Senator astray.

It also has played a part in creating a misconception overseas that Bourbon is just another name for all American brown spirits. This misconception appears even in popular culture. In the movie *Goldeneye*, you'll hear James Bond's boss M say she likes Bourbon. Then she pulls out the iconic square bottle of Jack Daniel's Tennessee Sour Mash Whiskey. When American single malt or rye whiskey hits store shelves in Europe, will they call those Bourbon too?

It also serves to minimize the connection with its birthplace. Every time a tour guide has to explain that Bourbon can be made anywhere in the United States instead of just Kentucky, it feels like they're willingly giving away their heritage. Not to mention how strange a feeling I got while writing *The Lost History of Tennessee Whiskey*, when I realized I was putting a Kentucky county name on

Tennessee spirits. Placing this county's name on Colorado or California spirits seems awkward.

As you will find out throughout this book, language matters. When it is imprecise, it leads to misunderstandings, false narratives, weak foundations for historical arguments, and, of course, plenty of lore.

Upon Further Review...

Whether "America's Native Spirit" is or isn't an accurate descriptor for Bourbon, it can be said with great confidence that the joint resolution of Congress did not declare it as such in 1964.

However, that doesn't mean Bourbon fans can't claim it as such today. In an unexpected twist, the 2007 resolution that contained the senator's error turned out to be the slogan's best friend. While it is true Bunning incorrectly interpreted the 1964 act's intention in the body of the 2007 document, the official statement in its resolving clause declared "that the Senate (2)- recognizes bourbon as America's Native Spirit and reinforces its heritage and tradition and its place in the history of the United States."[9]

It's a bit of dumb luck, but this statement gave an official position for the senate—Bourbon is America's Native Spirit. However, before touting this piece of information to your friends, make sure your language is pinpoint and precise. When saying Congress made this declaration, either don't give the date or say it was in 2007, not 1964.

On this matter, his execution wasn't perfect. But then, as Senator Bunning knew, perfection isn't easily obtained.

Reality: True. The Senate did "eventually" declare it.

Canadian Scotch

Myth: American and Canadian distillers make Scotch.

AI: False

In a ramshackle building near the gentle waters of the Tay, a Scotsman named Robert McLaren set up a copper pot still and applied the trade so well-known to his countrymen—the art of distilling malt whisky. His skills were genuine and his spirits were prized by the stonemasons and military men who built his home village of Perth.

Contrary to how it may sound, the waters that fed McLaren's distillery were not from the River Tay in Perthshire, Scotland. Instead, his makeshift distillery was near the growing village of Perth in Upper Canada (now Ontario), along the Tay River.

It's no accident that the waterway and town name were nearly identical to those in Scotland. It was a tradition of European settlers to bring with them a little slice of home to the New World. Ontario alone is home to several European city names, including London, Dublin, Paris, and Berlin (renamed Kitchener during World War I).

Selling a Taste of the Old World

With so many immigrants across Southwestern Ontario desiring a taste of home, any whisky that brought back memories of their native land was sure to be prized. So Robert's old world skills at distilling malt whisky endeared him to the other Scotsmen in the area. But his output showed was nothing more than a local favorite while Robert was alive. Under the stewardship of his son, John Alexander McLaren, the family spirit was able to spread across the region and then the country.

Embracing his father's passion for their ancestral home, John made sure his whisky was closely associated with the great whiskies of the Old World. When he began distributing his spirits in Ottawa, he advertised his McLaren's Pure Malt Whiskey as "genuine usquebaugh or small still whiskey," emphasizing that the style was "celebrated in Scotland and Ireland"—two countries known for their fanaticism over claiming the best whisky.

He wasn't lying. Malt whisky did traditionally have a sterling reputation in these Celtic regions, but without careful scrutiny, a reader of one of his advertisements could easily be led to believe John was referring to his own whisky's reputation abroad. Playing into the illusion, he quoted scientist Edward Smith, a Fellow of the Royal College of Physicians in London, saying "Small Still Whiskey has always been regarded as the better kind." To head off any talk of deception, he divulged in small letters, "this is the kind of whisky the subscriber makes."[10]

These kinds of slick claims would earn a lawsuit today. But in the 19th century, sleight-of-hand advertising was everywhere. This lack of marketing regulation is why alcohol-heavy snake oil with no healing powers whatsoever (beyond the placebo effect) could be legally sold as cure-alls. It was also the era when whisky was openly sold as medicinal, with distillers claiming their spirits cured rheumatism, aided digestion and restored vigor. It was a free-for-all.

With these elevated advertising campaigns, McLaren's grew a reputation as one of the finest whiskies in Canada. Throughout the 1870s and 1880s, barrels of John's spirit spread across the Canadian plains[11] and over the Rocky Mountains to Vancouver.

With the invention of semi-automatic bottling machines, John embraced the new technology and began bottling his whisky in the 1890s. This gave him the opportunity to make a direct impression on his customer, without a bartender or wholesaler as the middleman. Using the words "pure malt whiskey" on his bottles, he added a tag line "The Genuine Usquebaugh-the Old Fashioned Small Still Whiskey so celebrated in Scotland and Ireland. Warranted Free from Fusel Oil."[12] Soon, liquor stores like Bate & Co in Ottawa were advertising McLaren's Perth Malt as Scotch Whiskey, right next to famous authentic Scottish brands like Usher's and Walker's.[13]

Eventually the words "Scotch whisky" made their way to McLaren's bottles. But it was clear by the label that John wasn't trying to claim his whisky was made in Scotland. Not only did the bottle use a beaver as its icon, below the brand name, it clearly stated, "John A. McLaren Distiller. Perth, Ontario."[14] In other words, he felt Scotch whisky was a style, not a spirit made in a specific country. Interestingly, John faced no backlash from Scotland's distillers, even with Tommy Dewar traveling across Canada in the 1890s.

Then, sadly, John passed away unexpectedly in 1901.[15] The brand's future was put in doubt when they discovered John, a lifelong bachelor, didn't have a will. Several people attempted to lay claim to the distillery and his fortune. In the end, the money and property would go mostly to his nephew Mayor J.A. Stewart of Perth.[16] As for the whisky, it remained on the market as McLaren's Scotch Whisky into the 1910s.[17]

Giving Scotch Back to the Scots

With the death of the McLaren brand, the concept of Canadian Scotch faded from use by distilleries in Canada. But it didn't die out completely. During American Prohibition, west coasters in Seattle and San Francisco often referred to bootlegged spirits from the Great White North as Canadian Scotch.[18] But after the repeal of Prohibition, future generations rarely repeated those words.

However, with no regulations, there was nothing to stop other countries from using the name Scotch. But, when bottles of whisky labeled German Scotch entered the United Kingdom in the early 1930s, Britain's parliament took action.[19] For half a century, the Spirits Act of 1880 regulated the kingdom's rules. After a full review of the older law, they passed the Finance Act of 1933 in June, making it illegal to sell any whisky distilled outside of Scotland as Scotch whisky.[20] After that, a watchdog group called the Whisky Association (later the Scotch Whisky Association or SWA) kept this act in its back pocket as a way to defend Scotch's good name.

The Finance Act of 1933 created a domino effect as other countries moved to protect their own national spirits. The French government recognized Cognac, Armagnac, and Champagne as distinctive of their regions in 1936, and then recognized Calvados in 1942. Over the next couple of decades, Tequila (Mexico), Irish Whiskey and Poitín (Ireland and Northern Ireland), Genever or Jenever (Belgium and Netherlands), and Grappa (Italian) were also protected under geographical indicators (GIs).

It seemed everyone was onboard with countries locking down their spirits' reputations by not letting their names be used across borders. To the Scots, it appeared their name was safe and never again would there be a German or Canadian Scotch. All was right with the world.

Down in the Glen

By the late 1980s, Canadian whisky had made quite a name for itself—especially in the American market. Legendary Canadian blends like Canadian Club, Seagram's VO, and Seagram's Crown Royal led the way. People thought of Bourbon as too strong or stodgy. The 7 & 7, a simple highball cocktail made with Seagram's 7 Crown whisky and 7UP, had replaced the Bourbon Old Fashioned in the hearts of Americans who were looking for something lighter and more refreshing. Bourbon, rye, and Scotch single malts had a hard time competing in the marketplace—and the Canadians saw no reason to mimic these out-of-fashion spirits.

Then came Canadian entrepreneur Bruce Jardine, who stepped into the scene with a bold announcement: he intended to produce Canada's first single malt whisky (apparently he was unaware of the history of McLaren's pure malt). His distillery was developed in a province with deep Scottish roots. Its name, Nova Scotia, means "New Scotland." It dates back to 1621, when King James I of England (also James VI of Scotland) granted Sir William Alexander a charter to establish a Scottish colony in Canada, hoping to attract Scottish settlers to the area.

To get his distillery off on a good foot, Bruce worked with distillers at Bowmore Distillery on the island of Islay in Scotland. They generously offered him advice on the right distilling equipment to purchase. With the help of local architects, he built the distillery along Maclelland's Brook near the North Cape Highlands on the island of Cape Breton. It was a true throwback to the spring-fed burns of Highland Scotland. He named it the Glenora Distillery, and topped the building off with a pagoda chimney, giving it the iconic feel of a Scottish distillery.

If Bruce wanted to link single malt whisky to its rich Scottish heritage, he couldn't have chosen a better location outside Scotland. Cape Breton's rugged coastline, deep-rooted Celtic and Acadian cultures, and stunning natural beauty make it feel like a North American version of the Scottish Hebrides. With town names like Inverness, Glencoe, and Dunvegan, frequent references to "Highlands" for its mountainous areas, and strong Scottish influences in music and dance, it's enough to make a Scottish visitor feel at home.

But the road to profitability was rough. Nature and the used whiskey barrels needed for aging required time to work their magic in the cool Canadian climate. To supplement their income, the group produced Smuggler's Cove Rum, as Jamaican rum was popular in Canada at the time, and also sold Morrison Bowmore's whiskies. Still, the distillery went into receivership while waiting for spirits to age. The struggling business was reorganized, but after converting debt into equity and recapitalization, cash flow problems forced a sale. In 1994, the third owners, a group of investors led by Bedford entrepreneur Lauchie MacLean, purchased the distillery, tightened up the business, and improved the marketing around Smugglers Cove.

When the decision was made in 2000 to release their first single malt, the investors were well aware of Scotland's protective nature over the word Scotch. No Canadian distillery had dared stumble into that territory. Glenora steered clear, releasing their eight-year-old whisky as Glen Breton Rare Canadian Single Malt Whisky. The dark label featured a red maple leaf, to signify their Canadian roots. The name was a mashup of "glen" for the distillery's home in Glenville and Cape Breton.

It was quite a surprise to Lauchie and his team when the Scotch Whisky Association went to court to stop them from using their product name. Glenora went about business as usual following up their eight-year Glen Breton with a ten-year-old single malt. With no luck in the courts, in 2004, the SWA took the complaint to the Canadian trademark office. It seems the organization took exception to the word "glen," feeling it was the Canadian distillery's way of confusing customers of Scotch brands like Glenmorangie and Glenfiddich into buying their product. They deemed it "unfair competition."[21] Yet the bottles clearly stated the whisky was from Canada and sported the iconic maple leaf symbol on its label. It seems ironic that an area settled as New Scotland, hoping to attract Scottish settlers, would see one of its businesses punished for using a common Scottish word in its brand.

Neither side budged, and the case dragged on for years. Eventually, Glenora won the legal battle in the courts. Unsatisfied, the SWA appealed the decision all the way to the Canadian Supreme Court. In June 2009, the high court refused to hear the case, leaving the lower court's ruling in place. Glenora was granted full rights to use their trademark.

Five months later, the British parliament took a curious step of reviewing the rules of Scotch whisky. Coincidence?

The last time they were reviewed and adjusted was with the Scotch Whisky Act of 1988. Back then, the concern was Scottish blenders selling under-proofed spirits, yet still labeling them as Scotch. Titled "An Act to make provision as to the definition of Scotch whisky and as to the production and sale of whisky; and for connected purposes," it gave the clearest picture yet of what could be sold as Scotch whisky, including definitions of the types of acceptable blends and proof levels.[22] The act passed with royal assent on June 28, 1988.

Now parliament wanted to go a step further to protect not only the name of Scotch, but its regions as well. The Scotch Whisky Regulations 2009 (SWR) act repealed the Scotch Whisky Act of 1988 and replaced it with rules that put limits on advertising, production, and the packaging of Scotch whisky. It also blocked the use of the names of Scottish distilling locales like Campbeltown and Islay, and regions like the Highlands, Lowlands, and Speyside, by making them geographically protected areas.[23]

It's hard not to assume this action was brought on by the Scotch Whisky Association's battle over the word "glen." Perhaps the SWA thought Glenora might consider incorporating the local Cape Breton Highlands into the name of one of their future spirits.

But it wouldn't be the Canadians that would trip into this minefield.

There Can Be Only One

Enter the Virginia Distilling Company. Built along the edge of the Blue Ridge Mountains, a region steeped in Scots-Irish heritage, the distillery set out to honor this connection by distilling single malt whisky. In 2016, they launched their flagship Virginia Highland Malt Whisky to wide acclaim, catching the attention of magazines and spirits competitions on both sides of the Atlantic.

This didn't sit well with the Scotch Whisky Association, and with the SWR 2009 ruling on their side, they took action. The SWA went to Delaware and opened a legal case in U.S. Federal Court. They pointed to the Virginia distillery's use of the word "Highland" and the spelling of whisky without an "e" as confusing to customers.[24]

This time, cooler heads prevailed and the two parties reached an amicable resolution. The Virginia Distilling Company would sell off their current supply of bottles and all future bottlings would no longer include the word Highland—although they kept the spelling of whisky without an "e."

Today, geographical indicators are well respected, and corporations know better than to cross that line. However, there are still people who think Scotch is just a term for any single malt or blend. Unfortunately, there is no way to contain it. But if you ever utter the words Canadian Scotch, may it be in raising a toast to Robert and John Alexander McLaren, whose passion for their Scotch heritage let them get away with the coup of the millennia—the only known legal bottling of something they called Canadian Scotch.

Reality: False. Scotch is not a style but instead a geographical indicator, so it must be made in Scotland.

"Master" Distiller

Myth: Master Distiller is a certification.

AI: False

Throughout history, few geniuses have shaped their art as profoundly as Johann Sebastian Bach.

Born in 1685 to a musical family in Eisenach, within the Duchy of Saxe-Eisenach (modern-day Germany), young Johann faced early challenges. Orphaned at a young age, he was taken in by his brother, Johann Christoph Bach, who immersed him in rigorous musical training. Under his brother's guidance, Johann absorbed the compositions of Italian, French, and German masters, decoding their styles and techniques.

With his remarkable talent, it wasn't long before Johann grew frustrated with the skill level of those around him. At court, he ran afoul of several musicians that he felt were mediocre talents. While they were satisfied with the conventional seven note major and minor scales, Bach, in his heart, saw music's deeper potential for moving and elevating the soul.

Finding the range of contemporary keyboards limiting, Bach sought ways to expand the instrument's potential. Tunings favored certain tones in the scale and notes went out of tune as you climbed to the next octave. To solve this,

Bach envisioned a new tuning—equal temperament—where each octave would double the frequency of the lower octave's C, with the 12 tones evenly spaced. This meant that, for the first time, any key played across multiple octaves would resonate in harmony, enabling richer, more complex compositions. With this simple yet revolutionary change, Bach unlocked music's potential, opening the door to new heights of harmony, melody, color, and dissonance.

To show the power of his innovations, he created a two-volume masterwork called the *Well-Tempered Clavier*. Its 24 preludes and fugues in all major and minor keys explored the possibilities of a tuned instrument and showcased Bach's mastery of counterpoint and harmony.

Driven by his passion for elevating music, his love of God, and deep religious devotion, Bach composed over 1,000 pieces across a wide range of genres, from sacred music and orchestral works to solo keyboard compositions. But it wasn't only his prolific output that set him apart—his expansion of the musical palate laid a foundation for future musical geniuses, including Mozart, Haydn, and Beethoven.

If ever there was a true master of music, it was Johann Sebastian Bach.

The Evolution of Mastery

History abounds with great masters who helped shape science and the arts. Albert Einstein and Sir Isaac Newton were masters of physics. Leonardo di Vinci was a master of engineering, art, and science. Michelangelo Buonarroti was a master of both painting and sculpture. Aristotle and Socrates were masters of philosophy. William Shakespeare, Charles Dickens, and Jane Austen were masters of English literature, and so on. These high achievers took the accepted norms of their fields, absorbed them, and then expanded the potential of their craft for generations to come.

This definition of master is one that the world embraced for millennia. Whether learning as an apprentice or on their own, they gather knowledge and survey the world around them. Then, through their own skills, knowledge, and creativity, they elevate their craft or industry, creating a new foundation for future generations to marvel at, be inspired by, and build upon.

In the 9th century, the concept of mastery evolved from one-on-one interaction to organized instruction for two or more individuals. In the Muslim world, this new form came into being at the University of al-Qarawiyyin (Morocco). Here, a formalized education developed through a structuralized curriculum taught by instructors. In this environment, the masters were "teachers" or "educators." Christendom embraced this same methodology with the rise of the Schola Medica Salernitana (School of Salerno) in the Duchy of Benevento. Here, students mastered the art of medicine, which eventually included the art of distillation.

Within a couple of centuries, advancements in medicine and an increasingly complex society created demand for degrees with more extensive training, skills, and specialized knowledge. The University of Bologna (then part of the Holy Roman Empire, now in modern Italy) responded by developing advanced courses in civil and canon law. To signify this elevated mastery, they introduced the doctorate degree. Today, the doctorate remains the highest level of achievement in the university system, with the master's degree just below it.

With the invention of the printing press, formal education for the masses, and greater access to information, a new form of mastery emerged—one rooted in individual initiative. Now, mastering a language, cooking, or photography could be achieved with just a book or internet access, putting mastery within reach for many.

While genuine achievement remains inspiring, the democratization of knowledge and the liberal use of the term "master" have diminished some of its weight as a unique and powerful designation. Mastering piano scales, after all, isn't quite the same as Bach redefining music.

In the world of whiskey, a certain mystique surrounds legendary distillers and blenders of the past. For whiskey fans, figures like James C. Crow, Jack Daniel, and Johnnie Walker are akin to the Beethovens, Shakespeares, and Teslas of their craft. It's easy, by modern standards, to attribute titles like "master distiller" or "master blender" to these figures.

But what of modern-day master distillers and master blenders? How do they earn that title? Is it through apprenticeships, school certifications, or is it self-proclaimed? And what of the masters of the past—how did they earn their titles?

Mastery in Whiskey

From its inception until the mid-17th century, distillation was practiced by alchemists, monks, religious orders, and apothecaries. Seeing the distillation process as a form of purification, our ancestors used spirits as a base for herbal medicines, tonics, and treatments for various ailments. These healing waters earned the name *aqua vitae*—Latin for "water of life."

After Britain's King Henry VIII broke from Catholicism, he dissolved the monasteries and forced the monks out of their sanctuaries. Practiced in the art of distillation, the monks helped spread this knowledge to the masses. Distilling spread among farmers, clergymen, and small landowners as a way to pay rent, create medicines, and for enjoyment. The rise of taxation curbed the practice for some, while others continued to distill illegally.

Eventually, the Industrial Revolution reshaped society, drawing people to towns, increasing goods production, and creating a greater need for cash and trade. Distilling became a cash business, while farmers continued to distill to pay rent, barter, and preserve perishable fruits and grains.

During this period, when farms and rural distilleries were the primary sources of spirit production, *aqua vitae* remained a local affair. A distiller's reputation only traveled as far as a horse and buggy or a sailing ship could carry it. For

17th- and 18th-century distillers, mastering the craft wasn't the objective; it was about survival and securing a profit. Their spirits, often unaged and harsh, needed additives or dilution just to be drinkable. They definitely were not yet worthy of legend.

The distiller's reputation began to develop with the advent of the railroad and steamship. In the early 1800s, changes in British tax laws and the spread of the railroad in the United States increased the amount of whiskey making its way from region to region. Before long, unscrupulous wholesalers started doctoring spirits to boost profits, leading to a decline in whiskey quality. Many times, tainted whiskey found its way into unsuspecting communities, which prompted the use of branding by distillers and distilleries to instill trust in a spirit's quality.

In America, a select few gained reputations as "celebrated" distillers—among them James A. Miller and James C. Crow in Kentucky and George Smith's Glenlivet and John Jameson's Bow Street distillery in Scotland and Ireland respectively. Yet, contemporary records show that they were not referred to as master distillers. In fact, modern whiskey fans may be surprised to find the terms "master distiller" and "master blender" conspicuously absent from 19th-century records.

Take Alfred Barnard's landmark book, *The Whisky Distilleries of the United Kingdom* (1887), for example. After visiting 160 distilleries across Ireland, Scotland, and England, Barnard provided detailed profiles that captured each distillery's layout, machinery, processes, and heritage. He also focused on the people involved, listing directors, distillers, malt men, coopers, bookkeepers, and more—yet he never once used the title "master distiller." A search through American newspapers from the same era yields similar results. It appears the term "master distiller" has been applied retroactively to 19th-century distillers through oral tradition.

In other words, distilling in the 19th century was simply an occupation. The names we remember today were often those of distillery owners or individuals whose names survived by luck or chance. Many of the figures we think of as distillers were actually owners who relied on skilled workers to ensure quality. James C. Crow is one of the rare exceptions—never owning a distillery but still earning a reputation for his whiskey. However, there's no record of him being called a "master" during his lifetime. Today, there are many ways to gain fame and glory through marketing and creative skill, but back then, distillers didn't see themselves as having any importance to future generations. They were just striving to make the best product they could.

Now, think of the impact this realization has on the narratives written around these historic distillers today. Our obsession with finding firsts and greats become clouded in terminology that wasn't historically significant (and possibly didn't even exist) in the 19th century or before.

So where did the term "master distiller" come from and what does it actually mean?

The Birth of the Master Distiller

To understand the term "master distiller," let's look at its earliest appearances in the industry.

The first mentions trace back to the years just before American Prohibition, although it wasn't used in the way we recognize today. The first references are not for an individual title, but for a distinction within a group of contemporaries. Take Kentucky's Green River Whiskey, for example. In 1904, an ad declared it was "Made by McCulloch, the master distiller of Kentucky."[25] This didn't mean he was the master distiller for all of Kentucky—in fact, like other distillery owners, he likely wasn't the one doing the distilling. Instead, this phrase was competitive marketing, suggesting McCulloch's mastery over other Kentucky distillers. Similarly, Old Still Creek Kentucky Whiskey advertised that its whisky was made by "a master distiller," not "the master distiller."[26] V.O.S. Armor Brands described their whiskey as "far removed from the commonplace, and of the finest inspiration of America's Master Distillers."[27] This early marketing of distillers as "masters" helped pave the way for the title we know today by highlighting the impact of having an expert distiller.

After Prohibition, the term found sporadic use. In most cases, it was used to show a bridge of quality between a distillery's pre-Prohibition and post-Prohibition whiskey. In 1937, Joseph Bernard Dant became one of the first to be singled out—being referred to as the oldest "master distiller" in the country.[28] However, this feels less like a title and more like his part of a rarified group of distillers—there is no evidence throughout his long career that he was referred to as "the master distiller."

The modern concept of individual titles like "master distiller" and "master blender" didn't take shape until the 1960s and '70s. The title attached itself to legendary whisky blender Richard Paterson after he started speaking to large audiences. It was a way to convey to laymen the level of expertise achieved by the individual. Similarly, when Booker Noe coined terms like "Kentucky Hug" and promoted his spirits at public events, the title "master distiller" underscored his significance within the Jim Beam hierarchy.[29]

The Modern Master Distiller

Today, the titles of "master distiller" and "master blender" have become commonplace. In the United States, most distilleries have one, while in Scotland and Ireland, the titles are less prevalent, possibly because of a more European sensibility of masters in other pursuits. In those countries, it is often replaced by more modest titles like "production director" or "lead distiller."

The expertise, responsibilities, and education of master distillers vary widely depending on the size of the distillery.

In larger corporations, most master distillers follow an apprentice-to-master path, spending years refining their skills as assistants or working through various departments. Once they reach this esteemed title, only a few continue working directly with the stills—pushing the boundaries of distilling. Instead, most oversee recipe development, cask management, quality control, blending, compliance, safety, and team management. Some simply serve as ambassadors, representing their brand around the world, while never touching a still.

In smaller craft distilleries, the education and experience level of the master distiller can range from expert to self-taught enthusiasts, like Phil Prichard of Prichard's Distillery in Kelso, Tennessee, who started out distilling rum in his kitchen sink.

And between these extremes lie countless unique paths to the title.

No degree, certification, or time apprenticing is required to become a master distiller—much like mastering a language through books and videos, distilling is something you can learn with practice. It doesn't mean what you create is going to be great. Nor does it put you in the league of Eddie Russell (Wild Turkey) or Dr. Bill Lumsden (Glenmorangie). For many, "master distiller" is simply a title, covering a wide range of experience levels as diverse as those in other fields.

And sadly, for those who want to place master distillers in a historical context, the extreme variety of skills and responsibilities, the modern business structure, and the technological innovations over the last century or two makes comparing today's master distiller to the distillers of the past nearly impossible—not to mention how little we know about the advances they individually brought to the industry.

As the industry evolves, the title of master distiller may eventually fade or be reserved only for those who have truly mastered the art through monumental achievement—much like Bach's mastery of music through a lifetime of study and self-discovery. Perhaps, a hundred years from now, people will look back and marvel at the widespread use of the term today and its lack of formal requirements. Just as the absence of the term in 19th-century distilling reflects that era's perspective on the distiller's role, today's liberal use may reveal ours.

The spirit of our ancestors is always hiding in the details.

Reality: False. Buy a still and you can call yourself a master distiller.

The Sour Mash Doctor

Myth: Dr. James C. Crow invented the sour mash process.

AI: Complicated

> *"Beneath the bluegrass sod of a country burying-ground near the little hamlet of Millville, in Woodford county, sleeps James Crow, who originated the process of distilling whisky by chemical proportions. To Crow more than to any other man or men is due the international reputation that Kentucky whisky enjoys." - Louisville Courier-Journal* (Sept 5, 1897)

In a state filled with whiskey legends, that is quite a statement. This paragraph is the preamble to one of the most fascinating—and exaggerated—biographies ever written about a 19th-century distiller. Drawn from the mind of staff writer Daniel Mayes Bowmar, it portrays Kentucky distilling legend James Crow in grandiose terms: a man of Herculean build, with a sharp scientific mind, an innovative spirit, and a philosophical outlook. His achievements, according to Bowmar, are too numerous to mention. To read it, one might think the good doctor was more than a distiller—he was the savior of Kentucky whiskey.

I must admit, I too am fascinated by the life and whiskey of James C. Crow. In the 19th century, his namesake Old Crow whiskey held a stellar reputation, counting generals, statesmen, authors, poets, and even presidents among its fans. Yet the true story of the man and the secrets of his whiskey have puzzled writers, marketers, and historians for generations. Some simply shake their heads, while others, like Bowmar, embellish and weave fantastical stories to build a legend worthy of the whiskey that bears Crow's name.

When I started the *Whiskey Lore* podcast, Crow became the subject of multiple episodes. The sheer amount of myths surrounding him is staggering. Unfortunately, much of the information available online only led me further astray in my storytelling. For someone seeking the truth, the conflicting information I found was aggravating. Did he create or just improve the sour-mash process? Was he born in Inverness or Edinburgh? Was he truly a doctor?

In my work of dispelling whiskey lore, there may be no better subject than James Crow. It's time to set the record straight—at least as accurately as the available information allows.

To illustrate how far the truth veers from the legend, let's begin with a condensed version of the mythical James C. Crow before diving into reality.

The Legend of Dr. Crow

Born in 1789 in Edinburgh, Scotland, James Crow pursued his passion for science and medicine from a young age, attending the University of Edinburgh College of Medicine and Surgery. He began his career as a physician and surgeon but eventually saw a greater path to success in America. Upon arriving in Philadelphia in 1822 with his brother Douglas, the two opened a mercantile business. However, when the business failed, James set out to rebuild his fortune by establishing himself as a distiller in Kentucky.

Arriving in Frankfort in 1823, he attended a session of the state legislature and met Colonel Willis Field. Impressed with James's scientific mind, Field hired him to run his whisky distillery along Griers Creek in Woodford County. What Dr. Crow didn't know about distilling, he quickly learned from reading "what was said to have been the most extensive library in Kentucky at that period...and it gave to him the secret of correct distilling." James spent weeks poring over his books, determined not only to make a great spirit but to make the process repeatable—at a time when Kentucky distillers were famous for using a pinch of this and a gallon of that.

James tested the balance of limestone water, the quality of the beer, varying levels of heat, and searched for the right balance of ingredients. What he created made him so renowned that "orders poured in from everywhere—much faster than it was possible to fill them." Soon, casks of "Crow's whisky" were making their way to "Washington, Philadelphia, New York and Boston, and to England, Scotland and other foreign countries." Influential figures like Daniel Webster and Henry Clay swore by "Crow's whisky."

Few outside his local community truly knew this legendary distiller. During his years at Oscar Pepper's distillery, James kept close to the modest, one-story stone stillhouse along Glenns Creek. The only thing that could draw him from his daily work was his devotion to the local poor; he often walked miles to provide them with medical care, never accepting a penny in return.

After later taking a position at the Burgess Yancey and Anderson Johnson distillery, James passed away at the controls in 1859. Despite his success and enduring reputation, Dr. James C. Crow died penniless, with only his family at his side.

How History Went So Wrong

What you've just read is a somewhat restrained, condensed version of James Crow's life as portrayed by historians and reporters like Bowmar. I left out some of Bowmar's more grandiose claims, such as "Crow was one of the most celebrated characters of the West," or that he was "a noted conversationalist, always sent for to entertain visitors to Versailles like [Henry] Clay, [John J.] Crittenden, [Charles] Morehead, and other distinguished statesmen."[30] If James was such a man about town, why was he never in the papers? This also contradicts the idea he only went out to tend to the rural poor. Perhaps the most bizarre part of Bowmar's account is his assertion that James abandoned a wife and child in Scotland, only to have them track him down when a barrel bearing his brand arrived in their Scottish village.

When it comes to his whiskey production, marketers and historians often point to James Crow's scientific acumen as the reason for his success. They credit him with moving Kentucky distilling from the barn to the stillhouse, introducing measuring tools like hydrometers and saccharometers to ensure consistency, and his mastery of the sour mash process producing a whiskey that far surpassed his competitors. A few even credit him with inventing the sour mash process.

Very little of what we think we know about this legendary distiller and the spirits he produced are actually true, due to what historians call historiographical errors. This type of error arises when a historian introduces incorrect information into their work—whether through poor research, misunderstandings, or exaggerated oral tradition. Another historian uses this inaccurate information, passing it on and causing a ripple effect. With each retelling, the lore gains weight and perceived validity. An article like Mr. Bowmar's, if repeated, can mislead future historians, leading to false conclusions and dead ends. People ultimately accept these myths as truth because they become so deeply embedded.

It's time to deconstruct the life of James Crow and put it back together, using legal documents, sworn testimony, and birth records. You're about to see firsthand how far embedded lore may have pushed us from reality. We'll also move closer to discovering the secrets of his success and his true impact on Kentucky whiskey.

The Search for the Real James Crow

Our search begins with the 1850 U.S. census, where we encounter 63-year-old James Christopher Crow, husband to Elizabeth (aged 56), and father to Catharine (aged 30). Born in Scotland on June 11, 1787, he was the son of William and Cathrine Crow of Dirleton, a village 20 miles east of Edinburgh.[31]

Contrary to popular belief, it seems James was neither a doctor nor an aspiring scientist, if the account of James E. Pepper, the son of his employer Oscar Pepper, can be trusted. Instead of attending the University of Edinburgh School of Medicine, Pepper recounts that James Crow honed his craft working in grain distilleries in the Lowlands of Scotland before taking his expertise to France's renowned brandy distilleries.[32]

Other details of James's early life and his arrival in America remain a mystery. Did he sail the Atlantic with his brother? Did they establish a mercantile business in New York or Philadelphia and go bankrupt? It's all possible. But this is where the 1850 census records fall short. Elizabeth's birthplace appears to be New York, though the handwriting is difficult to decipher. The census suggested their daughter Catharine was born in 1820, though her gravestone states 1812, adding to the mystery of James's actual timeline. It is her gravestone that led historians to believe Catharine was born in Scotland, but the census doesn't agree. If she was indeed born in 1812, then James would have arrived in America much earlier than the long-touted 1822 or 1823. If the 1820 census date is correct, it is conceivable the couple traveled to Elizabeth's family home for support during the birth, but this raises questions about the Philadelphia narrative.

Ahhh, the joys of genealogical research.

The 1812 date is intriguing for another reason: it coincides with Willis Fields Sr.'s purchase of a plot of land known as "Airy Mount," where he established a distillery on Griers Creek.[33] Historians have identified this location as the likely starting point of James Crow's Kentucky distilling career. Unfortunately, James never owned property in the United States, and census records before 1850 only list heads of households, so we cannot verify his exact location between 1820 and 1840 through those records. However, we do know that by the summer of 1820, James was in Versailles, Kentucky, as evidenced by a notice in the *Kentucky Gazette* showing he had mail waiting at the post office.[34]

Whatever year he arrived, it didn't take long for his talents as a distiller to shine through. By the mid-to-late 1820s, people who knew James and worked with him said he was an in-demand distiller, working on various farms around the area, including the Edwards and Henry farms.[35]

While history often casts him as both scientist and physician, James's real expertise likely came from his hands-on experience in Europe. Scottish grain distilleries would have exposed him to scientific measuring tools, orderly facilities, and the concept of consistency—skills that would set him apart in the rugged landscape of frontier Kentucky. His time in the brandy distilleries of France may have introduced him to fermentation control and aging techniques unfamiliar to most Kentuckians. As Bowmar suggests, he probably learned through books as well, but they were probably Willis Fields; James's final inventory after his death contained no personal library.

The first sign of James's distilling prowess appeared in an 1835 advertisement by Frankfort wholesalers Anderson & Stevenson, who touted his "superior whis key."[36] Not long after, he caught the attention of Oscar Pepper, a 26-year-old who had recently inherited his family's farm, mill, and distillery on Glenns Creek from his father, Elijah. In 1838, a new limestone stillhouse was built, perhaps with James's arrival in mind. James settled into his role at Oscar Pepper's distillery (today's Woodford Reserve Distillery), entering what would become the most successful period of his career.

Eventually, his name stretched beyond Kentucky. In 1846, Crow's celebrated whiskey was spotted in a Vicksburg, Mississippi newspaper advertisement.[37] It is one of the earliest mentions of a Kentucky distiller's name regarding his whiskey.

Within a short period, it simply became Crow whiskey, New Crow whiskey, or Old Crow.

In 1855, James Crow left Oscar Pepper behind and moved a few miles down Glenns Creek to the Anderson Johnson distillery.[38] However, he didn't leave Oscar high and dry. James had passed his skills on to his assistant, William Mitchell, who continued making whiskey using Crow's techniques—though a neighbor distiller Thomas S. Edwards noted Oscar marketed this whiskey as Old Oscar Pepper's,[39] rather than Old Crow's or Mitchell's. Whether James ever put his name on a barrel at Johnson's distillery remains a mystery.

Historical accounts vary on the date of James's death, placing it between 1855 and 1859, but his tombstone at the Versailles Cemetery confirms April 20, 1856. Multiple accounts have the 68-year-old James Crow passing away while doing what he loved—making whiskey.[40] A romantic end for a legendary figure. Yet, strangely, no obituary appeared at the time of his death. If he was truly the folk hero of "the West" that Bowmar describes, his passing in relative obscurity raises more questions than it answers.

Much of his life will forever remain shrouded in mystery.

What Made Crow's Whiskey So Special?

While little is known about James Crow the man, we have slightly more to go on regarding his whiskey. Unfortunately for historians, James left no written record of his recipes or techniques. Apart from his apprentice, William Mitchell, no one appears to have had firsthand knowledge of how to replicate the old master's work.

However, a few years after Bowmar's article appeared in the *Courier-Journal*, a legal dispute over the use of the name Old Crow brought together distillers, friends, and area residents who had known or worked with James Crow. Although oral tradition has its limitations in proving historical facts, the legal risks of false testimony lend some credibility to these accounts—though memory's natural biases still obscure and embellish details. The insights they shared through their testimony paints a picture of Crow's whiskey quite different from the popular stories.

The case began in 1905, when W.A. Gaines & Company, the producer of Old Crow whiskey, started legal action against a Missouri-based company for unauthorized use of the "Old Crow" trademark. The case, known as *Rock Spring Distilling Co. v. W.A. Gaines & Co.*, forced W.A. Gaines to prove their own legitimacy of using the mark, since James Crow never worked for them. Their connection came through the hiring of William Mitchell, James's old assistant, who brought his methods of distilling to the company.

During these depositions, several men provided valuable insights into what the old master considered vital for creating his unique spirit.

While the testimony agrees with historians' assessment that it was James Crow's sour mash that set him apart, it wasn't because he invented it or even improved it. It was because he didn't abandon it.

This may be a confusing statement if you're a fan of modern sour mash whiskeys. It was for me, too. The reality is, what James Crow was making was an old-style, *traditional* sour mash, whereas the industrialized distilleries moved into making "sweet mash." But don't get their definition of sweet mash mixed up with the modern definition. After Prohibition, the original concept of sweet mash was lost for generations. Is your head hurting yet? Unfortunately, this is one problem with doing historical research—sometimes whiskey definitions change, leading to the wrong conclusions.

Let's break it down.

In the modern world, sour mashing involves reusing spent mash from a previous distillation, similar to how sourdough bread uses a starter. Distillers add this spent mash to the next batch of cooked grains to help control pH levels and bacteria before adding a cultivated yeast strain. In the 19th century, this was considered the sweet mash process. This is different from the modern use of the term sweet mash, which only uses added yeast and no backset sour mash in the fermenting process.

Traditional sour mashing, used in James Crow's day and before, didn't allow for the addition of cultivated yeast or chemical additives.[41] This meant spent mash and wild yeast from the atmosphere had to do all the work. Rather than mashing in one large vessel, James used 30 small tubs on wheels. These were hand-stirred by two of Oscar Pepper's enslaved workers, Dick and Albert. Once the wild yeast took hold, usually after two days, they added the mash to the fermenters. After fermentation, the spent mash was put aside for the next batch. This process continued until the end of the distilling season, usually in May. The fermented grains were distilled in traditional one-chamber copper pot stills. This would later be sold as "copper-distilled sour mash." [42]

As important to James's reputation as his traditional sour mashing was, he wasn't the only one doing it. Henry McKenna, T.W. Samuels, W.F. Bond, and James's Woodford County neighbor J.W. Lillard also produced "copper-distilled sour m ash."[43] So there has to be more to his distilling story than just this one technique.

This is where historians might point to James's use of scientific equipment and his demand for a clean stillhouse. However, neither of these was mentioned in the depositions.

Instead, three other factors for his success rose to the top. First, he insisted on using only the highest quality grains and ensured they were thoroughly cleaned before processing.[44] Second, he took advantage of the limestone water flowing from a spring above Glenns Creek, considered some of the finest for whiskey-making in the country.[45] And third, James went completely old school. While many of his contemporaries had switched to distilling using steam to heat the stills, James insisted on direct flame, a traditional method many had abandoned because of the risk of scorching the grain and imparting a burnt flavor. To counteract this, James and his distillers took a slow distilling approach, carefully monitoring temperatures and adjusting the fires below the pot still to prevent scorching. The copper pot would then allow for more control over reflux allowing him fine tune his spirit.

It is a way of making whiskey that would give a modern stockholder or accountant a heart attack. These techniques were a slow and deliberate way of making whiskey. Not only did it cost time, it reduced yields. While other distillers were getting 4 ½ gallons of spirits per bushel of grain, James was only getting 3 ½.[46] The result was a full-bodied, oily whiskey that no other distiller could match.

So it wasn't just one thing that made James Crow's whiskey so amazing—it was the perfect collection of old-school methods—along with a boss in Oscar Pepper who ignored the accountants for the sake of making the best whiskey possible.

The Lasting Legacy of Crow

Sadly, this legendary distiller never lived to see the height of his own fame. Highly prized in central Kentucky, James Crow's renown didn't make it far beyond Louisville during his lifetime. It wasn't until the Civil War, five years later, that barrels with his name on them started finding their way down the Ohio and Mississippi Rivers, growing older and rarer with time, with some barrels aging up to ten years.

His name and reputation revived in 1869 when William Mitchell brought his knowledge to W.A. Gaines's new Old Crow Distillery on Glenns Creek. The company's leadership—William A. Gaines, Hiram Berry, and Edmund H. Taylor—recognized the promise of the Old Crow name and shipped it as far away as California and New York, taking advantage of the growing railroad network. They also hired William Mitchell's cousin, Van Johnson, as an apprentice. Van would become head distiller in 1872[47] and hold the position until 1899.

By 1890, Old Crow had become one of the most respected brands in the country. However, around 1895, as demand increased, the original 30 small tubs were replaced by larger vessels. The copper pot stills remained, though when they stopped using natural flame is unclear.

After Prohibition, Old Crow renewed its legendary status under the ownership of National Distillers. By that time, the copper pot distilling had been replaced by more efficient column stills. Eventually, Jim Beam acquired the brand from National Distillers.

One tale often told about the brand's fall from grace in the 1970s involves a story about how an accident damaged the historic yeast strain, leading to its abandonment. Its a story with impact on the importance of the post-Prohibition yeast strain, but it bares little impact on the yeast strain of James Crow, seeing as he was a traditional sour mash distiller who used the atmosphere for his yeast, rather than something preserved in a yeast jug.

Today's Old Crow is a lower-proof, budget-friendly version of the spirit, perfect as a Jim Beam replacement in a Jim and ginger. But it's a distant echo of its former self. Perhaps someday, Suntory Global, its current owners, will look to recapture the magic of that old traditional sour mash whiskey. Whether the accountants could take it is another matter. But I'm sure whiskey fans wouldn't mind it.

Reality: False. James C. Crow didn't invent the sour mash process. He simply stuck with it and added some old country flair.

Lincoln County Process

Myth: One of Jack Daniel's mentors—either Alfred Eaton or Nathan "Nearest" Green—invented the Lincoln County Process.

AI: True

For fans of Tennessee whiskey, 2009 was a year to celebrate. Seeing a potential for job creation and increasing agricultural production, legislators passed a law that opened up a large swath of the state to distilling. For years, Tennessee had only two distilleries, with Phil Prichard's being the third to open in the year 2000. The issue was, only three counties were open to legal distilling. But with the passage of 2009's Tennessee House Bill 1084, 41 additional counties were granted permission to explore the manufacture of whiskey, moonshine, and other distilled spirits. Soon after, Corsair in Nashville and Ole Smoky in Gatlinburg became the vanguard of a booming Tennessee craft distillery scene.

Then, in 2013, the celebratory mood hit a snag as a rift developed between a handful of distillers and their legislators. Ironically, the cause of contention was a bill, recently signed into law by Governor Bill Haslam, intended to protect the good name of Tennessee whiskey. But to some, it was a law that too closely mirrored the distilling practices of the state's largest distillery.

At the heart of the dispute was the fifth line of the bill, requiring that any product labeled Tennessee Whiskey be filtered through maple charcoal before barreling. Referred to by the distilling community as the Lincoln County Process, this filtering method was a hallmark of the brand that lobbied for the bill—Jack Daniel's. Opponents questioned its historic authenticity as a statewide practice.

For Phil Prichard, the issue was personal. He argued that his distilling ancestor Benjamin Prichard didn't use the Lincoln County Process, so why should he? When the bill was introduced, he successfully lobbied the Tennessee State Assembly for an exemption, as he had been producing unfiltered Tennessee Whiskey at his Lincoln County distillery long before the bill came up for debate. The assembly granted his distillery a grandfathered exemption. The matter seemed settled, until Prichard sought to open a second distillery in Nashville. Because the exemption was location specific, he would have to filter the whiskey he made there to keep the Tennessee whiskey designation. Two more distilleries joined in the complaint—Full Throttle and George Dickel. The surprising part was Dickel also used and promoted charcoal filtering, but they claimed they were fighting for the little guy. Soon, articles appeared in newspapers, and the Tennessee whiskey community found itself divided.

Jack Daniel's defended the bill, reminding the community their goal was to protect the good name of Tennessee whiskey, which was a legitimate concern. At the time, American whiskey regulations allowed new distilleries in Tennessee to use any grains they liked, age whiskey in used or uncharred barrels, distill at a higher proof, and even add colorants and flavorings. When George Dickel and Jack Daniel's were the only major players in the state, maintaining quality control around the Tennessee Whiskey name was straightforward. But with the rise of new craft distilleries, a few corner cutters could easily tarnish the reputation they put so much effort into creating.

One of Jack Daniel's challenges lay in the process's nickname. For as long as anyone could remember, Jack promoted their charcoal mellowing as the Lincoln

County Process. It was a technique they said their founder embraced when he began distilling in Lincoln County in 1866.

Stories abound about where Jack Daniel learned the method, including connections to Alfred Eaton, an early Lincoln County distiller who is thought to have distilled at the Cave Spring Hollow where Jack Daniel's currently resides; Nathan "Nearest" Green, an enslaved man who later worked for Daniel as a distiller; and Reverend Dan Call, Daniel's first and only business partner. Each has been connected to the technique in their own right. Unfortunately, when Jack Daniel's Old Time Distillery burned down in 1930, historical records were lost, leaving hard evidence elusive. Oral tradition offers clues, but shifts with each new discovery. There is however one thing these figures shared: a connection to Lincoln County. If this was indeed a local technique tied specifically to Jack Daniel's, opponents of the bill had grounds to question making it a statewide requirement.

Yet, when the law was debated, Tennessee's broader distilling history was unknown. That history revolved around two books written about Jack Daniel and the modern marketing of George Dickel. The only one that touched on the wider distilling industry was historian Kay Baker Gaston. Her research into Robertson County's heritage and the real story behind George Dickel in the *Tennessee Historical Quarterly* were eye-opening, but it's a good bet few lawmakers knew of their existence. Andy and Charlie Nelson were reviving historic Tennessee whiskey brands related to their family at that time, but Belle Meade Bourbon was just getting to market. Lacking a deeper understanding of Tennessee whiskey's past, the debate hinged on untenable marketing lore rather than historical evidence.

It is time to seek the truth: Was charcoal mellowing truly what set Tennessee whiskey apart from Kentucky Bourbon and other competitors? And who created it? Was it Alfred Eaton, Nathan "Nearest" Green, Dan Call, or someone yet mentioned?

Charcoal Mellowing's Early Roots

Before we can explore the origins of the Lincoln County Process, we need to understand what it is and what benefits it brings to whiskey.

A good starting point is a tour of the Jack Daniel's Distillery in Lynchburg. On most tours visitors stop by a cabin where employees work with stacks of sugar maple wood arranged in pallet-like blocks. They start by saturating the wood with high-proof new make spirit, then they set it alight. After the wood burns down to charcoal, they collect the char and take it to the filtering room. Here, the charcoal is emptied into large wooden vats, where new make spirit is piped in, slowly filtering through over several days before emerging at the bottom. The old-timers call this process "leaching," while younger folks and marketers know it as "charcoal mellowing." It is thought the brilliant marketing of Jack Daniel's tied the name Lincoln County Process to charcoal mellowing and, once firmly established, newspaper reporters and new distilleries latched onto it as well.

The history of charcoal mellowing goes back to a time before barrels were commonly used for aging. Today, we expect most whiskey to spend at least a couple of years in a barrel, which imparts color and additional flavors. Barrels also help smooth out rough edges in the spirit by oxidizing it, which reduces headache-inducing fusel oils.

But before governments offered tax breaks for aging whiskey in barrels, farmers found other ways to rid their spirits of those unwanted fusel oils—a process they called "rectifying."

Rectifying has a centuries-old history, though today it has developed a negative reputation due to the practices of unscrupulous distillers and wholesalers in the late 19th century. These rectifiers took high proof, virtually flavorless grain neutral spirits and added flavorings and substances to mimic a whiskey. Mostly it was done with skill, but when it wasn't, the results could lead to sickness and death. Yet in earlier times, before corporate greed and devious practices rose in the industry, rectifying was a more innocent practice. The word itself simply means to clean the spirit and farmers and early distillers found many ways to do this.

In the early days, farmers distilled with efficiency in mind, aiming to get spirits to market quickly. Stills were expensive, and owning more than one was rare, making double distilling time-consuming and less profitable because of spirit loss in the second run. This single distilled whiskey often yielded a harsher taste. To smooth these rough edges without adding color, which was less desirable in the early days, distillers used methods like distilling a second time, adding milk to counteract oils before redistilling, or filtering through charcoal.[48] Of these techniques, charcoal mellowing was the most economical, as it didn't require the purchase of additional machinery, or fuel to run a still a second time.

Charcoal filtering was not a new technique, nor was it exclusive to whiskey. People have used charcoal for water purification for centuries, possibly even since the dawn of humankind. One piece of charcoal has an incredible amount of surface area and can be used over and over, making it a highly effective and affordable purifying method.

The Rise of the Process

So, who was the first distiller to adapt this technique for whiskey production? Unfortunately, we may never definitively answer that question. What we do know, however, is that it wasn't invented in Lincoln County. This conclusion rests on two key pieces of information. First, a patent for this whiskey rectifying technique was filed by preacher and inventor Burgess Allison of New Jersey in 1802—eight years before Lincoln County even existed.[49] Second, future U.S. President John Quincy Adams called Allison's application "an abuse of the patent system," pointing out that the method was already well-established.[50]

With the technique clearly predating Lincoln County, the next question is how and when the two became inexorably linked. The search for an answer begins with old newspaper records. The first known mention of the "Lincoln County Process" appears in an 1896 *Louisville Courier-Journal* profile of Robertson County, Tennessee. At that time, both Robertson and Lincoln counties enjoyed the strongest reputations for whiskey quality in the state. The article hinted at regional distinctions, noting that while people considered Robertson County whiskey higher quality, they preferred the whiskey made using "the Lincoln County process."[51] Notably, "process" was not capitalized, suggesting it was not yet a formally defined concept.

The next known reference appears in a 1905 advertisement for Old White Oak Whisky, produced by E.R. Betterton & Co. of Chattanooga. The advertisement described their product as "Copper Distilled Lincoln County process, Tennessee Whiskey of the highest grade." Again, "process" was written in lowercase, reinforcing that the term had not yet become a standardized label.[52]

It wasn't until October 1952 that the phrase "Old Lincoln County Process" appeared in print, in an advertisement from the Ellis Wholesale Drug Company of Springfield, MO. Selling bottles of Jack Daniel's, it mentioned the distillery used the expensive process the same way it had been "by the same family for seven generations."[53] This time the entire phrase, including "Process," was capitalized. So it appears Jack Daniel's was the first to market an official process by 1952. The word "old" makes it appear they used the term internally, or that it was familiar to the community, rather than originating as a creation of the marketing team.

But what was the process? The ad didn't say.

In 1954, however, an ad in the *Albuquerque Journal* provided a bit more detail, declaring, "Jack Daniel's is frankly, EXPENSIVE!" as part of a unique sales pitch. The ad described the whiskey's "leaching of every drop through powdered sugar maple charcoal," calling it "the rarest whiskey in the world."[54]

It is obvious Jack Daniel's is the source for the connection between the term and the leaching process, but why wasn't it mentioned before 1952? There had certainly been opportunities. In 1909, Jack Daniel's nephew, Spoon Motlow, operated a wholesale house in Chattanooga and laid out the history of Lincoln County whiskey. But when he mentioned charcoal mellowing, he called it by its common name, "leaching," attributing its origins to "Africans working at the distillery." [55]

The real reason may be that 20th-century marketing misread what it was that made 19th-century Lincoln County whiskey so special. After all, Tennessee's distilling was shut down in 1909 and didn't return until 1938. With almost a thirty-year hiatus, some old techniques were sure to have been forgotten. I decided it was time to go back through old newspapers and see if I could detect what it was that made Lincoln County whiskey so special. Was it just leaching, or was there something more?

Lincoln County Whiskey

Just as Bourbon County whiskey's reputation was built on the backs of forgotten distillers named Spears, Shawhan, and Miller, Lincoln County's reputation was built through names like Eaton, Fanning, and Kelso. While their names have faded from memory, the legend of their quality whiskey shows up in newspapers as early as 1852—a century before Jack Daniel's began actively using the term Lincoln County Process. Newspapers of that bygone era don't use the process name, instead they refer to these spirits generically as Lincoln County whiskey. What I discovered after scouring Tennessee newspapers from 1850 to 1910, is that writers have left us a few clues as to what set Lincoln County whiskey apart. In the final analysis there are three commonalities that repeat through the years.

The first was a commitment to slow, natural fermentation using the old-fashioned sour mash process, just like James C. Crow. In nary an article is there a mention of sweet mash and Lincoln County distillers, in fact, most of the time they were touting their superior product over the sweet mash produced by Robertson County and Bourbon County distillers. Of course, there were also sour mash distillers in those two areas, including Nelson's Greenbrier, but 19th century marketers never let the truth get in the way of a good story. Their boasting worked, because to this day, sour mash is still associated with Jack and George, albeit not the same process that Crow, Eaton, or Nearest Green used which is too expensive and time and labor intensive for modern distilleries.

Equipment was another defining characteristic. These early distillers, often poor and reliant on ancestral techniques, preferred low-cost multi-chamber log stills. Log stills were exactly that—hollowed-out logs where steam heated the mash, eliminating the danger of scorching with an open flame. This was the primary difference between James C. Crow and Lincoln County produced whiskey. It is also the reason modern Jack Daniel's will never 100% replicate what Nearest made, due to the distillery's dropping of log stills and the shift to using larger column stills.

The third technique that made Lincoln County whiskey special was indeed charcoal mellowing. But it wasn't the only place in the state that used this technique. Distillers from Memphis to Bristol, Nashville to Chattanooga and everywhere in between leached their whiskey. While some used it outside the state, it is truly what set Tennessee apart. In fact, Tennessee distillers thought it worked so well at cleaning up the spirit, they skipped the barrel completely and sold their unaged product as Tennessee White Whiskey. According to William Mida, a 19th-century wholesale whiskey expert, Tennesseans had such a preference for white liquor that, unlike Kentuckians who charred their barrels for color, Tennessee distillers often used uncharred barrels to avoid adding color.[56]

So it's clear that neither Reverend Dan Call, Nathan "Nearest" Green, or Alfred Eaton invented the charcoal mellowing process. But it is a good bet they used it, along with log stills, and old-fashioned sour mash fermentations. Perhaps future historians will credit them not just with one aspect, but with the broader tradition of Lincoln County whiskey.

With this deeper knowledge of the origins of the charcoal mellowing process, maybe it's time to retire the name Lincoln County Process as a marketing term.

Its existence only leads to confusion, and it is far from historically accurate. Thankfully, it didn't trip up the 2013 Tennessee General Assembly. And to their credit, they clearly defined in item five that the whiskey must be filtered through "maple charcoal prior to aging," rather than referring to it as the Lincoln County Process.[57] They were also right, almost by chance, at singling out charcoal mellowing as something their state was once known for as a whole.

In the end, the requests for rule changes were dropped. And Phil Prichard's first distillery is still the only one in the state that doesn't have to use the process. Ironically, his distillery is in Lincoln County. But this raises another question: now that the genuine history of Tennessee whiskey is better understood, will other rules, such as allowing uncharred barrels, be considered? Or will a desire to avoid future conflicts keep things as they are?

Only time will tell.

Reality: False. Not only was it not invented by these historic figures, the Lincoln County Process name holds no historical meaning beyond Jack Daniel's.

THE SPEAKEASY

MYTH: THE NAME "SPEAKEASY" DEVELOPED OUT OF PROHIBITION-ERA DRINKING ESTABLISHMENTS.

AI: True

It was early September 1838, and the small town of Dedham, Massachusetts, was preparing for a gathering of men with muskets. It was the annual mustering of the local militia, where citizens would account for their weaponry and readiness to defend, should the need arise. Seeing an opportunity to quench the men's thirst, a man known only as "a Yankee from Dedham" approached the town council to request a license to exhibit his striped pig at the event. As *The New Yorker* newspaper reported, "the magistrates, not suspecting his pig to be related to the wooden horse of Trojan fame, could see no reason for denying his modest request."

It seems a recently passed law in the State of Massachusetts didn't allow for the sale of alcohol under 15 gallons. The state legislature and temperance leaders were trying to rid the state of rowdy drinking establishments. But this clever Yankee had found a way around the law.

On the day of the muster, the Yankee erected his tent and disappeared inside as the men marched into town with muskets slung over their shoulders. As curious onlookers gathered around, he announced an invitation to see a wonderful marvel—a striped pig. At first, all seemed innocent enough. But as more and more staggering soldiers exited the tent, the ruse became clear: The Yankee was collecting a fee to see the pig, then passing out sips of brandy, gin, and whisky to his guests, free of charge.

The *New Yorker* noted, "So great was the interest felt in this department of Natural History that many visited him eight or ten times in the course of the day until the four-legged animal was the most rational and well-behaved of the lot."[58]

The striped pig story became one of many inventive responses to the tightening of liquor laws across the country. It proved the old adage: wherever there's a thirst for spirits, an industrious person will find a way to quench it—legislatures and temperance leaders be damned.

Tackling Intemperance

From its earliest days, America has proudly been a land of spirited imbibers. Massachusetts' first colonial governor, John Winthrop, had a fascination with distilling corn beer. When the Dutch settled New Amsterdam (now New York City), distilleries sprang up and thrived making genever and brandy.

Pioneer drinking habits varied widely, from sipping hard cider after a day in the fields to downing Madeira wine, rum, or rye whiskey at taverns and tippling houses. In a wild and untamed land, a pint of grog or bottle of rum made a hard life bearable, naturally integrating into everyday life. Having settled down into their new American habits, the idea of legislating alcohol consumption seemed as inconceivable to them as bowing to a king.

But in the first two decades of the 19th century, several societal changes occurred that nearly doubled the consumption of hard alcohol, giving rise to concerns about intemperance.

It all started as the Industrial Revolution found its way to American shores. The agrarian lifestyle gave way to people moving into crowded cities and towns.

Men's drinking moved from sips from a home distilled jug of spirits or a mug of beer or cider from a barrel by the door to drinking houses in town. Spirits like rum and whiskey became more accessible as production increased and access to transportation improved. So more and more men began losing weekly wages to the local public house.

By the 1820s, the average American was consuming an astonishing seven gallons (26.5 liters) of pure alcohol per year—three times today's standards.[59] As alcohol abuse became increasingly problematic, temperance societies began popping up across the country.

The citizens of Massachusetts took matters into their own hands. Formed in 1813, the Massachusetts Society for the Suppression of Intemperance aimed to enlist influential men as members. Publishing a temperance newspaper and hosting meetings statewide—their mission was to curtail the use of "ardent spirits" like rum and whiskey. Their message resonated with certain segments of the population, and the organization quickly grew.

But despite the society's growth, distilleries and grog shops continued to thrive, and stories of broken families and public drunkenness still echoed across the Bay State. Pleas evolved from having "philanthropists and patriots" lead the way to better men's health through abstinence in 1830 to a call for all-out abstinence in 1833. Still, the organization saw little progress.[60]

The Rise of the Pig

In 1838, the leaders of the Boston Temperance Society had seen enough, and they lobbied the state legislature to pass a highly controversial bill. Signed by Governor Edward Everett, the Fifteen Gallon Law mandated a minimum purchase of fifteen gallons of alcohol at one time, aiming to limit spirits consumption in local taverns.[61] Although it wasn't an outright prohibition, the law largely targeted the working-class and immigrant patrons who frequented these establishments.

Small tavern owners also felt the pinch. Meanwhile, wealthier citizens faced no issue, as they could afford to purchase and store large quantities of liquor.

But old John Barleycorn, the patron saint of alcohol imbibers, had secret forces looking for creative ways around the law. Pub owners asked patrons to pool their money so one person could buy the 15 gallons of alcohol and then share it with the others. Grog shops openly defied the law by selling 16 gallons of spirits, taking back 15 gallons immediately, and refunding the difference.

But the story that won over the hearts of American drinkers was the story of the Dedham striped pig—partially because the Yankee was sticking it to the law, but also because of the comical animal imagery associated with it. This clever act of defiance appeared in newspapers across the country, giving drinkers a symbol for their cause. *The St. Johnsburg Caledonian* joked that the striped pig was so popular, "some think of running him for president."[62] *The Dedham Patriot* predicted a new political party in the state, "the Striped Pig party," would join the Whigs and the Administration Party.[63] Meanwhile, *The Baltimore Sun* reported on the pig mania sweeping Boston, noting, "Every hotel and coffee house keeper now has one advertised, and the friends of the animal are starting a paper called 'the Striped Pig,' under the editorial management of Messrs. Chote & Hogg."[64]

Even in the nation's capital, *The Madisonian* observed that tavern signs, typically adorned with keys, bells, or eagles, were now decorated with striped pigs.[65]

But in the governor's mansion, the chief executive wasn't laughing so loud. Feeling he was becoming a laughingstock, Governor Everett changed course and pressured the legislature to repeal the law. When they didn't, the governor took the hit and was soundly defeated in the 1839 election. The striped pig had won the day and the Fifteen Gallon Law went the way of the dinosaur.

Out of Sight

It wouldn't be the last time a drinking establishment that skirted the law would be associated with a pig. Some speculate that the concept of the blind pig—an illegal drinking establishment frequented by the working class—was inspired by the Dedham striped pig story. However, the earliest uses of the term "blind pig" don't appear in the Midwest until the late 1870s, a generation and a half later.

The visually impaired porker made headlines when a group of women, wielding hatchets, went on a rampage in 1880, breaking up several "blind pigs" after one woman's husband took the family's savings and squandered it at these establish ments.[66]

While it's not impossible to think the memory of the Dedham porker may have influenced the name, it is just as likely that it came from the Southern term for illicit drinking spots—the blind tiger. This animal slang first appeared in a Tennessee newspaper in 1841, when a member of the legislature noted the introduction of several "destructive Blind Tigers" in Cannon County and another in Henry County.[67]

The rise of these illegal Tennessee drinking establishments came as a response to the legislature attempting to curb the sale of small quantities of liquor in tippling houses. A tippling house, unlike a tavern with lodgings and food, was a scaled-down, informal drinking spot that sold smaller quantities of alcohol. When the legislature attempted to put them out of business through a system of licensing and fines, tippling house owners realized their profits far outpaced the fines, so most paid them and operated illegally as blind tigers.

Over the next few decades, blind tigers and blind pigs would appear across the country, frustrating lawmakers and temperance advocates alike. This rise in unregulated establishments ultimately led to calls for full Prohibition in several states.

Epidemic in the 'Burgh

In 1888, another term for illegal drinking establishments appeared with a vengeance in Western Pennsylvania newspapers, with little to no warning. But for the first time, the association with animals disappeared. Pennsylvanians were dealing with a rash of illegal drinking houses called *speakeasies*.

The first mention appeared in the *Pittsburgh Post* in the September of that year, when two drunken men, Michael Scanlon and Baldy Brough, got into a street fight outside a Second Avenue speakeasy. During the altercation, Scanlon struck Brough over the head with a beer bottle, breaking his nose. The intoxicated Scanlon then wandered over to the rail yard, leaned against a train, and lost a finger to a moving boxcar.[68] That same day, the *Post* reported, "a number of speak-easy proprietors received the usual sentences." Apparently, Pittsburgh had an epidemic of these newly christened establishments. In fact, the prevalence of these "speak-easies" in the town of Jeannette, east of Pittsburgh led to the formation of an "Anti-Speak-Easy Society" to combat the 35 "speak-saloons" in a town of just 1,200 people.[69]

Wanting to know why the term "blind pig" wasn't sufficient for Pittsburghers, in the summer of 1889, the *Pittsburg Dispatch* conducted a major investigation into the speakeasy phenomenon. What they discovered was a diversity of establishments, rather than just the lower-class profile and clientele of the blind pig. They found that the speakeasies of Pittsburgh were quite diverse: some were modest rooms, while others were lavishly furnished, sometimes down alleyways or in basements of upscale homes. One establishment was described as having "choice paintings, a Brussels carpet, a heavy walnut table, rich curtains, and electric lights," with bartenders in the backroom ready to take drink orders. Some required code words for entry, others didn't, but their sense of flair made them acceptable for both men and women, setting them apart from the more utilitarian blind pig.[70]

So why did Pittsburgh suddenly see an explosion of speakeasies? Much like the striped pig in Dedham and the blind tiger in Tennessee, restrictive legislation fueled these establishments—in this case, it was Pennsylvania's High License Bill. Intended to eliminate lower-end saloons through high fees, the bill inadvertently pushed many into the shadows.[71]

As a result, Pittsburgh was overrun with more than 800 speakeasies. Initially, law enforcement tried to keep up, but the profits from speakeasies were so high that paying a $100 fine felt like a simple tax to proprietors. Even licensed saloons joined in, opening illegally on Sundays.[72] The legislature raised license fees as high as $1,000, but by 1891, Pittsburgh's illegal saloons had increased from 93 to over 380, demonstrating that the law had failed to curb demand.[73]

The Art of Speaking Softly

So where did the name speakeasy come from? Lore suggests it goes back to one of the earliest saloon keepers to ignore the law. Her name was Kate Hester, a widow, mother of nine children[74] and tavern owner in McKeesport, just south of Pittsburgh. Having lost her husband John in a tragic accident at the National Rolling Mill,[75] and struggling to pay the government's license fee, she let her license lapse and soon began inviting customers in, in secret. However, beer tends to slacken jaws, so she had to make sure her patrons didn't attract any unneeded attention from the law. At least a couple of times a night, she was forced to raise a finger to her lips and whisper, "speak easy, boys, speak easy."[76]

While Ms. Hester's use of the term might be the inception point for the use of the term "speak-easy" regarding Pennsylvania's use of the word, it wasn't the first time speakeasy was used to indicate a peddler of alcohol.

Newspapers reveal an even earlier use of the term speakeasy in late-1820s Australia. There, it was used in reference to private grog sellers, whose establishments were referred to by the upper classes as "speak easy shops."[77]

Going back even further, it's possible two English terms inspired the Australians. The first term is *speak-softly-shop*, which refers to the "house of a smuggler"—appearing in John Badcock's British slang dictionary from 1823.[78] The other term is *hush shop* (or crib), which as early as 1827 was used as slang referring to an illegal drinking house that served beer.[79] But how did these concepts reach Western Pennsylvania? According to the *Pittsburgh Times*, a Pittsburgh police detective named McTighe said he came across the terms in his copy of Badcock's English slang dictionary.[80]

While the problem continued in Pittsburgh and across Pennsylvania for many years, it was New York that spread the concept of the speakeasy to the country. With its lax law enforcement in the days of American Prohibition, the city fostered the growth of speakeasies in Manhattan. As a center of American culture, fashion, and media, news of New York's speakeasy scene overshadowed that of the nation's smaller cities.

Long gone is the temperance movement and America's need to escape the law for an illicit drink. The speakeasy has returned, but in name only, as these fun throwbacks to an earlier time remind us to stay in control of our alcohol intake so the law doesn't cut us off. But if they do, it is for sure some kind of spirituous animal revival will be on the way.

Reality: False. Speakeasies were running full steam 30 years before National Prohibition.

Irish Coffey

Myth: Rejection of Aeneas Coffey's continuous patent still nearly drove Irish whiskey to extinction.

AI: True

Out of the haze of unconsciousness, a man stirred. His body twisted uncomfortably, his shirt clinging damp and sticky to his skin. Disoriented, he fought to clear the cobwebs clouding his mind, struggling to piece together what had happened before everything went dark. Then, with a shiver, he remembered the sharp sting of a blade piercing his side. He wasn't sure how long he had been unconscious. Fear kept his eyes shut, but the warm orange glow filtering through his eyelids tempted him. He knew this wasn't heaven, but wasn't quite certain he'd escaped hell.

A muffled voice trickled into his ears, distant yet comforting. Then came the sound of footsteps and crushing leaves. Suddenly, a warm hand touched his shoulder. Startled, he opened his eyes to see a dark figure silhouetted against a bright blue sky. For a moment, the man's mind flashed with the previous night's chaos: savage men swarming around him, cold steel biting into his skin from every angle. Was this person hovering over him another attacker?

The figure's face softened into a gentle smile. Relief washed over the man as one word surfaced in his mind: saved.

The Misunderstood Legend

History is filled with turning points and "what ifs." And in the world of whiskey, there may not have been a greater turning point than on that cool November morning in 1810, in a field near Carthage in County Donegal, when a 30-year-old excise man named Aeneas Coffey was left for dead—but miraculously survived what should have been fatal wounds.[81]

Although his name might not be widely recognized, Aeneas Coffey's influence caused two major shifts that brought the whiskey industry into the modern age. Yet in Ireland, he's often associated with the downfall of Irish whiskey.

Who was Aeneas Coffey? And what did he do that led to this belief? It's time to meet one of the most important, enigmatic, and often maligned figures in the whiskey world.

The Early Life of Aeneas Coffey

Aeneas Coffey's early years are cloaked in mystery. He was born in Ireland—or perhaps Calais, France—with claims he attended Trinity College, though no records remain to confirm it. In his 20s, he began working as a gauger for the King's excise. Unlike many of his colleagues, who saw the job as merely a paycheck or an opportunity for graft, Aeneas developed a deep fascination with the art of distilling and dedicated himself to understanding its every nuance.

His commitment made him highly skilled at spotting the subtle tax-evasion tactics used by distillers—a talent that earned him favor with his superiors. Yet he also witnessed the hardship faced by the rural poor, many of whom were driven into illicit distilling by cost-prohibitive regulations. Aeneas believed solutions existed that could serve both the government's needs and those of the common distiller.

As Aeneas traveled across Ireland, from the ancient Midlands to Cork, Ulster, and the rugged terrain of Donegal, he grew increasingly troubled by how Parliamentary policies seemed to foster abuses rather than resolve them. Embezzlement schemes among excise officers ran rampant, yet perpetrators faced no consequences, receiving government amnesty instead. This lack of accountability only emboldened further misconduct.

Then parliament, eager to preserve grain for the war against Napoleon, restricted legitimate distillers from obtaining grain. It was a perfect outcome for illicit distillers, who kept the best grain for their own spirits. This pushed more distillers into the illicit trade and angered those that held licenses and paid taxes. Meanwhile, tax revenue dwindled, leaving the treasury in a perilous state. Illicit distillers thrived, capitalizing on a lack of regulation, access to premium grains, and no tax burden—they just needed a place to hide from the prying eyes of the revenue. Many moved deep into the remote hills and valleys of Donegal, Connacht, and the Inishowen Peninsula—Aeneas Coffey's newly assigned territory.

In Inishowen, resentment toward revenue agents was intense, with locals viewing them as corrupt, self-serving opportunists. To the people here, excise officers were public enemy number one. They only tolerated the officers' embezzlement schemes, knowing a simple payoff meant they had enough left over to pay the landlord their rent.

Although Aeneas Coffey opposed these corrupt practices, refusing to pocket anything beyond his modest salary, the frontier distillers of Inishowen had no reason to see him differently from any other excise officer. To them, he was simply another scoundrel in uniform.

Fully aware of the dangers, Aeneas took four of the king's soldiers along as he ventured toward Carthage Mountain at the northern end of the peninsula to investigate a rumored illicit still. However, as he and his men approached, they were suddenly surrounded by what Aeneas later recalled as around 50 locals, armed with an array of weapons. The group swiftly disarmed the soldiers, stealing their caps, before turning their fury on Aeneas. They beat him severely and stabbed him multiple times with their bayonets. Believing Aeneas dead, the king's soldiers fled into the woods.

Found bloody, beaten and near death, Aeneas barely survived the attack on that November day. He was sent home to his wife Susanna to convalesce.

The Pragmatic Change Agent

During Aeneas' absence from the field, the government ratcheted up efforts to crack down on illicit distilling by bypassing distillers and instead punishing landlords and entire communities through "townland fines." A townland was an Irish term for a group of tenant farmers, typically under a single landlord's control. This structure, developed under Gaelic rule, persists in a modified form to this day. By fining an entire townland for a single distiller's transgression, parliament's aim was to pressure landlords and local constables to do the work of suppressing illegal distilling within their jurisdictions.

But not every landlord wanted the practice stopped. For many, distilling was the only way their renters made enough money to satisfy their debts. Rather than halting the practice, these landlords simply passed the fines down to the distillers. Fortunately for the distillers, their spirits were gaining a solid reputation through the use of top-quality grains, allowing them to fetch premium prices at market and to absorb the higher rents. By Aeneas' own account, hundreds of illicit stills operated unabated in the Barony of Inishowen, where fines in the region far exceeded those in any other part of the kingdom. Parliament's systematic pressure wasn't working.

As parliament saw their coffers emptying, excisemen became increasingly aggressive. In the rugged hills and valleys of Inishowen, bands of illicit distillers devised strategies to keep government agents away from their stills. The most defiant rebellion took place in a valley called Urris, in the peninsula's western reaches. Citizens took up arms and lined the mountains, blocking the main road through the valley and thwarting multiple attempts by excise officers and their military escorts to enter. With the British government unable to control them, they formed their own government and informally became known as the "Poitín Republic," after the illicit moonshine spirit they made from grain and/or potatoes.

This united, isolated community held out for a couple of years. But after Napoleon's defeat at Waterloo, the British Army was able to mobilize enough troops to put serious pressure on Urris. When a detachment was stationed nearby at Lough Foyle, the Poitín Republic's resistance ended. Yet Aeneas understood that these issues would rise again without reform to the townland fines and the tax system.

Over the next couple of years, Aeneas rose through the ranks and took the position of Acting Inspector General of the Irish Excise, which he held outright by 1820. During his tenure, he introduced new technologies to curb distilling abuses. The spirit safe—a device that ensured honest distilling practices through a padlocked system—became a mainstay under his guidance. Coffey also advocated for tax reform, playing a key role in the passage of the Excise Act of 1823.[82] The act allowed for stills as small as 40 gallons in size and dropped the license fee to a manageable £10. It also shifted the payment of tax from when the spirit left to the still to when it left the warehouse, which allowed distilleries to age their spirits longer without being penalized for evaporation during maturation.[83]

Of course, not everyone was happy with the change. Fifteen large-scale distillers, including John Jameson, John Power, Robert Haig, and others from around Ireland, tried to delay the implementation of the new regulations. They claimed that if they had time, they could show the act would not be profitable for the excise, might harm spirit quality, and wouldn't end illicit distilling.[84] Their crocodile tears, however, were transparent, and the act passed easily. It accomplished the very thing the larger distillers feared. It brought illicit distillers out of the shadows and increased competition.

With Aeneas' help, the Excise Act ushered in the modern age of distilling in both Ireland and Scotland. For Scottish distillers, several of today's largest brands of

Scotch advertise the year of their founding as 1823. For Irish distillers, if not for the interruption of the Great Irish Potato Famine and a great temperance movement across the island, the results for their whiskey brands might be the same. Still, after a slow start, the Irish eventually surpassed the Scots in both demand and reputation.

As for Aeneas, he could have easily rested on his laurels and lived out his days behind a desk, basking in the glory of his achievements. But his creative mind wouldn't let him rest and he handed in his resignation by the end of the year—preparing to pursue a new challenge in Kilkenny.

Challenging the Art of Distilling

What Aeneas Coffey wanted to do was experiment and put his knowledge of the distilling industry to good use, maybe making a little profit along the way. He needed a distillery—a place to apply everything he had learned from working with distillers and to innovate. His first aim was to improve the speed and efficiency of distilling. He moved to Kilkenny and partnered in the development of a distillery at Alexander Gray's brewery on John Street.[85] He disappears from the record until 1828, when he establishes Aeneas Coffey & Co at 27 South King Street, Dublin—the site of the Dock Distillery. It is here he developed a piece of equipment that accomplished his goals and again changed the industry.

Aeneas's quest for faster, more efficient distilling was nothing new. Over the years, distillers had tested various methods to create chains of pot stills, hoping to transition from individual batch distillation to a continuous flow system. Aeneas had studied the work of Jean Baptiste Cellier Blumenthal, a Frenchman who in 1813 pioneered the development of a vertical multi-chamber column still. Using the Dock Distillery as his testing ground, Aeneas explored these ideas. Meanwhile, across the Irish Sea, another distiller, Robert Stein, was conducting similar experiments and, in 1828, installed a working column still at his Cameronbridge Distillery in Scotland.

Although Aeneas was impressed by Stein's technological advancement, he noted flaws in the operational flow and consistency of Stein's still. One of the primary issues was that it lacked an efficient way to regulate reflux—the process by which steam, once it reaches the condenser, is returned to the still for redistillation. The plates inside the still didn't allow for sufficient contact between the condensed liquid descending from above and the rising steam, lowering the spirit's strength and leaving impurities in the final product. The still also had a tendency to clog. Taking these matters into account, Aeneas developed his own column still, supplying it with perforated plates that let condensed liquid flow more easily from top to bottom, enhancing reflux efficiency. When he applied for his patent in 1830, his invention marked the beginning of a new era of low-cost distilling with improved dependability and efficiency.[86]

It has long been said, Irish distillers shunned their countryman's still, but that is far from the truth. The first Coffey patent still he sold went to the Watt's Distillery in Derry, and over the next three decades, his still became a fixture in many Irish distilleries, including James Haig Millar Distillery in County Wexford, Dixon and Company, James Moore's in County Tyrone, Sligo Distillery, Bann Distillery in County Antrim, Belfast Distillery, and Drogheda Distillery. In 1835, the company added a second office in the Bromley borough outside London[87] to enlist both local gin distilleries and distillers in Scotland.

Surprisingly, it also gained popularity among smaller distilleries across Ireland, including the remaining illicit distillers in Donegal.[88] Though more complex than traditional pot stills, Aeneas' still's faster output, fuel efficiency, compact design, and reduced labor needs were an advantage the smaller Irish distillers.[89] Yes, the flavor of the spirit took a hit versus the pot still, but because less desirable fusel oils were removed as part of the process, the resulting spirit was sold as purer and healthier than pot distilled whiskey.

Initially, Dublin's leading distillers saw this tall pair of stills as nothing more than an annoyance. In their view, these lighter spirits could never match the depth and quality of traditional pot still whiskey. Consumers from all over the United

Kingdom and Irish immigrants in the United States praised Dublin whiskey. What the Dublin distillers didn't anticipate was a shift in the laws of the kingdom that were about to supercharge the value of Aeneas' invention.

The Dublin War on Blends

For William Ewart Gladstone, simplifying government through reform and championing free trade were longtime passions. To open trade, as Britain's Chancellor of the Exchequer, he committed to removing "every protective, differential, or discriminating duty"[90] obstructing his mission. His 1860 budget led to a sweeping reduction in duties, cutting them from 419 to just 48.

By summer, Gladstone's reformist eye had turned to British spirits. The Spirits Act of 1860, formally titled "An Act to reduce into one act and to amend the Excise regulations relating to the distilling, rectifying, and dealing in spirits," granted distillers the ability to store whisky in bonded warehouses without paying duties up front and eased regulatory constraints. This allowed whisky to age without taxing the portion lost to evaporation—commonly known as the angel's share. Gladstone's reform ultimately benefited both distillers and whisky enthusiasts, increasing the availability of aged whisky on the market. It also brought in more revenue to the treasury.[91]

Three years later, Gladstone took further steps to refine the system with the Customs and Inland Revenue Act of 1863, bringing more advantages to British spirits through reduced regulation. Prior to this act, blenders could only combine malt whiskies with other malt whiskies—a practice known as vatting. With the new legislation, however, blenders like John Dewar, John Walker, and Andrew Usher were permitted to blend pot-distilled malt whisky with grain-neutral spirits produced from Coffey or Stein patent stills.[92] For the British whisky industry, this marked the dawn of the blended whisky boom.

Almost overnight, the businesses of Walker, Usher, and Dewar transformed. With grain neutral spirits as a base, single malt whisky became, essentially, a flavoring agent. The lower-cost grain spirits produced by the Coffey still drove down prices for customers while increasing profits for producers—a transformation that would have made the late Aeneas Coffey proud. Sadly, he had passed away a decade earlier in Bromley.[93] However, for large Dublin pot-still distillers, it was the beginning of a nightmare, as customer preferences changed before their eyes.

By the mid-1870s, Irish pot still whiskey supporters began pushing back in Parliament. One prominent voice was Mr. O'Sullivan, an M.P. from Limerick, who was alarmed at what he saw as a decline in quality. He recounted how a friend described a Scotch whisky as a "torchlight procession going down his throat." O'Sullivan called the grain spirit used in the blend "silent spirit" and warned it was "poisonous and deleterious stuff." His aim was to amend the Adulteration of Food and Drugs Bill to exclude grain whisky from being marketed as whisky, arguing that blending silent spirit with malt whisky was adulteration and harming genuine Irish whiskey sales. In April 1876, he introduced a resolution in the House of Commons, sparking a heated debate.

In the defense of blending, Mr. Anderson pointed out that Scotch blended whiskies outsold Irish pot still whiskey. He accused O'Sullivan and Dublin distillers of trying to protect their profits by legislating against the more affordable Scotch whisky. He also pointed out that Irish distillers in Belfast had been blending between five and six million gallons of whisky annually since 1860.[94]

Newspapers seized upon this debate, fanning flames as Irish and Scottish distillers squared off. Scottish distillers claimed the differences in prices between the Scots and Irish were merely what the distillers charged. They also pointed out that Irish distillers overvalued their spirits, charged merchants a greater amount than necessary, while the Scots were more interested in selling their product at a reasonable rate. Because of this, the merchants were buying more of the Scottish-made product.[95]

By 1878, the Big Four Dublin distillers—Jameson, Jameson, Roe, and Powers—had heard enough. They authored a pamphlet called *Truths About Whisky*, seeking to put an end to "silent spirit" being classified as whisky. They underscored the integrity of the Irish whiskey tradition and the time-honored quality of pot-still production. The pamphlet framed the issue as one of quality over quantity, suggesting the Coffey still enabled a cheaper product focused more on profit than on preserving whisky's integrity.[96]

While the Big Four's appeal did little to stem the spread of blends, their commitment to quality helped usher in a golden era for Irish spirits, with Dublin reigning as the whiskey capital of the world during the 1880s. However, their narrative inadvertently created the impression that Ireland wasn't producing grain-neutral spirits on Coffey stills—which was far from the truth. Distilleries like Brown of Dundalk, Walker of Limerick, and Watt's of Derry, along with eight others, were actively producing Coffey patent still whiskey. By 1904, it was said "vendors of patent spirits have been every year gaining firmer foothold, and Belfast has become more noted for its success in this respect than for the quality of its whisky."[97]

By 1909, the Big Four had lost their battle over what defines whiskey. A royal commission, appointed years earlier, concluded that blended whiskey—incorporating a substantial amount of the so-called "silent spirit"—was legitimized as whisky by its popularity with consumers. The fact was, it outsold both single malt and traditional Irish pot-still whiskey.

Over the next four decades, Irish whiskey struggled, with the industry nearly collapsing. Many sought a scapegoat, and the popularity of Scotch blends made with Coffey's patent still, combined with the Big Four's refusal to adopt it, made Aeneas Coffey a convenient target for blame in Irish whiskey's decline.[98]

But the truth behind Irish whiskey's decline is much more complex.

What Took Down Irish Whiskey?

The story of the decline of Irish whiskey begins in Scotland, but competition with blends wasn't the main problem. The trouble began with two brothers, Robert and Walter Pattison, who, recognizing the profit potential in whisky speculation, transformed their family's dairy business into a whisky enterprise. They acquired several distilleries and spent heavily on advertising, but behind the scenes were inflating company assets, engaging in speculative trading, and manipulating financial records. Their actions contributed to a boom of overproduction across the industry, leading to a market flooded with whisky and a dangerous bubble. In 1898, this bubble burst in what became known as the Pattison Crash, bringing the whisky markets across the United Kingdom to their knees.

As the industry reeled, the Distillers Company Limited (DCL), led by Chairman William Ross, acquired struggling distilleries. Originally formed in 1877 from a merger of six Scotch whisky distilleries, DCL was one of the few entities with the financial strength to buy up failing operations. They soon targeted prominent Irish distilleries, including Jameson, Power, and Roe, for acquisition. These distilleries resisted, fighting to maintain their independence, but with the market weakened and DCL holding monopolistic influence, independent Irish distilleries were left in a precarious position.

Then, in 1916, unrest with British rule reached a fever pitch in Ireland, and the Easter Uprising in Dublin marked the start of a violent march toward the dividing of the country. After Ireland was split by treaty into Northern Ireland (remaining part of the United Kingdom) and the Irish Free State (later the Republic of Ireland), the Irish Civil War erupted in 1922. If war wasn't bad enough to disrupt trade, in 1932, the Irish government fought an economic war against the British Empire, leading to crippling tariffs on Irish whiskey and other goods.

Irish whiskey lost another prime market in the United States because of Prohibition. Yet it wasn't just the immediate revenue loss that hurt—it was also the blow to its reputation, as barrels of rotgut or watered-down, adulterated spirits were fraudulently labeled as "pure Irish whiskey."

Then in late 1933, when it appeared America's long drought was ending, the Scots took advantage, making a deal with New York's Somerset Importers[99] to sell preorders of Haig and Haig and Dewars in anticipation of Repeal. The first Irish brands to reach the U.S. were Bushmills and Dunville's from Northern Ireland and Jameson and Paddy's from the Free State. Then, just as the Irish Republic was achieved, the onset of World War II brought on an isolationist policy under the de Valera government. Further tariffs through the 1950s brought about the end of all but a handful of distilleries. In 1966, led by John Clement Ryan of the Powers family, the few remaining distilleries in the Republic merged into a single company. This move may have been the only thing that saved Irish whiskey from total extinction.

So the reality is, Aeneas Coffey had little to no direct impact on the downfall of Irish whiskey. Rather than blaming *him*, the emphasis should be on elements out of the industry's control and the comedy of errors that took place during governmental transitions and war.

It's time to give Aeneas a break—and rather than tearing him down, he should be recognized for the several positive contributions he brought to the industry. Not only did he help tackle the issue of illicit distilling, he played a part in modernizing the industry through the Excise Act of 1823 and the creation of his patent still. If not for that patent still, the blended Irish whiskey that brought the country back from obscurity—Jameson—might not have been the success that it became.

It may be a bold statement, but Aeneas Coffey isn't the villain of Irish whiskey—he is actually one of its greatest unsung heroes.

Reality: False. The unfair lore surrounding Aeneas keeps us from celebrating his positive impact on modern whiskey.

Bottle Aging

Myth: Whiskey continues to age in the bottle.

AI: False

For the whiskey lover in me, it was a dream trip—a cross-country adventure culminating in the sampling of whiskeys from one of the largest pre-Prohibition whiskey finds in history.

It all began when a listener of my *Whiskey Lore* podcast reached out, asking me to help analyze nearly two dozen carboys (large glass jugs) of whiskey discovered in a family vault alongside unopened, 100-year-old bottles of Bourbon. It was an invitation I could not turn down. It ended up being an incredible moment, sampling some of the most unique spirits ever to cross my lips. I was tasting a true legacy of American whiskey, preserved for a century in glass. As a reward for me coming all the way out west, I went home with a couple of pints and half-pints of pre-Prohibition Old Taylor and Hermitage whiskeys from their collection.

Some people would have locked the bottles away, watching their value rise or using them as showpieces. Others might have sold them. But for me, whiskey is meant for sharing. So, I contacted two whiskey-history-loving friends in Kentucky and invited them to join me at Colonel Edmund Haynes Taylor's gravesite in Frankfort. Taylor was not only the namesake of Old Taylor whiskey, but also had connections to the Hermitage Distillery. What better way to enjoy these whiskeys than to enjoy them with friends while toasting the legacy of the man himself?

Before meeting up with my friends Jerry and Todd, I had a long drive ahead from Los Angeles to Kentucky and decided to stop at a few distilleries along the way.

One of my visits was to the Huber family's Starlight Distillery in Southern Indiana. A family-run distillery and winery, I'd learned about them through fans of my Instagram account and was excited to see what the buzz was about. They took me on a tour of the farm, the stillhouse, and the warehouse, where I sampled some of their experimental whiskeys. After meeting the whole family, I couldn't think of a better way to show my appreciation than by cracking open that 100-year-old bottle of Old Taylor to share with them.

Before opening the bottle, everyone gathered around with glasses in hand, eager to taste this piece of Bourbon history. Opening it felt like an event in itself, knowing we were releasing alcohol vapors that had been trapped since 1917. After a toast, we raised our glasses, not knowing exactly what to expect. It was a surreal moment, drinking the fruits of someone's labor from a century ago.

Before heading on to Frankfort, I had one more stop in Louisville. Jerry Daniels, who runs Stone Fences Tours out of central Kentucky, invited me to meet him at the Frazier Museum for a behind-the-scenes tour with Stephen Yates, the museum's sales manager and host of their tasting series on YouTube. With the museum serving as the head of the Kentucky Bourbon Trail, it seemed fitting to bring my bottle of Old Taylor there to share.

Watching Jerry and Stephen experience that same moment of reverence was a joy. But as we took a sip, something was different for me. Beyond the deep respect for the spirit and its history, my palate seemed to engage more fully with the spirit this second time, and I couldn't escape the oddest feeling. I thought, "this whiskey tastes a bit young." What I was tasting were pronounced notes of alcohol and bready yeast—flavors that age out of a whiskey, the longer it stays in a barrel. I kept my thoughts to myself, letting my friends savor the moment.

But now I was perplexed; how could a 100-year-old whiskey taste young? Dusty bottles of historic whiskey are highly prized and go for sky-high prices. Something didn't add up.

What I was being reminded of was that whisky, once placed in an air tight bottle, stops maturing.

It was a lesson I'd learned back in my 20s, when my father-in-law gifted me with a bottle of Chivas Regal 16 year old blended Scotch whisky. Not being a whisky drinker himself, he'd held onto the bottle for a couple of years but had no intention of drinking it. When he gave it to me, my first assumption was that I had just been gifted a Scotch that was now around 18 years old. I decided to hold onto it a bit longer. After a year and a half went by, I finally decided to open it.

The problem was, I had no idea what a 16 year old whisky tasted like, let alone a 20 year old whisky. As a beer drinker I found it harsh, but thought that was what a refined 18-year-old whisky was supposed to taste like. Still, I had to tame it down and bought some whiskey sour mix to make it palatable. Yeah, yeah, I know. I was young, okay?

I started telling that story to my non-whiskey drinking compatriots, but one day I told the story in front of a whiskey enthusiast. He shook his head knowingly and then lowered the boom. "You know whiskey doesn't age in a bottle."

Talk about being disappointed. It was my first brush with the myths surrounding whiskey. I honestly didn't want to believe it at first. After all, wine and champagne connoisseurs talk about vintages and how wine develops as it spends year after year tucked away in cool dry cellars. Why wouldn't a bottle of whiskey age like a bottle of wine?

Those bottles of Chivas and Old Taylor were about to send me on a mission of discovery.

Whiskey and Wine

To understand what happens to whiskey in a bottle, it helps to start with the differences between wine and whiskey. Although both are alcoholic beverages, they undergo distinct processes. Wine develops low levels of alcohol through fermentation alone, much like beer. Whiskey starts as a fermented "beer" but is then distilled to a higher alcohol level, similar to how brandy is made by distilling wine. This transformation in character from low to high alcohol content has a profound effect on how these beverages age.

In a bottle, wine's delicate mix of acids, sugars, and other compounds remain active and continue to evolve in a low-oxygen environment. Corks allow tiny amounts of oxygen to interact with the wine, a controlled oxidation process that softens tannins and develops the wine's flavors. This bottle-aging process creates more complex aromas and flavors as esters and other compounds change over time, with red wines benefiting particularly from this method thanks to their higher tannin and acid content. For wine, conditions like cool temperatures, high humidity, and minimal light exposure are essential to its aging process.

Whiskey, on the other hand, relies on the barrel for its character development, beyond the flavors of the original distillate. As whiskey ages, it interacts with the wood, soaking in and out of it as temperatures fluctuate. The porous wood provides just the right amount of oxidation, while simultaneously mellowing harsher elements like fusel oils through contact with the wood itself. This unique aging environment encourages the high-proof whiskey to gain complexity, color, and reduces or eliminates youthful notes. Once whiskey is placed in a bottle, however, its high alcohol content (usually over 40% ABV) keeps it stable and resistant to further oxidation. If sealed with airtight caps, a bottle of whiskey essentially becomes a time capsule, locking in the personality of a whiskey.

Yet, even whiskey doesn't remain unchanged indefinitely. Take my "young" tasting bottle of Old Taylor, for example. While a sealed bottle is mostly airtight, over a century, some evaporation is inevitable, allowing oxygen to slowly seep in. When I visited the California family who invited me to sample their pre-Prohibition whiskey, they showed me several bottles the auction house had rejected because of excessive evaporation. With heat or dry conditions over time, whiskey caps lose their seal—especially if made with cork, and without the presence of wood, oxidation leads to a gradual decline in quality. Whether it's the alcohol or the water evaporating, the whiskey's character changes, and not for the better.

To minimize these effects, it's best to store bottles in a cool place away from extremes. High humidity can cause mustiness, while excessive dryness leads to evaporation. For opened bottles, a wine preserver can be useful. These cans of inert gas replace oxygen in the bottle with argon or nitrogen, which helps maintain the whiskey's peak condition for a decade or more.

With this knowledge, I revisited my experience with that "young" tasting Old Taylor. My first thought was the whiskey had spoiled through oxidation, as at least 20% of the spirit had evaporated over the century it sat in the bottle. But why would this make it taste young and unpolished? But then I looked at the tax stamp: this whiskey had been distilled in 1914 and bottled in 1917. Unlike today's young craft whiskeys, most Bourbons back then aged for at least six years. I thought about that year 1917 and how the country was heading toward Prohibition. It is highly likely Col. Taylor was bottling and selling his supply as fast as possible to save being stuck with inventory when Prohibition hit. By bottling the whiskey early, he had taken a time-capsule snapshot of what a young whiskey would have tasted like back in the 1910s. Once bottled, time could only take away from the spirit, rather than doing anything to improve it. Lesson learned.

So next time you're offered a chance to taste whiskey that was bottled 20, 40, or 100 years ago, celebrate the people whose efforts of long ago have transcended time to meet your nose and lips. But if you're considering purchasing such a bottle to taste the magic of the spirit, remember: it's the time in the barrel that enhances flavor, not the time in the bottle.

Reality: False. Whiskey does not live by the same aging rules as wine.

Bourbon Street Whiskey

Myth: Bourbon got its name from Bourbon Street in New Orleans

AI: False

To the American soldiers in attendance, it seemed the sun had never shone so brightly as it did that day. High in his saddle sat the man they called the American Cincinnatus, General George Washington, awaiting the approach of British General Charles O'Hara on a plot of land that would come to be known as Surrender Field. Days earlier, American and French forces had stormed the ramparts at Yorktown, Virginia, just three miles to the north, bringing British General Lord Cornwallis' forces to heel.

On this day, October 19, 1781, Washington's troops, standing side by side with their French allies, formed disciplined ranks, their eyes fixed on the advancing British. As the redcoats marched past the American forces, the victors broke into a spirited rendition of "Yankee Doodle," a tune the British had originally fashioned during the French and Indian War. The macaroni mentioned in the song was the name of a fashionable hat worn by the British aristocracy. The song was meant to mock colonial soldiers like Washington, who they felt fancied themselves noble simply by sticking a feather in their caps. On this day, however, the once rabble turned Yankee victors wore the tune like a badge of honor.

On any other day, it would have been Cornwallis himself offering the formal surrender, but he claimed a sudden illness, leaving O'Hara to face the victorious American commander. Approaching Washington, O'Hara made an unexpected turn toward the French commander, Comte de Rochambeau, who promptly redirected him back to Washington. Taking Cornwallis' absence as an affront, Washington instructed O'Hara to surrender instead to his own second-in-command, General Benjamin Lincoln. The ceremony concluded with each British soldier laying down his weapon before returning to the British camp.

When the war had begun six years earlier, few could have imagined the Continental Army—a ragtag group by all appearances—holding its own against the world's most powerful army and navy. The fledgling American forces desperately needed support from an outside power. Benjamin Franklin was sent to Versailles as ambassador to appeal to King Louis XVI for aid. When Generals Horatio Gates and Benedict Arnold secured a crucial victory over the British at Saratoga, the French saw promise and agreed to back the Americans. The Marquis de Lafayette was among the greatest gifts they sent, aiding Washington in battles across Pennsylvania and New Jersey. Yet, it would be four years before the French offered their fleet for support.

When they finally did, General Washington presented Rochambeau with his plans to capture New York, but the French, whose ships were stationed in the West Indies, recommended targeting the Chesapeake Bay instead. Their objective was Lord Cornwallis, who had just been pushed out of the South by Continental General Nathanial Greene. Under orders from commanding British General Henry Clinton, Cornwallis built a port fortification on the York River at Yorktown. Joint forces under Washington and Rochambeau moved south into Virginia to meet him.

What followed was a perfect storm. Desperate for assistance, Cornwallis sent plea after plea to Clinton in New York. For reasons unknown, the commander of British forces remained idle, leaving Cornwallis to fend for himself. As French and American troops advanced on the British fortifications, Admiral François de

Grasse used his fleet to fend off British warships under Admiral Lord Thomas Graves, setting up a blockade that cut off Cornwallis' forces from further aid or supplies. With French warships and troops bolstering their efforts, the Americans succeeded in ending major hostilities with the British, paving the way for independence.

After the war, Americans celebrated their partnership with the French, hailing the Marquis de Lafayette, Admiral de Grasse, and Comte de Rochambeau as heroes. A trend emerged in which newly founded American towns adopted French-style names, becoming -villes rather than English -boros. Amid this period of Franco-American camaraderie, Virginia carved out a new western county, naming it after King Louis XVI's House of Bourbon in 1785. When Virginia ceded its western territories to the Federal government to form a new state in 1792, Bourbon County, Kentucky, was born.

Running From the Obvious

When it comes to naming Bourbon whiskey, one fact is undisputed—it traces back to the French House of Bourbon. Yet, for over 60 years, historians have debated which landmark truly inspired the whiskey moniker. Was it the source of the spirit, Bourbon County, Kentucky, or Bourbon Street in New Orleans?

To you and me, the answer might seem obvious. Yet, when I traveled to Kentucky, I was surprised at how many distillery tour guides attributed the name to Bourbon Street in New Orleans. It seemed strange that they were so willing to give away a piece of Kentucky's legacy to a street in Louisiana. I wondered, what was the smoking gun that made Bourbon Street a more compelling option than Bourbon County?

Their narrative suggests that while Bourbon was regarded as Kentucky whiskey, the name evolved after barrels of the stuff made its way down to Louisiana on flatboats, and then into the taverns and public houses along Bourbon Street in the early 19th century. Although French Creoles favored Cognac and French brandy, shortages led them to accept Kentucky's "red likker" as an alternative. Soon, visitors traveling up the Mississippi requested "Bourbon Street whiskey"—later shortened to just Bourbon whiskey.

It's a good story, but it felt awkward.

On the other hand, the Bourbon County theory talked about on other tours also had its awkward points. Rather than attributing the name to Bourbon County as it existed in the 1820s (when the words Bourbon and whiskey first appeared together), some suggest it referred to the entire region once encompassed by the original 1785 Bourbon County borders, which later split into several smaller counties.

It had me shaking my head. Why couldn't it just come from Bourbon County?

To get clarity, I needed to explore both theories further.

First, I went to New Orleans to investigate the Bourbon Street theory. I met up with *Drink and Learn* podcast host Elizabeth Pearce, anticipating her to support the idea. Instead, I did a double-take when she immediately dismissed it. She explained that the Bourbon Street connection originally came from the words of Kentucky historians.[100] One particular piece of speculation came from Kentucky Bourbon Hall of Fame historian Michael Veach, who suggested the Tarascon Brothers—French traders who established a trade route between Louisville and New Orleans in the 1810s—might have been the source of this desirable Bourbon Street spirit.[101][102] However, Elizabeth pointed me to the research of Bourbon Street historian Richard Campanella. His book *Bourbon Street: A History*, details the famous throughfare as a residential area, where barrels of Bourbon rolling down the street in the early 1800s would be out of place—especially with French Creoles as inhabitants who had little fondness for anything American. [103]

As for the idea of Bourbon referring to multiple counties rather than just Bourbon County—this theory arose from multiple historian's speculation. In *The Social History of Bourbon* (1963), author Gerald Carson expanded the use of the name "Bourbon" to describe northeast Kentucky as a whole. Eight years later, author Henry Crowgey speculated in his book *Kentucky Bourbon: The Early Years of Whiskeymaking* that the term "Old Bourbon" was stamped on barrels of whiskey that came from any county that used to be part of the original Bourbon County dimensions. This bit of creative thinking was picked up by future writers and eventually made its way into the mouths of distillery tour guides around the state.

It seems one of these theories had to be wrong. I decided to investigate further and pieced together two podcast episodes—one investigating the Bourbon County theory and the other digging into the New Orleans connection. By the time I released the two episodes, I felt like I'd found the answers. But as I've reached deeper into the history of whiskey, I've found bits of my own speculation falling apart as I uncovered new information. It was my first big example of how history has a way of humbling researchers and their eager need to uncover something new.

So now I'm on a mission. It is time to get to the bottom of this once and for all. The best place to start is with the flimsier of the two theories—the Bourbon Street connection. To get closer to the truth, let's explore the history, culture, and people of New Orleans.

New Orleans and the Long Struggle for the Mississippi

The origins of New Orleans and Louisiana trace back to an expedition in 1682 by French explorer René-Robert Cavelier, Sieur de La Salle. Hoping to expand France's territory in the New World, he journeyed down the Ohio and Mississippi Rivers to the Gulf of Mexico, claiming the land for King Louis XIV and naming it "Louisiane" in his honor. The first capital was established in Mobile, later relocating to Biloxi, but frequent flooding made it an unstable choice for a government. In 1718, Jean-Baptiste Le Moyne, Sieur de Bienville, saw the potential for trade on the Mississippi River and established New Orleans, which he made the capital four years later. From that point until the French ceded the territory to the Spanish at the end of the French and Indian War, New Orleans operated as a French-only trading post.

When the Spanish took control in 1763, New Orleans became a key base for the Spanish Navy, shielding shipping routes from British interference. The town's trade now shifted from French to Spanish, but the French Creoles—cut off from France—refused to embrace Spanish culture. They thought of the Spanish as nothing but interlopers and refused to learn the language.

As for river access, while the Spanish controlled the Mississippi, a treaty allowed British ships access north of New Orleans. It wasn't until 1778 that Governor Galvez expanded New Orleans trade—adding the 13 breakaway colonies and France.

After the Revolutionary War, settlers began pushing into the Ohio River Valley, creating new trade prospects with New Orleans. In 1782, early French traders Tardivean and Honore made their first trip down the Monongahela River from Redstone Old Fort in Pennsylvania to New Orleans. That same year, Captain Jacob Yoder took a similar path—he eventually moved to Kentucky, foreshadowing the state's future as a trade partner.[104]

But travel down the Ohio and Mississippi in those days was rife with obstacles and peril. At Louisville, the Falls of the Ohio created a natural barrier that required seasonal travel or the loading and unloading of boats on either side of the falls. If a flatboat made it past, the strong currents of the Mississippi played havoc with the boats. Sawyers, sand bars, and snags beached or ripped boats apart at unsuspecting moments. Night travel was out of the question, but there were no ports along the route and there was always the danger of Indian attacks. It was no peaceful glory ride. It's estimated that 20% of the boats that made the journey never reached New Orleans. It didn't help that in 1786, after the Treaty of Ghent settled the Revolutionary War, the Spanish ignored agreements that allowed British and American ships open access to the Mississippi.

Among the most frustrated was General James Wilkinson, a war hero who served under Benedict Arnold and as aid-to-camp to Horatio Gates at Saratoga. Established as a Philadelphia merchant, in 1784 he saw an opportunity to expand his fortunes by opening a store in the developing town of Lexington. Access to the Mississippi was critical if he was to be successful in his endeavor. In 1787, he reached out to Spanish Governor Miro and made a trade agreement to renew flatboat traffic to New Orleans.

Wilkinson's early cargo lists didn't include whiskey, but by the end of the 1780s, official records show the spirit traveling on pirogues and flatboats heading south. But when the Spanish cut off trade again, Kentucky settlers grew frustrated with the newly established American Congress, who seemed disinterested in Mississippi trade issues. This led to several intrigues, including a scheme by Genet, the French foreign minister, to take New Orleans by force, for the benefit of Kentuckians. There were even some who talked of Kentucky succession and an alliance with France. Meanwhile, Louisiana's Spanish Governor Carondelet began negotiating a treaty with the Kentuckians at New Madrid.

Then in 1795, a treaty with Spain finally granted Americans full navigation rights on the Mississippi and three years of duty-free storage in New Orleans. This sparked a trade boom with cotton, sugar, indigo, tobacco, and timber as top exports. But when the agreement expired, Spanish Intendant Morales revoked America's right to deposit, reigniting tensions upriver. Thousands of gallons of whiskey and peach brandy sat idle in Louisville.[105]

To Americans, Morales was stonewalling, but what they didn't realize was that things were out of his control. A secret treaty between the Spanish and the French in October 1800 gave Louisiana to Napoleon in trade for a kingdom in the Italian peninsula. Besides gaining a foothold on the North American continent, Napoleon also had interest in the sugar trade in Saint-Domingue (now Haiti). But when the Haitian Revolution broke out in 1803, he quickly looked to off-load his American holdings. Napoleon's $15 million sale of Louisiana to the American's finally opened free trade on the Mississippi.[106]

New Orleans and Kentucky Whiskey

Stories abound of how New Orleans embraced the whiskey coming down on flatboats from Kentucky. They suggest the rocking of the spirit on these simple sailing vessels turned the spirit red and the French Creoles, who loved their French brandy, took it as an adequate substitute.

Enter the Tarascon Brothers—Frenchmen with experience in selling wine and brandy. At the beginning of the 19th century, the brothers, John and Louis, owned a wholesale business in Pittsburgh and two ships—the Amity and the Pittsburg. These two ships made frequent trips to St. Thomas in the West Indies and their first journeys were down the Ohio and Mississippi rivers to New Orleans.[107] However, travel in those days was difficult. Flatboats were the most economical. These boats rode down the river, were disassembled, and then sold for scrap. The sailors then had to walk north along the river until they reached Natchez, then braving the wilderness, robbers, and Indian attacks along the Natchez Trace, before reaching Nashville and heading into Kentucky. For larger unpowered ships like the Amity and Pittsburg, there was no way back up the river, so they sailed into the Gulf of Mexico and up the Atlantic coast. Any additional cargo was unloaded and any passengers had to make their way back to Pittsburgh by horse or wagon.

The other treacherous situation was getting goods past the Falls of the Ohio at Louisville. Larger vessels could only pass when waters were high, usually after the Spring run-off. When the falls were active, ships would be unloaded on one side of the falls with cargo reloaded on the other side. The brothers decided to remove this obstacle from their path and moved to Louisville in 1806, establishing a warehouse, flour mill, and wharf at Shippingport near the falls.

What they didn't anticipate was a great technological advancement that would be a boon to their business. It came in the form of a ship named *New Orleans.* It was this vessel in 1811, that opened the era of steamship travel along the

Mississippi. For the first time, powered vessels easily navigated both downstream and upstream. Soon steamships joined the flotilla of flatboats making their way south opening up a lucrative trade. If ever the Tarascon's were going to talk French Creoles into converting to Kentucky whiskey, the time was now.

However, there is no evidence New Orleans had great interest in whiskey from Kentucky or elsewhere in the 1810s. A wholesale price list in the 1810 Louisiana State Gazette showed generic whiskey only fetching 50 to 65 cents per gallon—on par with locally distilled "taffia," an unaged spirit made from sugarcane juice. In comparison, Peach brandy held a little more value at 75 cents while French fourth-proof brandy sold for $2 per gallon.

In 1811, W.M. Brown, at 74 Levee Street, was one of the first merchants in the area to advertise whiskey. His shop, far from the French Quarter, had on offer 200 barrels of Old Rye Whiskey—origin unknown.[108] White & Morris was another of the early merchants to publicly advertise barrels of whiskey, though they mentioned neither origin nor type in these early notices. It wasn't for a lack of products baring geographical indicators. Smiths & Morrisons offered 2,150 barrels Monongahela & Kentucky flour for sale, yet they didn't give the same consideration to their "179 barrels of Whiskey."[109] It wouldn't be until 1820 that a geographical indicator for whiskey appeared in New Orleans, when Wm. F. Osborn on Canal Street advertised "25 Bbls (Beer Barrels) Pennsylvania Whis key."[110] "Kentucky whiskey" followed a year later, when William Brooke offered 250 barrels of it in his Paulding's Row shop. Still, none of these establishments were in or near Bourbon Street or the French Quarter.

Connecting Bourbon to Bourbon Street

So when did the term "Bourbon whiskey" finally show up in a New Orleans newspaper? The first documented mention appeared in April 1842 when H. McKinnell & Co., located at 70 Camp Street, placed an ad in the New Orleans Times Picayune for "Common Whisky and Old Bourbon Whiskey."[111] Six months later, Fetter & Lonsdale at 71 Tchoupitoulas Street advertised "10-year-old Bourbon Whiskey." Neither of these merchants were in the French Quarter.[112] In fact, the evidence shows no use of "Bourbon whiskey" in New Orleans between 1811 and 1842.

It's wasn't that "Bourbon whiskey" wasn't gaining traction elsewhere. The earliest known mention appeared in the Bourbon County newspaper, the *Western Citizen*, in 1821. It surfaced later in Natchez, Mississippi, in 1826,[113] then again in 1837 and 1838 in Mississippi and Alabama respectively. Could someone have brought the name back up the Natchez Trace to Bourbon County, inspiring the *Western Citizen* mention? It's a stretch.

So, how about the suggestion that Bourbon Street was strictly residential in the early 19th century? This isn't entirely accurate. In the 1820s, Bourdin & Co. ran a short-lived taffia distillery there, and there was also a soap factory. But most of the businesses were smaller and typical of 19th century towns—doctors, butchers, and grocers. One of interest is Mr. Sinnett's store at 7 Bourbon Street. In 1821, local merchants Hartman & Schmidt moved their offices to this Bourbon Street location and offered for sale Holland gin, Madeira wine, and cases of half pint and pint tumblers.[114] If whiskey was sold on Bourbon Street, this might have been the place—but there is no mention and the business shuttered its doors two years later.

Even if Bourbon Street had welcomed barrels of spirits, it's unlikely they included American whiskey. The Creoles, who never warmed to Spanish culture when they were in control, felt the same about American culture. This disdain ran so deep that in 1836 tensions between the groups led to segregating of New Orleans into three districts: the French Quarter and Faubourg Tremé; Uptown; and the rest of the city from Esplanade Avenue downriver. Each had separate governance, with the mayor the only unifying figure. It would be nearly a generation before the old hostilities faded and a downturn in the economy gave enough reason for the city to reunite just before the Civil War. Perhaps with cooler heads and city unity

Kentucky Bourbon whiskey had a chance to cross into the French Quarter in the 1850s, but it's less likely before that.

This leaves Bourbon County, Kentucky, as the more likely namesake for the spirit. But was the name really tied to the "old" dimensions of Bourbon County? That's another story for another piece of lore.

As for the Bourbon Street connection, I have one more piece of evidence, which I believe puts a final nail in this lore's coffin. It starts with a reexamination of the first wholesale advertisement for Bourbon outside of Kentucky. It occurs in an 1826 J.W. Trembly wholesale advertisement in the Natchez Weekly Democrat, which offers for sale "50 gallons of Old Bourbon County Whiskey."[115] This early phrasing, "Bourbon *County* whiskey," was quite common in the two decades before the Civil War. And how many times does "Bourbon *Street* whiskey" appear in seven decades of pre-Civil War history? Not once.

Reality: False. Sometimes the easiest answer is the right answer. Bourbon is named after Bourbon County, Kentucky.

Canadian v American

Myth: Canadian whisky rules are less strict than American whiskey rules

AI: Complicated

What a glorious day it must have been—the day Noah Webster first held a copy of his landmark work, *An American Dictionary of the English Language*. After nearly 30 years of research and toil, followed by months of rallying financial support for the two-volume set, December 1826 marked the moment Webster's vision of a distinctly American English language reached the public.

The *Boston Daily Advertiser* hailed it as "an extraordinary novelty in the literary world. That any Yankee should have hardihood enough to propose the establishment of his standard for the regulation of the English language, is indeed surprising." As to "the minor wits beyond the water," the article went on, "we congratulate them on the opportunity that is now afforded them of throwing up a good deal of the acrimonious bile with which they are usually troubled ... whenever a production of any merit is generated on this side of the Atlantic."[116]

It was a point of American pride and an intellectual feat. For over 70 years, Samuel Johnson's *A Dictionary of the English Language* was the last word on English grammar and language: a comprehensive set of books with over 40,000 entries with detailed definitions. Challenging it seemed audacious. But Webster, a patriotic American, believed true independence meant developing a unique cultural identity—one defined by its own customs, history, political discourse, food, arts, and literature, all expressed in a distinctly American English.

Initially, friends doubted his ambitious project and he found several critics. Patriot Thomas Jefferson was lukewarm about the idea. Jefferson admired Webster's earlier work, *The American Spelling Book* (1783), finding its morality-guided reading lessons beneficial for children. But altering the English language itself, as Webster proposed, seemed to him a step too far.

Undeterred, Webster built a massive list of words, eventually discarding thousands he deemed obsolete or unhelpful. He mastered 26 languages to trace the origins of English words, scoured American and British texts for examples, and delved into science to document newer terms Samuel Johnson hadn't included. He took a special interest in regional dialects and colloquial language. And he separated letters that were once used interchangeably like I and J, and U and V, to solidify a list of new words.

One of the most controversial things Webster did was change the spelling of a large number of English words. His goal was to simplify the language by trimming the fat. Words like colour and honour lost their "u." Where double letters existed, like in traveller, he reduced them to one letter. He dropped silent letters, spelling ax and whisky without an "e." He moved letters to better match phonetic sounds, transforming theatre and centre to theater and center.

Once released, Webster's dictionary became one of the most influential works produced by an American. As American influence spread, just as Webster hoped, it gave the United States a unique identity and voice on the world stage.

Under the Influence

In the two centuries since Noah Webster redefined the English language for Americans, much of the country has had limited interaction with British words and dialects, particularly in the South. Not until the 20th century—through wars, film, radio, television, and immigration—did exposure to British English increase. However, along the northern border with Canada, American citizens had a different experience. Because of Canada's long-standing relationship with the British Empire, their language was filled with British influence.

Growing up just 35 miles away from the Canadian border, many of these influences made their way into my education and everyday life. It felt natural having a country across the border with different words, higher speed limits, and the metric system.

Then these fun little differences became issues when my family moved south to North Carolina. In school, my teachers marked up my papers whenever I spelled words like dialogue, catalogue, colour, defence, grey, and theatre. What were natural spellings for me were out of place in a world focused only on American English. Feeling like a stranger in a strange land, it took me a long time to train myself out of using Canadian spellings—some I have never been able to shake. As I grew older, these contrasts only stoked my curiosity about Canada and its culture.

When I started doing whiskey tastings with my Carolina friends, I decided to think outside the box and went to the store to find a Canadian whisky for one of our first tastings. Unfortunately there wasn't a big selection; most options were blends my parents used for cocktails, like Canadian Club or Seagrams 7 & 7. I needed something more exotic, so I asked the store owner for a suggestion. He handed me a rectangular box with the words *Caribou Crossing* on it. The packaging looked promising. The bottle came in a velvet bag and the square bottle was topped with a golden moose atop the cork. He told me it was a "single barrel" rather than blended Canadian whisky. He called it "the Canadian Blanton's," nodding his approval. Sadly, I was so new to whisky, I didn't know what that meant, but he seemed to think it was good. Later I learned about Blanton's cult following.

While my friends admired the presentation, I sensed some skepticism about Canadian whisky before they even tasted it. I almost felt the need to apologize for not bringing a Scotch or Bourbon. It felt like I was cheating everyone with my mid-shelf pick. But we were all pleasantly surprised by what we tasted. It felt like I'd scored a mini-victory for Canada.

Schooled in Canadian Whisky

Over the next few years, as I explored Bourbon and Scotch, my interest in Canadian whisky faded. After bringing up Canadian whisky to a few Bourbon fans, the universal opinion seemed to be that because of Canada's allowance of non-whisky additives to their blends, it just wasn't as good as American whiskey. I let it taint my opinion and I moved on to explore whiskies from other countries and regions.

Then one day, I received a message from two Canadian podcasters from Nova Scotia who invited me to be a guest on their show. To prepare, I listened to a few episodes to get a feel for their content. One of their guests was Canadian whisky expert Davin DeKergommeaux. I realized I knew his name because I have a copy of his book *Canadian Whisky*, though I was embarrassed to admit I'd only skimmed through it. After the podcast was recorded I asked if they could put me in touch with Davin. It was time to get past American opinions and delve deeper into the world of Canadian whisky.

During my interview with Davin, I told him "what confuses me and confuses a lot of people is that some of the rules for Canadian whisky feel very liberal. And I think it causes some people to think, oh, is this really good-quality stuff or not?"[117]

What I was referring to is Canada's 9.09% rule, which allows for the blending of a specific percentage of flavorings into whisky. This regulation stems from long-standing Canadian distilling and blending traditions. Specifically, it permits up to 1/11th (or 9.09%) of a blended Canadian whisky's alcohol content to consist of non-Canadian whisky or other flavorings.

If that number seems oddly specific, it dates back to a time when Canadian blenders were allowed to add an additional 10% over the absolute alcohol content in a blend—resulting in a total of 110%. To make things simpler (although this is debatable coming from someone not so great at math), they worked out a formula to scale the measurement back to 100%. The math: 10 divided by 110 equals 9.09%.

Since most Canadian whisky sold in the United States is blended and falls under this rule, many Americans assume that it's somehow inferior to U.S. spirits because of the added flavorings.

Expecting Davin to offer some concessions or marketing spin, I was surprised when he passionately argued the opposite—that Canadian whisky's standards offered a unique advantage over American whiskey.

He pointed out that the rules for Canadian and American blended whiskey were essentially the same thing. Both are bottled at a minimum of 40% alcohol by volume (ABV). They can both be distilled to 190 proof or over, as long as it still possesses the taste, aroma, and characteristics generally attributed to whisky.

What gave the Canadians the advantage, he said, was they have to age their spirits for three years in small wood to call it whisky;[118] the American whiskey standard, except corn whisky, says the spirit only have to touch the inside of an oak barrel—there is no age requirement. This may be splitting hairs to some, but it is hard to deny that whiskies do gain benefits from aging.

Apples to Apples; Bourbon to Canadian

Now, I hear my Bourbon drinking friends saying, "hold on, wait a minute! Bourbon has an age requirement—doesn't it?"

Well, that is just it. What Davin is comparing is the Canadian whisky standard to the "generic" American whiskey standard—not to Bourbon. And usually what we think of is the regulation for "straight" Bourbon rather than standard Bourbon.

To be labeled as "straight," Bourbon must age at least two years in new charred oak barrels (with an age statement if under four years). On the other hand, standard Bourbon only needs to be put in a new charred oak barrel—nothing states for how long. Both straight and standard Bourbon cannot be distilled above 160 proof (80% alcohol by volume), a rule that helps retain flavors that would be lost at higher proofs. Additionally, Bourbon must enter the barrel at no more than 125 proof (62.5% ABV) and include at least 51% corn in the mash bill. Bourbon also doesn't allow for added grain neutral spirits, flavorings, or colorants.

In this case, straight Bourbon appears to have a higher production rule set than the Canadian whisky standard, so his suggestion was that generic American whiskey rules provide a more direct, apples-to-apples comparison.

Something else to consider is that, just because there are minimum requirements, it doesn't mean distillers are hanging onto the lowest rung on the ladder. Plenty of Canadian whiskies are distilled and aged to meet or even exceed standards comparable to those for straight Bourbon. The only lingering issue remains transparency regarding added flavorings which is allowed in both Canadian and generic American whiskeys—something neither are required to disclose.

Then, after a chat with Dr. Don Livermore, Master Blender for J.P. Wiser's in Windsor, Ontario, I realized I'd misunderstood Canada's 9.09% rule and its relationship to American whiskey flavoring rules. American whiskey allows additives like caramel, fruit juice, sugar, spices, grain neutral spirits, and wine—capped at 2.5% by volume. If they add more, it must be labeled "flavored whiskey." Canada's rules are much stricter. In Canada, flavorings are limited to spirits and wine. The spirits used must be aged at least two years in small wood casks, which includes options like Bourbon and Tennessee whiskey, while many non-U.S. produced whiskies, by default, will be aged three years. Beyond wine—rum, tequila, sherry, and other spirits are also allowed as flavorings, but they must meet the two year aged in small wood requirement. So as Don points out, these are not sugars and spices, they are fermented and distilled spirits meant to elevate the quality of the spirit, not just work as an inexpensive flavor enhancer.

The reality is, comparing Canadian whisky rules to generic American whiskey standards isn't a fair fight. The term *blend* might seem universal, but Canadian whisky operates at a higher baseline. Between the three-year aging minimum, precise flavoring standards, and the 9.09% rule, there's a clear effort to elevate the spirit.

But flavoring isn't the only thing different about Canadian blends. What I am about to unveil is a time honored technique that is a slice of genius. It is a natural process with flexibility that might turn a few Bourbon distillers heads.

How Canadian Blends Outsmart Bourbon

Thinking back to my school days, I remember how frustrated I was that some of my teachers thought I simply couldn't spell. Growing up in the South, they were unaware of my prior education and assumed I was the problem. In that same way, American whiskey fans assume the Canadians approach blending whisky the same way as the Americans, Scots and Irish—by taking a high-proof grain spirit and flavoring it with single malt or pot-still whisky. This assumption allows those who have misunderstood the 9.09% rule to see that as the only differentiator in Canadian blends—thus making Canadian blends inferior to other country's blends.

The truth is, Canadians have a completely unique way of approaching their blends. And when I learned about, it started me thinking how hamstrung Bourbon distillers are in the way they make whiskey, while the Canadians have found a more flexible path to natural flavor creation.

In American distilling, distillers choose their grains and create a "mash bill" upfront—before cooking, fermenting, and distilling. In the case of Bourbon, at least 51% of that recipe needs to be corn. Traditional three-grain Bourbons typically contain malted barley to help the conversion process, and a flavoring grain (usually rye or wheat). The proportions directly affect the flavor of the spirit. For instance, distilleries that use over 15% rye in their mash bill are looking to spice up their Bourbon. Those that use wheat instead of rye tend to want softer notes.

The Canadians take a different approach to creating flavor. Rather than choosing the grains at the beginning, instead they just distill all the grains separately. What they are left with is a 99-100% corn, wheat, rye, or malted barley whisky. After distillation, they are aged separately and then blended together in the desired proportions. In a way, this gives much more control over the final product.

With Bourbon, you have a single spirit aging over a single span of time. With Canadian blends, you can let your rye spirit age for a shorter time than your wheat or corn whisky. You can age your corn for 20 years and add a five-year old rye to it, if you like.

So with a Bourbon, if you use 80% corn, 15% rye, and 5% malted barley, aging and warehouse location are your options for controlling how the barrel interacts with a spirit. With the Canadian system, you can age all of the grain whiskies separately to get the best advantage out of each of them. Then you can blend 80% 20-year-old corn whisky, 15% 5-year-old rye whisky, and 5% 12-year-old single malt whisky to arrive at the same formula. But the whisky will be different, because it aged differently. In this way, a Canadian blend could be said to use a technique that is more sophisticated than even straight Bourbon.[119]

While the rest of the world needs to take a second look at Canadian whisky and set aside some long-held assumptions, this misunderstanding does highlight one major weakness for their whiskies.

Bourbon's strict rules make it relatively easy to know what you're getting—look for an age statement or the *straight* designation, and you'll have a solid understanding of what's in the bottle. With Canadian blends, unless the distillery openly shares the details of their blend or any flavoring agents used, you're often left guessing, limited by the broad scope of the regulations.

After Don walked me through some of the intricate formulas and blending techniques, I realized there simply might not be room for every nuance to be detailed on a label. It creates a sense of a lack to transparency and hides the true creativity and craft behind the spirits.

Avoiding the World of Assumptions

The lesson in this? Lets stop judging a book by its cover and assuming everyone does things the way our country does. Just because a bottle of Canadian whisky says its a blend and flavoring is part of its rule set, don't assume it is automatically inferior. And understand there are things you may not realize about a whisky and the culture behind it. It is good to learn a little more before dismissing it. Distillers and blenders are using fascinating techniques—both globally and within individual nations. Allow them to challenge our expectations, give us a sense of their cultural heritage, and bring us some surprises.

The Bostonians knew Noah Webster probably wasn't going to be taken seriously by the British when he revised the English language for Americans. But his work led to the development of an American culture and value system that sets us apart. And isn't that what makes the world so fascinating to explore? It's the same with whisky.

Reality: False. Versus the generic American whiskey standards Canadian's aging requirements and flavoring restrictions are more strict. It is when comparing to Bourbon and straight whiskeys it becomes more complicated.

Triple Distilled

Myth: All Irish whiskey is triple distilled

AI: False

In an industry brimming with myths and legends due to a lack of clear documentation, one of the greatest gifts to whiskey historians is an epic work by journalist-turned-distillery-explorer Alfred Barnard. After writing a popular series of articles on breweries, Barnard set off across Great Britain to document the whisky industry to show the public just how important it had become. This effort was compiled in the book *The Whisky Distilleries of the United Kingdom* (1887). In it, Barnard documented 163 distilleries across Scotland, Ireland, and England, meticulously cataloging as many details about the facilities as possible. His work has become an invaluable resource, offering a vivid snapshot of the era.

Each chapter in Barnard's book reads like a travelogue as he and his entourage zig-zag across each country. Along the way, he describes the cities and villages they visit, sharing details about the community and its history before delving into the distillery background and ownership. He then dives into descriptions of the buildings, equipment, processes, and the spirits each distillery was producing. The only thing he typically avoids is tasting notes or specifics about the whiskies themselves. It is an invaluable resource for truth seekers.

Armed with Barnard's book, I set out to explore one of the enduring legacies of Irish whiskey—the tradition of triple distillation. Often seen as integral to the "Irish style," triple distillation is so strongly associated with Irish whiskey that it's practically a hallmark of the category. I wanted to know: Were Irish distilleries in the 19th century truly using this method, or is it a more recent concept?

The challenge in using Barnard's work, however, is that he usually lists only the types and number of stills each distillery used, rarely specifying how many distillations each whiskey underwent. To complicate things further, some distilleries had more than three stills.

Luckily, while examining his profile of George Roe & Co's Thomas Street Distillery, I bumped into some evidence:

> *From [the] Washbacks the wash is pumped up into a Wash Charger, a large wooden vessel, holding 40,000 gallons; from here it goes by gravitation into the Wash Stills, each having a capacity of 20,000 gallons, and, after undergoing three distillations, the spirit is pumped into the Vats in the Racking Stores, which holds 11,784 and 11,901 gallons respectively. Here the spirit is reduced to 25 over proof, and racked into puncheons or casks, weighed, branded, and sent to the Warehouse. The Still Houses contain eight Pot Stills - there are no patent stills on the premises - holding from 12,000 to 20,000 gallons respectively.*[120]

In this case, Barnard explicitly states that they distilled their spirits three times, confirming it was a technique in use during the 19th century.

But was triple distillation common practice for all Irish distilleries of that time? And is there any modern-day requirement that all Irish whiskey must be triple distilled? When I took a look bottles of Irish whiskey on my local store shelf—Jameson, Redbreast, Bushmills, and Tullamore D.E.W.—they all seem to say yes. Was I just witnessing a coincidence?

A Modern Day Barnard

I realized my knowledge of Irish whiskey was a little lacking, so I planned an epic journey around Ireland and Northern Ireland to learn about the industry, its techniques, and whether all distilleries practiced triple distilling or just a select few. I also wanted to understand why the Irish embraced it and what benefits they believed it brought to their whiskey.

As I traveled from Dublin up to Belfast, over to Donegal, further south to Galway, West Cork, and everywhere in between, I found a great diversity in Irish distilling. Some distilleries were producing Irish pot still whiskey (using both malted and unmalted barley), while others focused on single malt, rye, or Irish blended whiskey (which can combine pot still, single malt, and grain spirit). I even encountered a few distilleries producing peated whiskey, challenging the long-held belief that only Scots make peat-smoked whisky. One distillery was even peat-smoking oats, and another was experimenting with potato spirits.

As for triple distilling, many distilleries indeed practiced it, but quite a few opted for double distillation instead. So, it clearly wasn't a regulation, but more of a tradition. According to the distillers and tour guides I spoke with, triple distilling was a longstanding practice, though few could pinpoint exactly when it became an "Irish tradition."

The reasons distilleries gave for triple distilling varied. Some mentioned it created a lighter spirit; others said it allowed more copper contact, which helps clean the spirit. And some simply stated that was the way it was always done. Each distillery had different ways of employing the technique.

To explain more, let's break down the pot still distillation process.

It all starts with the wash still receiving wash from the fermenters—a liquid that has gone through fermentation and typically reaches 4-8% alcohol by volume (ABV). Once in the first still (known as a wash still), heat is applied by steam or fire. The wash boils and lets off steam. The goal is to get the steam making contact with the copper to clean the spirit. Eventually the steam makes its way out of the top of the still into the Lyne Arm, where it touches more copper. Next, it travels through a copper condenser coil and is cooled back to liquid form. The entire process goes by the name of the wash run.

During the first distillation, the resultant spirit is referred to as low wines. Its alcohol content is usually between 20–30% ABV. The spirit is not yet proofed high enough to be considered for barreling and is filled with undesirable flavors and oils. This is where a second distillation is used to distill out the unwanted elements of the spirit while raising the alcohol level to the desired level.

The distiller repeats the process of distilling, but instead of using the first still, the liquid is pumped into a second still, known as a low-wines or spirit still. After distilling and condensing, the resultant liquid enters a gold and glass box called a spirit safe. Here, the distiller takes on an additional step known as making cuts.

A cut is the decision point during the run where the distiller uses a trough and handle to direct spirit into two or three receiving bowls within the spirit safe. The cuts include the heads, hearts, and tails of a spirit. The heads are the highest proof spirits that come off the still first. The initial part of the heads, referred to as the foreshots, are filled with poisonous methanol. As the spirit continues to flow, the alcohol level drops and the distiller determines where the heads end and the hearts begin. The hearts is the most desired part of the run and usually contains 65–75% alcohol. The distiller moves the lever to allow the hearts to flow into the bowl and into a spirits receiver. The rest of the run is known as the tails. Sometimes a distiller will allow a little of the tails to make its way into the spirits receiver. This is because some of the personality of the spirit might be hidden in the oils and congeners found at the beginning of the tails run. But eventually, they will move the trough on the spirit safe to the third or first bowl, depending on if they want to re-distill the heads and tails in the next batch or keep them separated. The result of the second distillation is a spirit good enough for most American, Japanese, and Scotch distillers to barrel, but a good number of Irish distillers go a step further.

The goal of triple distillation is to create the cleanest, mildest spirit possible while retaining enough flavor. Distillers can control how much flavor remains by deciding whether to make cuts only on the third run or on both the second and third runs. Modern Irish distillers use both methods: some cut only heads or tails on the second run and then perform standard cuts on the third. This final distillation produces a lighter, cleaner spirit that can reach an ABV of 80% or higher. Naturally, some of the spirit's robust flavor and complexity is lost in the third distillation, but for fans of light and easy-drinking whiskeys, it's an ideal choice.

The Marketed Myth

As I made my way around the Emerald Isle, I had a pretty good sense of why distilleries triple distill, but what I was still puzzled about was why people automatically assumed all Irish whiskey was triple distilled.

I thought my visit to the Midleton Distillery in East Cork might lend me some answers. After all, it is the home of triple-distilled powerhouses like Jameson, Redbreast, the Spots, and Powers. In the chapter about Aeneas Coffey, it was mentioned that the Irish whiskey industry almost collapsed at one point. It was saved in 1966, after a member of the Powers family, John Clement Ryan, suggested the best way for the Irish whiskey industry to survive was to have all the major remaining distilleries merged into one. After a century of fierce competition, a miracle happened. Dublin's Roe, Jameson, and Powers all agreed to merge into Irish Distillers Ltd (IDL). They also agreed to leave Dublin, with a state-of-the-art distillery being built in Midleton to house all three brands. Eventually, Bushmills would join the company, but would keep their own distillery in Northern Ireland.

While Midleton produced several labels, Jameson Irish Whiskey was the one they looked to establish in the export market.

As the most dominant Irish whiskey in the world, Jameson became synonymous with Irish whiskey. It should be of little surprise then that the Jameson style became the very definition of Irish whiskey. It's a blend; it's sold as a triple-distilled whiskey; and it's promoted as being smooth and easy to drink—all the characteristics that have morphed into the mythological Irish style. If someone spotted Bushmills on the shelf, it didn't dissuade people from the argument, as Bushmills' biggest seller was also a triple-distilled Irish whiskey.

I expected my tour guide at Midleton to squash this idea up-front—the same way Kentucky tour guides remind you that all Bourbon doesn't come from Kentucky. Instead, she doubled-down on it by giving us an easy way to remember, stating that all American whiskey is single distilled, Scotch whisky is double distilled, and Irish whiskey is triple distilled.

It was at that moment that I realized, the consolidation of the Irish whiskey industry into a single company allowed them to shape people's perceptions. All of their big sellers were triple distilled. The first modern double distilled Irish whiskeys didn't appear in the market until John Teeling opened the Cooley Distillery in the 1980s and growth was slow.[121] It made sense why people were coming away from trips to Ireland, with this false notion. As for the tour guide's rule, it is entirely flawed and discounts the diversity of spirits, not only in Ireland but also in Scotland and America.

As I established during my trip, there were several distilleries that were double distilling in Ireland. In Scotland, nearly all single malt whiskies are double distilled, though Springbank and Auchentoshan produce triple distilled expressions. And as for American whiskey, the claim of "single distilling" doesn't fit the bill either: Bourbon is typically distilled once in a column still and then a second time in a pot still called a thumper or doubler. And that doesn't account for American distilleries that still use old fashioned pot stills or hybrid stills. And what she was describing in terms of the process of making Jameson didn't strictly follow triple distillation either. Being a blend, it is made of a certain portion of triple-distilled pot still whiskey, but then it is blended with grain spirits that were sent through a Coffey patent still that I doubt they are using with only three perforated plates (if that can even be considered three separate official distillations).

When I returned home, I felt comfortable debunking the myth of universal triple distilling in Irish whiskey. But one question still lingered: When did triple distilling begin in Ireland, and was there ever a time when all Irish whiskey was made this way?

Triple Distillation in the Irish Golden Age

Answering those questions with certainty is nearly impossible, given the limited record-keeping in 18th and 19th century distilleries. However, thanks to Alfred Barnard's detailed documentation, I could investigate the distilleries that were still active in 1886.

I focused on the Dublin distilleries, which were regarded as some of the best in the world at the time. They proudly promoted a unique "Dublin style" of whiskey, claiming it to be superior to Scotch. Was it triple distilled? In George Roe's case, it was a clear yes. The rest would require a breakdown of the language in each profile. By examining his use of terms like "wash stills," "spirit stills," and "low-wine stills," I pieced together a clearer picture of the practices among Dublin distillers in the late 19th century.

Here are the five major Dublin distilleries Alfred Barnard and his mates cataloged:

1. JOHN JAMESON & SON (Bow Street Distillery)

- **Stills:** Four pot stills (two wash stills, two low-wines stills)
- **Distillation:** Double distilled (the low-wines still in this case could also be considered the spirit still, since it is the last still in a two step process)

- **Whiskey Type:** Pure Malt whiskey
- **Condensing:** Worm tubs

2. **GEORGE ROE & CO. (Thomas Street Distillery)**

- **Stills:** Eight pot stills
- **Distillation:** Triple distilled (explicitly stated in the text)
- **Whiskey Type:** Dublin Pot Still whiskey
- **Condensing:** Undefined

3. **WILLIAM JAMESON & CO. (Marrowbone Lane Distillery)**

- **Stills:** Four pot stills
- **Distillation:** Likely double distilled (explicitly states only wash and spirit stills)
- **Whiskey Type:** Undefined
- **Condensing:** Undefined

4. **JOHN POWER & SON (John's Lane Distillery)**

- **Stills:** Five pot stills
- **Distillation:** Triple distilled (mentions wash, low-wines, and spirit stills)
- **Whiskey Type:** Pot Still whiskey
- **Condensing:** Worm tubs

5. **DISTILLERS' COMPANY LTD. (Phoenix Park Distillery)**

- **Stills:** Four pot stills[122]
- **Distillation:** Double distilled
- **Whiskey Type:** Dublin whiskey
- **Condensing:** Worm tubs

This research shows that Irish distillers were not exclusively triple distilling. In fact, 40 to 60% of Dublin distilleries were double distilling. The great irony is that the one name most associated with modern-day triple distillation, John Jameson & Son's, was actually double distilling in 1886.

As for the origins of triple distilling, it isn't really mentioned in Irish newspapers in the 19th or most of the 20th century. In reality, triple distilling was just another tool in the toolbox—a further step in refining or rectifying a whiskey. Farm distillers likely only applied it when they felt it was necessary, rather than viewing it as a signature style. Stills were expensive, and it would have been challenging for most farmers to afford three. Instead, they would run the spirit through the same still multiple times. But this takes time that a farmer may not have. So they would only triple distill when absolutely necessary.

But why Ireland and not Scotland, the United States, or Japan? I believe (although this is pure speculation), it is related to another hallmark of Irish distilling—the Irish Pot Still style. Unlike Single Malt that uses only malted barley, the Irish Pot Still style adds in unmalted barley and other grains. The unmalted barley creates a much oilier and peppery spirit than during double distillation, creating a spirit that might be too heavy for some. The third distillation would remove some of this excessive oil and pepperiness, creating a more enjoyable spirit for the masses. I talked to several distillers in Ireland about this theory, and it seems plausible.

In the end, each distiller decides what makes a spirit great. If triple distillation produces the desired result, they'll use it. If their customers prefer a more robust, complex whiskey, double distillation might be the better choice. There is no simple rule and very few absolutes in whiskey production or history.

Ultimately, Ireland's whiskey heritage is as varied as its landscape. While triple distillation may be iconic for some brands, it's not the defining feature of all Irish whiskey.

Reality: False. It is up to the individual Irish distiller to choose how to distill their whisky.

Hair of the Dog

Myth: Renewed drinking in the morning cures a hangover.

AI: Subjective

For time immemorial people have searched for ways to reduce or remove pain. Many find comfort in knowing that a doctor, emergency room, website advice, or pill is readily available to keep them from suffering. The desire to avoid pain and illness is so ingrained that the pharmaceutical industry has created pills to prevent indigestion before it starts, while hospitals have rebranded as health centers, hoping to encourage visits by healthy patients, keen to avoid getting sick.

Our ancestors, however, didn't have anything resembling these modern safety nets. Out on the edge of a Scottish bog, in the cavernous valleys of Inishowen, or across the wild plains of the 19th-century American West, doctors didn't exist or were a luxury, and people learned to fend for themselves.

Nature abhors a vacuum, and so, up sprang a host of home remedies and miracle cures. While we may scoff at them today, for those living in desperation and willing to try anything, skepticizm turned into hope.

Hard Pills to Swallow

For people suffering from a fever, an Irish remedy required wrapping a large spider in dough or fruit preserves and swallowing it. If that remedy seems a bit harsh, the English suggested a mixture of stag-horn fungus spread on bread with butter and molasses—and for severe cases, this should be washed down with water from the nearest church baptismal font.

For babies suffering from mouth thrush—a painful fungal infection in the mouth—some believed that reading the Psalms 8 aloud could bring healing.

Warts had several odd cures: one remedy involved rubbing a bean pod on the wart and discarding it, with the idea that the wart would decay in sympathy with the pod. Another suggested rubbing the wart with a small snail and then impaling the snail on a thorn. Even if it was minimally helpful in taming the wart, it definitely isn't a positive outcome for the snail. Frogs were to blame for warts in some cultures, so the best suggestion was to avoid them all together.[123]

While modern readers scoff at these "so-called" cures, our ancestors lived in a world where bloodletting (draining blood to help drain the body of disease, and reduce inflammation or infection) of patients was standard practice by physicians. On his deathbed, George Washington was in so much pain from a throat infection that he allowed his doctors to drain him of 40% of his blood in a 12-hour period, likely hastening his decline. [124]

Like Cures Like

Thanks to advances in science and medicine—and the gradual rejection of superstition as a basis for cures—many dangerous practices and home remedies have faded from use. Yet, certain concepts from this era still find applications today. One of the enduring theories is the homeopathic principle of "like cures like."

Imagine if you could cure a wart by touching the frog that caused it? While that probably wouldn't work, it's not time to throw the baby out with the bathwater. Sometimes, seemingly crazy ideas can evolve into practical solutions.

In modern medicine, one of the more popular uses of the "like cures like" theory is in the development of vaccines. The goal of a vaccine is to help a person's immune system build up its defenses by introducing a weakened or attenuated form of a virus, causing only a mild reaction rather than the full-blown disease. Vaccines for measles, mumps, and chickenpox use this approach. The polio epidemic was halted thanks to a vaccine that uses a dead or inactive virus that couldn't replicate itself, thus again introducing the body to the disease without the risk of developing the disease. So there is a practical application for this concept.

The Hangover

For whiskey fans, one ailment nearly all of them encounter at some point is the annoying and sometimes painful hangover. This condition is familiar to most consumers of alcohol: at one point or another, people consume too much, and their bodies start to rebel. Naturally, in search of relief, the sufferer will turn to almost anything to alleviate the discomfort. This is where drinkers have created their own "like cures like" homeopathic solution, The curious phrase often used to describe this remedy—"hair of the dog"—is a metaphor rooted in antiquity, tracing back to a man named Gaius Plinius Secundus, better known as Pliny the Elder.

Born in the Roman Empire around 23 or 24 AD, Pliny had a keen curiosity about the natural world and set out to compile all known knowledge of his time. His magnum opus, *Naturalis Historia* (Natural History), spans 37 volumes and remains one of the largest works from the Roman Empire, documenting the natural world as it was understood in antiquity.

In one passage, Pliny offers a peculiar remedy for hydrophobia (fear of water) resulting from a rabid dog bite. He suggests applying "the ashes of a dog's head" to the wound, followed by ashes of the hair from the tail of the very dog that inflicted the bite.[125] It sounds gruesome, but the term "ashes" likely refers to remains from the dog, which may have been put down due to rabies.

Thanks to this being preserved in such an important volume, this so-called cure was talked about for centuries. Then in the 16th century, an Englishman John Heywood applied the idea as a metaphor for hangover relief, stating in his *A Dialogue Conteinyng the Nomber in Effect of All the Prouerbes in the Englishe Tongue* (1546), "I pray the leat me and my felow haue / A heare of the dog that bote vs last night / And bitten were we both to the braine aright / We sawe eche other drunke in the good ale glas."[126] To John, a little nip of the previous evening's libation was sure to do the trick. By the early 19th century, this had evolved into, "the hair of the dog good for the bite."

How widely Heywood's remedy was used is unclear, but by 1858, the *Baltimore Sun* reported the story of a German woman who firmly believed in the rabies cure. From her house on Albemarle Street, the woman watched in horror as her child was viciously attacked by a dog. With bloody bites on the child's legs and arms, the incensed woman grabbed the angry dog, held it down and ripped fistfuls of hair from its body. Then she pushed clumps of the dog's hair into her child's wounds. Unsurprisingly, the wounds began to fester and inflame. Concerned, she brought her child to Dr. A.W. Emory on Pratt Street. He had his own cure. Going about the laborious task of removing the clumps of hair from dried blood in the wound, he applied medically tested ointments. He asked the woman why she did it and with an innocent look on her face, she said she'd "always heard the hair of the dog was good for the bite!"[127]

So, applying a dog's hair to a dog bite doesn't really help in the healing process—not a big surprise. But what of John Heywood's great remedy for the hangover? Is it truly a case of "like cures like?" Or will it only fester like a dog bite clogged with a canine's lost coat?

The Modern Take on the Hangover Cure

Science suggests that drinking more alcohol to "cure" a hangover is largely a myth. While a small amount of alcohol might offer temporary relief, it can actually prolong or worsen symptoms, as alcohol itself is a diuretic and exacerbates dehydration.

Instead it's generally recommended to stay hydrated with water or electrolyte-rich drinks to alleviate symptoms of dehydration like headaches and fatigue. For those experiencing hangover symptoms, some find that a balanced breakfast with carbohydrates, potassium, and proteins may help stabilize blood sugar levels. Over-the-counter pain relievers might provide relief from headaches, but are not recommended for all patients as some can irritate the stomach. Since excessive alcohol may interrupt sleep patterns, some people find relief in a good nap.

There are several home remedies that should be avoided. These include eating raw eggs to get protein, drinking pickle juice to get electrolytes, eating burnt toast to ingest your own charcoal-filtering system, eating greasy food to absorb the alcohol, and going for an excessive workout to sweat out the alcohol. There is no proof any of these work and they may have adverse side effects like salmonella poisoning or severe dehydration. And sorry Bloody Mary fans, while tomato juice contains water, electrolytes (like sodium), and vitamins—particularly vitamin C and potassium—there is little evidence to support claims that having a Bloody Mary will alleviate hangover symptoms. At best, these remedies may offer a placebo effect, giving the impression of relief without addressing the underlying issues.

Of course, some may still be tempted to experiment with these cures. However, for those seeking a real solution, the best advice—similar to those pharmaceutical ads on TV—is to ask a healthcare professional, especially if symptoms are persistent or severe.

The most reliable way to avoid a hangover is simply to limit drinking. When a "buzz" signals that you're crossing the line, it's a good point to slow down or consider stopping altogether.

My personal favorite hangover avoidance trick is to walk away when someone yells "hey, let's do shots!" Bouncing back and forth between different types of alcohol almost always gets me in trouble. It's all part of being a responsible drinker.

Maybe someday, medical science will perfect a real hangover cure. But for now, the best advice? Leave the dog's hair where it belongs.

Reality: False. There is no known cure, and more alcohol only delays the recovery.

BRANDED

MYTH: THE MARKETING TERM BRANDING CAME FROM THE STAMPING OF THE WORD "BOURBON" ON WHISKY BARRELS.

AI: Complicated

How do you build a new distilling legacy after leaving your family's name in the hands of another corporation? That was the challenge Bill Samuels Sr. faced at the dawn of the 1950s.

The First Samuels Legacy

When talking about the origins of Kentucky's thriving Bourbon industry, the Samuels name is too often neglected. But the family's roots in Kentucky distilling stretch all the way back to the origins of the state itself. The first family member to arrive in central Kentucky was Revolutionary War soldier Robert Samuels. He and his son John were both farmer distillers who made whiskey to preserve grain and make a profit off of their crops. In 1844, it was Robert's grandson, Taylor William (T.W.) Samuels who built the family's first commercial distillery.[128]

Over the next 65 years, the Samuels family built a strong reputation for their Bourbon. They faced hardships, including the death of T.W. and his son William Isaac Samuels in 1898 and multiple fires—but each time, the family rebuilt. When Prohibition hit, the government moved the T.W. Samuels' stocks to a consolidation warehouse, and T.W. Samuels' grandson Leslie B. Samuels was forced to watch his family's business dissolve in the summer of 1923.[129] Leslie went on to become Mayor of Bardstown, but held onto the dream of someday reopening the distillery.

With Repeal in 1933, the opportunity arose and Leslie grabbed it. He raised money through investors from Cincinnati and rebuilt the distillery near its original location.[130] He served as Vice President of the T.W. Samuels Distillery in Deatsville until his passing in 1936. His son, T. William "Bill" Samuels Sr. served as General Manager.

In 1942, the company underwent significant changes, rebranding itself as Country Distillers Products under the leadership of President Robert L. Block. As Bill began considering his own future, he explored the idea of opening a new distillery under the Samuels family name. However, his plans were put on hold when duty called him to serve in World War II. When Bill returned, his desire to use the family name conflicted with Country Distillers ownership of the T.W. Samuels brand, so he took a semi-retirement—settling down in Bardstown with his wife, Margie.

Building a New Brand

Over the next few years, Margie noticed Bill growing more restless. He needed an outlet for his creative spirit and considered a return to the distilling business, but the Samuels' name was no longer available to him. It was time to write a new chapter in the Samuels' legacy—but where to start?

There are three bits of lore circulate about what happened next. The first story suggests Bill either had industry friends over to the house or just Margie in the room when he ceremoniously lit the old family recipe on fire, to demonstrate the need for a new direction. The second story suggests Bill was so enamored with the whiskey made at Stitzel-Weller that Pappy Van Winkle assisted him in the transition to a wheated mash bill. The third story suggests Margie was not a fan of the spicy nature of rye and asked for something different. As it is with lore, likely one or all of the stories have a measure of truth to them.

To separate themselves from the rest of the Bourbon market, they focused on creating a premium whiskey. Consumers were demanding something less aggressive and brands that delivered, like Stitzel-Weller's Old Fitzgerald developed a loyal following. One of the secrets behind the spirit's success was its use of wheat as the flavoring grain rather than rye. This was music to Margie's ears. To find the right type of wheat, they needed to try out several varietals. Margie, a graduate of the University of Louisville, and a homemaker brought a unique perspective to the process. She knew distilling up batches of whiskey would be time intensive and expensive. Instead, she suggested they try out the different types of grain by baking bread. She made several loaves before they settled on soft red winter wheat—a grain they chose for its subtle sweetness and mellow flavor.

But having a mash bill was not enough. They needed a new distillery and the old one in Deatsville was not an option. As luck would have it, Bill discovered the perfect location, the rundown historic Burks Spring Distillery in Loretto. Located 25 miles south of Bardstown, it was a little out of the way, but what attracted him to it was the surrounding land known as Star Hill Farm. The couple sold their property in Bardstown and moved out to the farm.

Next, they needed a new brand name. Margie knew that to create a premium Bourbon brand, it couldn't be named after a place or a distiller's name—those were already abundant in the market. As she brainstormed, inspiration struck when she thought of her collection of English pewter. Each piece was individually stamped with a logo and the name of its manufacturer, a unique identifier known as a "maker's mark." That was it—their whisky would be called Maker's Mark.

With the name in place, Margie then worked on designing a seal that would make this new spirit stand out. To honor the family's legacy, she incorporated an "S" for Samuels and "IV" to signify Bill's place as a fourth-generation distiller in the Samuels line. (Only later did they discover the generations before T.W. Samuels started commercially distilling.) She completed the seal with a star, a tribute to Star Hill Farms, the land where they had established both their home and the newly resurrected Burks Spring Distillery.

Next, Margie set her sights on the bottle design. While most Bourbon bottles had a tall, long-necked shape, she wanted something distinctive and sophisticated, reminiscent of elegant Cognac bottles. In her own collection, she noticed many bottles featured a wax seal, which she felt added a touch of class. She began experimenting with this idea, heating red wax in her deep fryer to test different dipping techniques.

Finally, Margie completed the design with a hand-torn label, putting added emphasis on the word "whisky," rather than Bourbon and spelling whisky without an 'e' as a nod to the Scottish spelling. I was another choice that set Maker's Mark apart in a crowded Bourbon market, giving it a unique identity.

The first hand-dipped and hand-labeled bottles hit the market in 1958. Their marketing positioned the whisky as a premium choice, with the tagline "tastes expensive and is." At over $6 a fifth, Maker's Mark stood out on the shelf alongside other premium brands like I.W. Harper and Old Taylor, while other Bourbons were going for gimmicky decanters to draw eyeballs. They further underscored the premium quality by noting that the whisky was made from an "original old sour mash recipe" and offered it at 90 and 101 proof.

Remarkably, Margie's design has remained virtually unchanged, even through decades of industry shifts. Her iconic red wax, bottle shape, and label design continue to stand as a testament to her vision and genius.

Margie Samuels passed away in 1985, but her influence endures through every bottle of Maker's Mark. Today, it is one of the most recognizable Bourbon brands worldwide. In 2014, Margie was honored by her home state when she was inducted into the Kentucky Bourbon Hall of Fame—following Bill Sr.'s induction twelve years earlier.

Bourbon Branding

The story of Margie's genius in building the Maker's Mark brand is truly inspiring. But while touring distilleries around Kentucky, I began hearing another branding story that was difficult to believe. The claim was that Kentucky Bourbon is where the concept of branding originated.

It's true that whiskey and other spirits have significantly influenced many aspects of modern life: income taxes, food safety regulations, licensing, and even women's suffrage have ties to whiskey. Spirits distillers also played a key role in the rise of brand identity, using logos, slogans, and eye-catching marketing in newspapers and signs. Whiskey and beer producers were early adopters of advertising paraphernalia, with beer barons and whiskey dealers promoting their brands by pairing logos with images of attractive women on signs, paintings, and calendars to encourage consumption.

But did Bourbon really create the first brand?

This idea ties back to the early days of Kentucky distilling, when flatboats left Maysville (then known as Limestone Landing) on the Ohio River, loaded with barrels stamped "Bourbon" or "Old Bourbon." As discussed in Chapter 9, some believe distillers in areas formerly part of Bourbon County continued to use the name because of the area's stellar reputation.

In reality, however, the story of "Old Bourbon" being stamped on barrels remains speculative. There's no evidence from 1821—the year of the first-known reference to Bourbon whiskey in connection with Maysville—to support this claim. Richard Whittingham, a friend of James Crow, suggested that branding barrels with stamps only became widespread after the Civil War, when the government required it to enforce the whiskey excise tax. Prior to this, Crow supposedly marked his barrels simply with chalk to denote his name.[131]

So if Kentucky Bourbon had anything to do with the invention of branding, it would have to have occurred after that year. So the only question that remains is—was there branding before then?

The Evolution of Branding

Determining the "first" to brand anything is as challenging as pinpointing who made the first coin. Branding was born out of necessity in the ancient world. The concept of placing a "brand" on something originated as a way to indicate ownership. Think of a red-hot branding iron searing a symbol into the hide of cattle. Depictions of cattle branding can be found in the tomb of Khnumhotep II, who lived in the ancient city of Beni Hasan during the 12th Dynasty of Egypt (circa 1900 BCE). Not only is that long before Kentucky Bourbon, it is centuries before the development of Ancient Greece.

Moreover, product manufacturers have long placed their names or symbols on their products. Maker's marks were burned into pottery, and ceramics were commonly stamped with identifying marks throughout antiquity. For these early manufacturers, it was less about showing ownership and more about demonstrating pride in their work or the product's origin.

As an advertising medium, the concept of brand names didn't really catch on until the invention of the printing press in the 15th century. Even then, packaging and logos were still a couple of centuries away. In the 17th and 18th centuries, choosing what to buy in a store was less about choosing a brand and more about selecting what was available—be it a pound of flour, a bushel of corn, or a dozen eggs. Most things were local and trusted.

With steamships and railroads, products came from farther afield, introducing a need for trust in unfamiliar goods. Branding soon evolved to signal quality, not just origin. In the 1840s, distillers with developing reputations like Crow and Miller saw their names used in newspapers to promote their superior spirits—but this was less about a distillery developing a brand and more about wholesalers taking advantage of a quality reputation.

As recipes for creating fake Bourbon out of grain-neutral spirits began showing up in books in the 1850s, distillery owners reacted and brands like Pike's Magnolia and Marcus Smith's Old Reserve Whisky out of Cincinnati emerged as distillers tried to set themselves apart from the flood of doctored whiskies. Soon the rest of the industry followed suit.

By the late 19th century, the rise of a consumer culture further cemented branding's impact, as companies created distinct logos and slogans to build loyalty. This era saw the rise of names like Coca-Cola, Ivory Soap, and Quaker Oats. In the whisky industry, as bottling and advertising moved from wholesalers to distillers after the Civil War, branding Bourbon and other whiskies became an artform.

So, while it's tempting to credit Bourbon with pioneering branding, by the time Bourbon became well known, branding had a history spanning millennia. That is not to discount the impact of marketing geniuses like Margie Samuels and Colonel E.H. Taylor, but rather than inventing the concept, they showed others how it should be done.

Reality: False. Bourbon mastered the art of branding, but it is an ancient practice.

Tennessee Bourbon

Myth: Jack Daniel's is Bourbon

AI: Complicated

Turn on a radio in 1978, and chances were good that a Bee Gees song would be playing—or would be soon. Barry, Robin, and Maurice Gibb's soulful harmonies and Barry's distinctive falsetto dominated the disco era. Their music, with five number-one songs on the *Saturday Night Fever* soundtrack (1977), helped make it the biggest-selling album in history until Michael Jackson's *Thriller* surpassed it in 1983. Their next album, *Spirits Having Flown* (1979), continued the streak with three more number ones, including "Tragedy," "Too Much Heaven," and "Love You Inside Out."

The Gibb family's success didn't stop with the trio. Their younger brother, Andy Gibb, achieved three consecutive number ones with "I Just Want to Be Your Everything," "Love Is Thicker Than Water," and "Shadow Dancing." Barry and Robin also co-wrote and sang on Samantha Sang's top 10 hit "Emotion." It seemed the brothers Gibb could do no wrong.

Then came the 1980s, and with it, a disco backlash. After Barry collaborated with Barbra Streisand on her album *Guilty*, the brothers shifted toward a more adult contemporary sound, aiming to step away from the disco label. *Living Eyes* (1981) reflected this pivot but met with limited success. Barry continued lending his vocals in support of artists like Dionne Warwick, Kenny Rogers, and Diana Ross, while the Bee Gees as a group took a backseat, distancing themselves from being a punchline for all that was wrong with disco. When they returned to the scene in 1987, they did their best to remind people that before disco, they were admired for their unique blend of singer-songwriter soulfulness and lush iconic harmonies. Finally, in 1989 the brothers reached the Top 10 with an adult contemporary crossover song called "One." It would be their last hit single on the pop charts.

Today, some still label the Bee Gees a "disco band." And while hits like "Stayin' Alive," "Night Fever," and "You Should Be Dancing" helped define the disco era, it was only a five-year segment of their 54-year career. Before their first funk-inspired album, *Main Course* (1975), the Bee Gees had already built a rich catalog of folk and soul hits, with 13 Top 40 entries, including "To Love Somebody," "Massachusetts," "Lonely Days," and their first number one, "How Can You Mend a Broken Heart." To pigeonhole them as "disco" downplays the legacy of a group whose versatility spanned decades and genres. How many listeners, turned away by one segment of their career, missed out on exploring music they might have enjoyed?

Now, I can already hear the groans from my friends in the Volunteer State: Drew, you're not about to compare Tennessee and Bourbon to the Bee Gees and disco, are you?

Stick with me. I promise it will be worth it. If only to spark further conversation.

What's in a Name

The seeds of this unusual comparison took root just weeks before the release of my book *The Lost History of Tennessee Whiskey*. After two years of digging through tax records, court filings, title deeds, and old newspapers, I was eager to share Tennessee's rich, 250-year distilling legacy. It felt like the state—often overshadowed by Kentucky in whiskey circles—was finally poised to get the recognition it deserved.

Then, scrolling through my Instagram feed, I stumbled on a photo of a Jack Daniel's bottle with a rough label, clearly an older release. Beneath the photo of the square black-label bottle was one word that grabbed my attention: "Bourbon." Writing Bourbon instead of Tennessee Whiskey on a bottle of Jack Daniel's isn't just a simple spelling error. Since all Jack Daniel's comes from Lynchburg, TN, I assumed it was either labeled that way for the export market or it was a counterfeit. It was a post on my friend Jacob Kiper's Instagram account (@comingwhiskey) and it looked like he was ready to stir up arguments pro and con as he added the playful caption, "Let the arguments begin."

Something about the image and the caption gnawed at me. I gave a passionate response reasoning out why Jack wasn't Bourbon. My friend replied, saying he had it on good authority from a long-time Tennessee distiller that Jack Daniel's could indeed be considered a Bourbon. Shortly after, I received a detailed message from that same distiller, explaining the technical distinctions and why he believed Jack Daniel's, although not labeled as Bourbon, met the requirements for it.

Most people might have been satisfied, but this clung to me like an itch I couldn't scratch. It felt like I had to defend Tennessee whiskey's honor.

My Defense

Let's start with the distiller's argument, which focuses on the technical distinctions. As I mentioned in Chapter 5, in 2013, the Tennessee General Assembly established rules for Tennessee whiskey, closely aligning them with Bourbon's standards, with only two differences: Tennessee whiskey must be made in Tennessee, and it must undergo charcoal mellowing before entering the barrel.

But therein lies the rub. If Tennessee whiskey can legally be sold as Bourbon but not all Bourbon can be sold as Tennessee whiskey, are they really the same? Take the comparison of a Jeep and a Mack Truck. Both are vehicles with bodies, engines, and gears, used to transport people or cargo, but they're designed with different purposes in mind, and people choose them based on specific needs.

Similarly, Tennessee whiskey has its own unique identity, thanks to the charcoal-mellowing process that softens the spirit before it enters the barrel.

In 1941, The U.S. Treasury Department agreed with this assessment when the Motlow family (owners of Jack Daniel's at the time), requested that they be allowed to label their product as Tennessee whiskey instead of Bourbon. The government concluded that Jack Daniel's was a distinct product with "neither the characteristics of bourbon or rye whiskey but rather is a distinctive product."[132]

The question I often here is, but how different is it—really? After all, there are bottles of Evan Williams that say they are charcoal filtered. The difference is, Evan Williams' filtering occurred after aging. This may seem insignificant, but charcoal filtering before barreling prepares the spirit by removing harsher congeners or fusel oils before interaction with the barrel, allowing oxidization of a cleaner spirit. Filtering after aging creates the potential for charcoal to strip out flavorful oils that matured and developed during oxidization. This loss of flavor is why a lot of distilleries are moving away from concepts like pre-bottling cold-filtration and charcoal filtering.

Let's say I've convinced a Kentucky distiller of the benefits of filtering before barreling, can they call their product Tennessee whiskey? No. If they simply put charcoal filtered on a bottle, would fans of Tennessee whiskey be drawn to it? Well, how many realized bottles of Evan Williams said charcoal filtered on them? Probably not many. It's easier to look for the Tennessee whiskey distinction, same as Bourbon fans look for Bourbon. And what about those people who are buying a Bourbon, only to find out in the fine print it has been mellowed like a Tennessee whiskey. Would they be disappointed after reading that? Think of a Coca-Cola fan. If they took home a bottle with that iconic red label on it, but read the fine print and found there is Pepsi in the bottle, would they be disappointed?

This leads to the question of Tennessee distillers labeling their whiskeys as Bourbon. Can they follow the rules of making a Tennessee whiskey, yet label it as a Tennessee Bourbon. Yes. But why? Again, you are confusing your customers.

You've just gone through the extra time and expense to create a spirit that has a stricter standard than Bourbon with a title no other state can claim. Does it make any sense to suggest your product is something less than it is? It would be like having the ability to call a spirit Cognac, yet opting to call it brandy.

The Harm of Calling Tennessee Whiskey Bourbon

Then there's the phrase often heard: "Tennessee whiskey is simply Bourbon that goes through an extra step of charcoal mellowing." Of all the misconceptions about Tennessee whiskey, this one frustrates me the most.

In 2009, Tennessee opened up half of the state to distilling, sparking a boom in craft whiskey. Distillers suddenly faced choices about the kinds of spirits they wanted to make. Some opted to bottle sourced Bourbon; others went for moonshine, distilling Bourbon, or experimented with charcoal mellowing. Yet, without knowing their own history, some resisted making Tennessee whiskey, fearing they'd just be mimicking Jack Daniel's and George Dickel—a fair point. But as these distilleries started selling their spirits, many defaulted to telling the story of Bourbon, Jack Daniel's, or American whiskey, unaware of Tennessee's rich distilling past.

This gap in knowledge partly stems from the impression that Tennessee had no whiskey history before Jack Daniel's. This was assisted by American whiskey authors who laser focused on Kentucky's Bourbon history while ignoring all but Jack Daniel in Tennessee. When the 2013 law codified Tennessee whiskey under rules similar to Bourbon, the "extra step" phrase started circulating. Ironically, in a moment when Tennesseans could have sparked curiosity in their own state's history, its legislators made a move to reinforce Bourbon's stature—as if Tennessee whiskey needed Bourbon as a crutch.

Am I being too harsh?

The next time you're in a bookstore, compare the number of books on Kentucky Bourbon to those on Tennessee whiskey. If Tennessee whiskey is just Bourbon, why would those numbers change? Yet, Tennessee whiskey boasts a 250-year history—distilling was flourishing in Tennessee even before Daniel Boone began carving the first trail into Kentucky. Reducing Tennessee whiskey to just being Bourbon, using a process that was defined a dozen years ago as an excuse—it's like, it's like... calling the Bee Gees a disco band.

If Tennessee distillers truly want to share their passion, they need to connect people to Tennessee's unique legacy—not bolster Kentucky Bourbon's.

After my social-media exchange about Jack Daniel's status, I revisited a Tennessee distillery I hadn't been to in a while. As I bought a tasting flight, the bartender walked me through their different expressions. When he got to the Tennessee whiskey, he said, "but the owner is thinking about getting rid of the Tennessee whiskey."

"What?" I asked, with a bit of shock and dismay in my voice. "Why?"

He said it was because people didn't understand what Tennessee whiskey was, so they were planning to default to Tennessee Bourbon.

On my way out, I started thinking. Would a Tennessee Volunteer fan tell a prospective college football fan to root for the Alabama Crimson Tide instead of Tennessee because more people know their history? Of course not. So why wouldn't they take the same pride they have in their football team and put it into helping people embrace Tennessee's whiskey legacy? This is an opportunity to tell a story—a story very different from that of Bourbon. If owned that distillery, I'd lean into the Tennessee whiskey and tell them, if they want Bourbon, there are distilleries across the state line that would be happy to share that story.

Heck, when Jack Daniel was marketing his spirits, do you think he would have even considered calling what he made Bourbon? Right or wrong, to him and others that made what they called Lincoln County whisky, it was far superior to Kentucky Bourbon. In fact, they were so competitive they even claimed it was better than the sweet mash whiskey from Tennessee's Robertson County—a strong competitor at the time. It was partly marketing, but mostly pride. Imagine telling a French vintner that California sparkling wine is the same as Champagne, or telling a New Yorker that the best New York-style pizza is from Chicago. Or tell a Coke drinker it is the same thing as Pepsi.

So I think it's time to honor Tennessee's great whiskey heritage without putting it in the context of Kentucky's heritage.

Of course, this is just one man's opinion. But what does Jack Daniel's have to say on the subject?

While there are rumors floating around about tour guides admitting that Jack is a Bourbon, the brand's official website states that Jack Daniel's "meets or exceeds Bourbon standards on every point." So "it's not Bourbon, it is Jack."[133]

I'll drink to that!

Reality: False. The ghosts of Lincoln County distillers, including Jack Daniel, would wholeheartedly disagree, as did the federal government in 1941.

WHISKEY OR WHISKY?

MYTH: FOUR DUBLIN DISTILLERS NAMED JAMESON, JAMESON, POWERS, AND ROE DECIDED THEIR IRISH WHISKEY SHOULD BE SPELLED WITH AN "E" TO DIFFERENTIATE IT FROM THE "SILENT SPIRIT" COMING OUT OF SCOTLAND.

AI: Complicated

"Argyle and Mar are gone to War
Which hath breed great confusion
For Church & State they do debate
Through Difference and Division"

These poetic lines open a broadsheet ballad titled *A Dialogue between his Grace the Duke of Argyle and the Earl of Mar* (1715). For the English working and lower-middle classes of the 18th century, the broadsheet ballad was a popular form of entertainment and news. Printed on one side of a sheet of paper, these ballads delivered stories of love, politics, history, and current events, all in simple, rhyming, easy to memorize verses. This made them accessible to both the literate and illiterate, as they were often sung aloud in public spaces like taverns or markets. This particular broadsheet brought news from the north, where the Scottish

Highlanders, led by "Bobbing" John Erskine, the Earl of Mar, were attempting to restore the Stuart kings to the British throne.

The battle wasn't going well for the Highlanders, who were surrounded by the Duke of Argyle's forces. Some drowned, others were described as running "like any hare." But Lord Mar was not about to give up. In the ballad, he warns his opponent that he's not through yet; though this battle may be lost, he's already considering raising a new force and arming his men with plenty of tobacco and liquid courage:

"We shall know how it goes Sir,
Whiskie shall put out Brains in Rage,
And Snuff shall Prime our Nose Sir,
With Sword and Guns into cur Hands
We'll stoutly Venture on Sir"[134]

Despite Mar's threats, the Jacobites would not reform under his command, and they lost "The Fifteen" (as this conflict came to be known) just a month later at the Battle of Preston in northern England. James, son of the deposed Stuart king James II, fled to France. Thirty years later, the Jacobites would try again under James's son, Bonnie Prince Charlie, in the rebellion of 1745 but that, too, would fail to restore the Stuarts to the British throne.

The Great Spelling Controversy

Though entertaining, this broadsheet was likely forgotten by its readers and listeners as soon as new news arrived from the north. But to fans of malt and grain spirits, it marked a seminal moment: the first known use of the word "whiskie" in print.

You may notice the unusual spelling here. While debates rage over "whiskey" and "whisky" today, "whiskie" never gained traction as a spelling. But having multiple spellings of a single word wasn't unusual for the time. This was still 40 years before Samuel Johnson's landmark book *A Dictionary of the English Language* created a British spelling standard. Even *usquebaugh*—the Gaelic term from which whiskey evolved—appeared with various spellings. In Irish Gaelic, *uisce beatha* (meaning "water of life," and akin to the Latin *aqua vitae*) contains a "c." In Scots Gaelic, which shares roots with Irish Gaelic, it's spelled *uisge beatha* with a "g." Samuel Johnson went in a different direction, spelling it as a single word—usquebaugh. His dictionary entry refers to it as an "Irish and Erse word" and suggests "the Highland sort, by corruption, they call it whiskey."[135] It is interesting to note that when Noah Webster compiled his American English dictionary, he followed his sense of simplifying words by spelling it "whisky."[136]

But wait—don't Americans spell it "whiskey," like the Irish? That's the modern trend and it has given rise to some clever mnemonic devices. One popular memory aid suggests that countries with an "e" in their names (Ireland and the United States) use "whiskey," while countries without an "e" (Scotland, Canada, and Japan) use "whisky." What about England, though? There is an "e" in England, but they seem to follow the Scots. And what about the number of American and Irish brands like Maker's Mark, George Dickel, and Blackwater[137] that don't follow this line of thinking? These exceptions show that while mnemonics can be helpful, they're often no match for the complexities of human culture—and are fertile ground for lore.

The reality is, while certain countries favor particular spellings, no law anywhere mandates "whisky" or "whiskey"—not even in Scotland, where the sight of "Scotch whiskey" can cause some finger wagging and a collective shudder among distillers, writers, and fans.

Many in Ireland have developed the same strict devotion to spelling whiskey with an "e." Why, you might ask? According to lore, it was thanks to four Dublin distillers (Jameson, Jameson, Powers, and Roe) who saw "silent spirit" flooding the market from Scotland and the Irish countryside. They took umbrage with the Scots making what they considered cheap blends with "silent spirit," and labeling it with the same name as fine Dublin whiskey. The addition of the "e" was to signify quality.

It's a clever marketing angle and a memorable story. And when you consider that modern bottles of Jameson, Powers, and Roe all feature the "e," the tale feels quite plausible.

But rather than taking their word for it, I decided to do a little sleuthing.

Seeking the "e" in Ireland

With a Newspapers.com subscription in hand, I dove into old newspaper articles, conducting searches that spanned a century before the Dublin Four's supposed "e" distinction. I wanted to look at whether anyone had snuck the "e" into Irish whiskey at an earlier date—and whether America followed suit soon after.

The results were quite surprising. In the mid-18th century, I found whiskey spelled with an "e" in English, American, and Scottish newspapers. The Scottish newspaper dropped the "e" a little over a dozen years later. So it's obvious that in the early days of whisky, Scotland had not yet stiffened its resolve to eradicate the "e," and the American colonies and the English were testing out both versions.

While visiting the Duke of York pub in Belfast, I looked at their walls filled with old whisky brand mirrors, noting many without the "e." This made sense, as Belfast's distillers leaned toward the "silent spirit" that the Dublin Four sought to differentiate themselves from. But then there was Bushmills—just an hour north of Belfast—consistently using the "e."

By the time I circled around to Waterford, the Dublin Four narrative was on life support. When I stopped into Blackwater Distillery, I talked to Peter Mulryan, the author of *The Whiskeys of Ireland* (2016) and he explained that Irish distillers of the 19th century sold through bonders, who listed the distiller's name as the source. If bonders controlled the labeling, how could the Dublin Four have set the standard for whiskey's spelling?

When I returned to America, I continued my newspaper search, determined to spot some trends. What I found shocked me. The first article I looked at was from the *Waterford Chronicle*. Dated Friday, August 15, 1777, it described an incident where a candle fell into a hogshead of whiskey in the Christ Church Yard, causing flames to burn down two adjoining houses. This article and all subsequent articles from the *Chronicle* spelled whiskey with an "e." This was over a century before the Dublin Four claim.

Not ready to pronounce the myth as dead, I expanded my search into Dublin. The first mention there came from a newspaper called *The Freeman's Journal*. In their March 12, 1785 edition, there is a story about an uprising on February 9 where excise gauger Barrington Lodge had his house attacked around 10 PM, by a mob in County Tipperary. Several bullets were fired into Lodge's house, the mob broke open the door, and they stole back five hogsheads of whiskey, distilled by Christopher Downes of Roscrea, which had been seized days earlier. Here whiskey is also spelled with an "e." As were other stories by the paper—again a century before the Dublin Four's claim.

The Historical Trend

The one place that held any consistency at all was Scotland. I am not sure where the almost militant love of the "whisky" spelling comes from, but it has held strong since the 1750s. With everyone else—all bets were off.

My search found that between 1800 and 1830, there were no less than 1033 articles in Dublin with whiskey spelled with an "e," plus 656 in Ulster, 253 in Cork and 250 in Waterford. As for the non "e" spelling, it only appeared 28 times countrywide between 1777 and 1829.

During this same time 1800 to 1830 time span, the Americans spelled it "whiskey" more than 26,000 times versus 71 instances of "whisky" during the period.

England was the biggest surprise, spelling it "whiskey" 70% of the time, but this made sense since they were following the advice of Samuel Johnson, while Scotland continued spelling it "whisky."

The next time period I studied was a couple years after Noah Webster released his Americanized dictionary, where he spelled whisky without the "e." Between 1830 and 1870 American distillers made a huge shift in spelling, with a 50/50 split between the two. Meanwhile, England turned 95% toward their northern neighbors, dropping the "e." Ulster, like the U.S., was evenly split, but the rest of Ireland was almost 80% spelling with an "e" in the years leading up to the Dublin Four's 1870s attack on "silent spirit."

The Dublin Four myth further unraveled with *Truths About Whisky*, a pamphlet by John Jameson & Sons, which was titled without an "e."[138] It made no mention of any campaign for the added letter.

Just for curiosity's sake, I decided to survey one more era—the one where Irish whiskey hit its peak and Bourbon and rye whiskey in the United States saw some of its greatest distilling legends. In the 1870s through 1890s, American publications used "whisky" two to one. With the rise of Old Forester and George Dickel at that time, it makes sense that they spelled whisky without an "e" and stuck with it. It makes more sense than the 20th-century lore that suggests George Dickel, a German-born American, spelled it without an "e" to celebrate Scotland's distilling tradition—especially since it wouldn't be until the time of Dickel's death that Scotch started making inroads in the American market thanks to the marketing of Tommy Dewar. It's fascinating to note that Ulster (much of which is today's Northern Ireland) spelled whisky in sympathy with their Scottish neighbors in the last two decades of the 19th century. Bushmills appears to be the one holdout. At one point, they suggested their use of the "e" was to align themselves with Dublin; this again is a dubious claim, as Bushmills started using the "e" at least in the early 1800s. The rest of Ireland, beyond Dublin and excluding Ulster, went 85% for whiskey with an "e." England followed Scotland with 80% spelling it whisky. However, when the subject of "silent spirit" was put under the microscope in 1909 by the British Royal Commission on Whiskey and Potable Spirits, they spelled whiskey with an "e."[139]

The results show conclusively that the Dublin Four did not introduce the "e" in Irish whiskey, and the idea of a rigid national spelling standard is a myth. The reality is, distilleries can spell it either way. They can even spell it with an "ie," as long as it is the plural "whiskies." However, if their country spells it "whiskey" the proper plural is "whiskeys."

It was lucky for the writers of broadsheet ballads that they didn't face such scrutiny!

As for me, I still get comments about my decision to go with an "e" in *Whiskey Lore*. I have second guessed myself about it a time or two—especially since I chose the spelling to signify I was based in the U.S., and officially the government doesn't spell it that way. I guess you could say, *Whiskey Lore* was a victim of whiskey lore.

Reality: False. It's not complicated. But one does have to wonder how much power Samuel Johnson and Noah Webster had, if even they couldn't control their country's spelling.

Better With Age

Myth: All whiskies taste better after ten or more years of aging

AI: Subjective

A man orders a neat 20-year-old Bourbon at a high-end restaurant, along with a steak. The drink arrives first, but he doesn't try it right away. When his steak is served, he checks if it's cooked to perfection, nods, and finally takes a sip of his Bourbon. He immediately stops the server and says, "Waiter! This Bourbon tastes like wood!" In an awkward attempt to lighten the mood, the waiter replies, "Well, at least you won't need a toothpick for your steak!"

It's a joke, of course, but for those who have ordered an overaged, long-in-the-tooth Bourbon, there might have been some sympathetic grimaces.

The Challenge of Age

How often have you seen someone overspend on whiskey just to impress friends? Sometimes it works out, but if you hear a non-convincing 'Oh, that's smooth,' they might be hiding their regret. Of course, some just shoot it like they're in an Old West saloon, so they likely didn't notice anything but an aftertaste.

Finding an exceptional, long-aged Bourbon can be as tricky as navigating an expensive cheese counter: price doesn't always equate to incredible flavor. Some older whiskies are like jewels of deep, complex flavors, like an aged Comté. But some are an acquired taste like Roquefort or have a pungent nature like Limburger and its air of sweaty gym socks. With whiskey, though, the stakes are higher, as even a single pour can run into the fifties or hundreds of dollars.

I don't mean to pick on Bourbon here, but ten years is a long time in a freshly charred barrel if it is aged on the top floor of a warehouse in Kentucky or Tennessee. Bourbons intended for longer aging are often moved to lower warehouse floors or stored in the cooler interior to slow the process and curb the loss of water (which evaporates before alcohol in warmer conditions). It is hard to know where a distillery stores its barrels, so an age statement only tells part of the story.

Scotch and Irish whiskey have two benefits that allow them to age longer: they are aged in less aggressive used barrels and they age in a climate that is cool and damp. Most of these whiskies reach maturity after around eight to 12 years and can handle another decade of aging without becoming overly woody. The problem with longer aged whiskies in these climates is the evaporation of flavorful alcohol. At 40 years of age, Scotch needs to be monitored to ensure it doesn't fall below 40% ABV. Usually Scotch and Irish whiskey mellow to a point where they take a highly trained palate to pull out flavors. The complexity can be off the charts, but not to the novice whiskey drinkers who are trying to impress their friends. But again, it's surprising how many people will knock back a $50 pour of Johnnie Walker Blue. Maybe they're taking their lead from James Bond, who in *Skyfall*, shoots a 50-year-old glass of Macallan.

What to Look For

So, what are the positive characteristics to look for, after you've purchased that 15-year-old Bourbon or 25-year-old Scotch?

A balanced array of flavors, where intriguing notes come forward without being overwhelmed by woodiness, is key. When some essence of the original new make spirit still shines through, it's a sign that the distiller, blender, or warehouse manager has carefully nurtured the cask. Fresh flavors from yeast, fermentation, and grains should blend with barrel-imparted notes like spices, caramel, vanilla, fruit, dark chocolate, or tobacco. Longer aging can mellow harshness, adding a perceived smoothness that appeals to first-time drinkers, while exotic casks—rum or tequila, for instance—introduce additional layers. But if oak, char, or sherry tannins dominate, the whiskey may be out of balance.

The "nose" (aroma) should also follow this balanced path. An older whisky might invite dried fruit, wood smoke, honey and spice, while younger whiskies might exhibit dominant yeasty, corn, fruit, or spicy grain notes.

Not everyone will experience an older whiskey in the same way. Some enjoy prominent oak notes in their whiskey—while some find it like "licking a fence," others relish its nutty, earthy qualities, or even feel comforted by the scent of fresh-cut wood or an old warehouse. After all, taste and smell are deeply personal, and any scent or flavor that triggers a positive memory can be a powerful part of the experience.

Smooth, How?

The term smooth is another point of subjectivity—and some ridicule. I have to admit, I've been guilty of giving a bit of a snooty glance when someone calls a whisky "smooth." Part of the reason is that smooth can be an imprecise term. Is the person saying the spirit has mellow flavors, lacks sharpness, or doesn't have an alcohol bite? I realize it is a beginner's crutch word, so I take it in that spirit now. To help them along, I usually ask, "What makes it smooth for you?"—a question that usually brings on a lightbulb moment, helping them think more deeply about their tasting experience.

Another issue with smooth is the misconception that it's always a compliment for an older whisky. I've had some whiskies that are so nondescript, I wondered why I didn't just have a glass of water instead of spending $80 on a glass of whisky.

Not All Grains Age the Same

Another thing to keep in mind is that there are particular styles of whisky that thrive with longer ages, while others quickly lose their personality. Wheat, for example, almost demands more barrel time to coax out personality, and, with the right treatment, it can benefit from long aging. Pappy Van Winkle famously built its reputation with complex 15- and 20-year wheat expressions in the late 1990s. Rye and peated whiskies develop their complexity at younger ages, with rye losing its spicy edge if left in a barrel too long. Similarly, peated whisky can reach peak character around eight to ten years, with layers of smoky and medicinal notes, but at 18 years and beyond, it can struggle to hold that same smoky essence.

Those Million-Dollar Bottles

What about Bourbons marketed at over 20-years-of-age and Scotches at 50 or older? How good could they be? They might surprise you. Distilleries in cooler climates have tricks to make whiskies survive longer to reach a desired age statement—including aging them in third- or fourth-use casks that have lost most of their ability to impart flavor. However, most of them are sold simply because of demand. The secondary market and auctions are full of people who buy and sell these long-aged spirits for thousands or millions of dollars. Because of the value, many of these bottles will never be consumed, so why worry about their taste? If the market craves it, distilleries would be foolish not to supply that need.

So let the buyer beware. Know what you're paying for. If it is to impress your friends or if you're out to hold it as an investment, then cost will be less of an issue. But if you are looking for an exceptional experience, it's good to know the pitfalls before blindly choosing a whisky simply because of its age.

Always remember—if a Bourbon and its buyer are 21 years of age, it doesn't mean either has developed into something beautiful and well-rounded.

Reality: False. The key word here is "all."

The Father of Bourbon

Myth: Elijah Craig is "The Father of Bourbon"

AI: Complicated

Under a brooding, overcast sky, a gray-haired man and his son stood in an open field, their eyes fixed on the dark clouds swirling above. The older man held a string tied to a small, homemade kite that danced and dipped as the winds grew angry; thunder rumbled distantly across the field.

Suddenly, the sky split open with a jagged flash of lightning, illuminating the man's determined face. A silver key, tied to the kite string just above his hand, threw a spark into a waiting jar—truly lightning in a bottle. And with that, a man and his son, standing fearlessly in the storm, were credited with one of humankind's great discoveries.

The "Lightning Tamer"

The story of Benjamin Franklin's famous kite experiment has been told and retold to children since that stormy day in June 1752. It's a classic tale, illustrated in school books with sketches and watercolor paintings. It's one of the stories that fascinated the French when Franklin traveled there in 1776 as an ambassador for the Continental Congress. To them, his curious nature as a scientist and his spirit of independence embodied the ideals of the Enlightenment.

But is the story true?

Well, partially. Franklin and his son did fly a kite in search of atmospheric electricity, but they were far from discovering electricity itself—that claim belongs to Greek philosopher Thales of Miletus, around 600 B.C. Thales noted static electricity when he rubbed amber (a fossilized tree resin) against wool, finding it could attract lightweight objects like straw or hair. This early experiment was so influential that the Greek word for amber, *elektron*, inspired the term electricity centuries later.

For the next two millennia a fascination built around the concept of electricity, with scientists like William Gilbert studying electric and magnetic phenomena and Otto von Guericke creating an electrostatic generator in 1663. Yet, by the 1750s, no one had tested whether electrical energy was present in the atmosphere during a lightning storm—enter Benjamin and his son William.

What is curious about the story is that most people take it at face value. It's amazing how few question the sanity of a man taking his son out in a lightning storm daring a sizzling bolt to strike their kite—let alone one with a metal key within arm's reach. But Franklin never intended the kite to be struck by lightning. He was interested in the clouds that produced it. Rather than waiting for a strike, he let the kite rise just high enough to capture static electricity from the storm clouds. The key was there to collect the static charge, which he directed into a Leyden jar lined with metal foil—a method he believed would isolate and store the energy. There was little danger to the boy, who actually wasn't a boy at all. William Franklin was in his early 20s.

The legend of Franklin's experiment, then, is partly a myth. He didn't discover electricity; he merely demonstrated its natural presence in the clouds above.

Patting the Wrong Back

The story of Ben Franklin and his son is a classic example of how the search for firsts and a single act can inspire myths and lore, often fueled by overzealous storytellers who stretch the original details far beyond their true scope.

There are numerous examples of individuals gaining fame for inventions that, in reality, were built upon others' ideas.

Thomas Edison, for instance, is often credited with inventing the incandescent light bulb. A master of self-promotion, Edison famously claimed to have failed 1,000 times before achieving success. In truth, a year before Edison introduced his bulb, English inventor Sir Joseph Swan had developed a light bulb with a carbonized paper filament that could burn for about 13½ hours, and even received a patent for it. However, Edison secured commercial success by developing a longer-lasting bamboo filament and refining the design for mass production, ensuring his place in history.

Similarly, Scotsman James Watt is often named as the inventor of the steam engine, a technology that eventually transformed whiskey distillation. Yet Thomas Newcomen had developed a basic steam engine well before Watt. Watt's true innovation was in adding a separate condenser, making the engine far more efficient and practical for widespread industrial use.

Whiskey has its own share of tall tales surrounding invention and discovery, and one of the most enduring involves Reverend Elijah Craig, a Baptist minister often hailed as "The Father of Bourbon." According to legend, Craig was the first to char the inside of a barrel and use it for aging his whiskey—thus he invented Bourbon. But did he truly make this groundbreaking discovery—and does he deserve claim to the title? Let's take a closer look at the man behind the legend.

The Story of Elijah Craig

Born in 1738, young Elijah Craig was raised on his family's tobacco farm in Orange County, Virginia. Instilled with a natural curiosity, inner passions, and a strong will, Elijah was an eager vessel waiting for a cause. His father, Toliver Craig, introduced the family to the Baptist faith—no small decision in early Colonial America. Under British rule, colonists were expected to attend the state-sanctioned Anglican Church (Church of England). Preaching outside the Anglican doctrine required a license. Of course, a Baptist license was out of the question. Nevertheless, Toliver and his sons Elijah, Joseph, and Lewis preached openly, running afoul of the law.[140]

Around 1771, Elijah organized his first ministry at the Blue Run Baptist Church in Orange County.[141] News of his powerful sermons spread quickly. Religious chronicler James Taylor described Elijah's preaching style in 1827: "His preaching was of the most solemn style, his appearance, as a man who had just come from the dead ... the sweet melody of his voice, both in preaching and singing, bore all down before it; and when his voice was extended, it was like the loud sound of a sweet trumpet." But his fervor brought him into conflict with the authorities, and he was jailed for preaching without a license in both Culpeper and Orange counties.[142] Feeling the spirit of his faith deep in his bones, Elijah preached so loudly from his jail cell that jailers in Orange County put him in solitary confinement to give their ears a rest.

Two items penned in 1776 by Virginian Thomas Jefferson would change Elijah's life. The Declaration of Independence proclaimed liberty from British rule, and the Declaration of Rights, incorporated into Virginia's new constitution, guaranteed the free exercise of religion, weakening the Anglican Church's control. This newfound freedom ignited Craig's passion for advocating Baptist interests, leading him to participate in the state's Revolutionary conventions[143] and work with the general assembly, where he became acquainted with influential figures like Patrick Henry and "the Father of the Constitution," James Madison. Yet, even with this pronounced new found freedom, Baptists remained outsiders in Virginia due to their anti-slavery stance—though Elijah and his immediate family were among the few who held exceptions to this belief.

While Elijah focused on political battles, his father Toliver ventured west into Kentucky country, driven by a mission to spread the Baptist faith. Not long after, Elijah's brother Rev. Lewis Craig followed his father, taking his Traveling Church out west. Elijah took his congregation to Fayette County, north of modern day Lexington, Kentucky, in 1786. Some see this move as Elijah's first link to Bourbon since Fayette County later became part of the area split into Bourbon County. However, his property went from Fayette, to Woodford, and later Scott County—never Bourbon County.

Elijah's home in Lebanon Town, later renamed Georgetown in honor of General Washington, sat on 1,000 acres along Royal Spring. It was here in the late 1780s that Elijah would become a Renaissance man of sorts. In 1786, his communications with James Madison included an early discussion of statehood and the need to divide Fayette County due to distance and inefficiencies—he suggested Versailles as the new county name. [144] He also took part in laying out the town of Lebanon. At the same time he founded the Great Crossing Church and established Kentucky's first classical school—nicknamed "Craig's Academy"—teaching Latin, Greek, and other classical studies.[145] He also demonstrated his entrepreneurial spirit, producing hemp rope, founding the area's first paper mill, and building a fulling mill for cloth production, a lumber mill, and a grist mill.[146]

The Legend of the Charred Barrel

In the pioneering days, where there was a grist mill, there was often a still nearby. Legend suggests Elijah Craig operated a distillery, but in the 1700s, industrialized distilling was still decades away from the frontier. Instead, he likely had a small-scale still set up in a barn or separate shed—away from the flammable dust produced by the milling process. One version of the legend claims his barn, where he kept empty barrels, caught fire but that Elijah quickly extinguished the flames. With the barrels now charred, Elijah, being either thrifty or low on funds, decided to use the burnt barrels to store his whiskey. When he later opened one, he noticed both a deeper color and a pleasant aroma. According to lore, he named this new liquid Bourbon.

It's a fun anecdote, perfect for marketing, but does it pass the sniff test?

It's true that Elijah had a still producing whiskey—and his son-in-law Josiah Pitts sold whiskey on trips down the Mississippi River—although whether they were Elijah's is more speculation than cold hard fact.[147] It's unlikely Elijah operated the distillery himself; with many other businesses to run, he would have relied on family, hired help, or enslaved workers to manage production. Perhaps he sampled what he distilled and managed casks, but there are no contemporary accounts to suggest this—nor are there contemporary accounts of his whiskey or its quality. Most likely he was distilling excess grain, as other pioneers did, for barter, and he possibly also distilled for others who brought their grain to him to grind. This means not only was he making corn whiskey, he was likely also distilling wheat, rye, or other grains.

There also isn't any logical reason he would have called a whiskey Bourbon in the 1780s, since his neighboring county's distilling heritage wasn't yet established. As mentioned in Chapter 9, the first time the words Bourbon and whiskey appear together in print was 1821, 13 years after Elijah's death. Post 1821, references were sparse and more geared toward Bourbon County proper, not the general area surrounding it. Even into the 1840s Bourbon was just one of several counties with reputations including Woodford and Nelson County. The 1850s saw a significant rise in the name Bourbon, most likely due to better transportation moving barrels around the country. It was at this time that recipes for creating "Bourbon" out of rectified spirits and flavorings began and people outside Bourbon County began usurping the name in large numbers.

As for the origins of charring barrels, that practice dates back well before the 1780s. The real question is whether charring was something early Kentucky distillers valued. According Samuel McHarry's 1809 publication *The Practical Distiller*, one of the era's essential handbooks for distillers, early distillers prioritized clarifying spirits, relying instead on rectifying through charcoal to improve quality. Color was added through the use of burnt sugar, not a charred barrel.[148] There's no early record of Kentucky distillers using charred barrels. The first known mention appears in an 1826 letter from a Lexington grocer, J.M. Pike to Bourbon County distiller John Corlis, almost two decades after Elijah's death.[149]

Friends, Neighbors, and Countrymen

One of the biggest strikes against the claim that Elijah Craig invented or produced Bourbon is the silence from those who knew him. Throughout the 19th century, he is frequently celebrated for his preaching, his school, and establishing the first paper mill. Yet, no mention of distilling Bourbon or the use of charred oak barrels surfaces from those familiar with him.

The best opportunity for someone to reveal Elijah's distilling would have been September 1828, during a dinner honoring General Andrew Jackson, who was making his second bid for the presidency. Amid toasts and resolutions of support, a 46-year-old cattle breeder from Gallatin County, Lewis Sanders, stood and raised his glass. "To the memory of Elijah Craig, the founder of Georgetown, Kentucky. A philosopher and Christian—a useful man in his day. He established the first fulling mill, the first paper mill, and the first rope walk in Kentucky. Honor to whom honor is done."[150]

It's not a surprise that Lewis would give such a tribute to Elijah Craig. Elijah was his uncle and he was named after Elijah's brother. A successful merchant and entrepreneur himself, Lewis built his empire, at the same time he was watching uncle Elijah fall on hard times. Always bad with money, Elijah spent many of his remaining years selling off property and trying to avoid debtors' prison.

Perhaps his toast was given to wipe away Elijah's rough final years and restore him to glory. But there is no mention of distilling—which runs counter to legend which suggests that Bourbon distillation brought him great acclaim.[151] Lewis also didn't mention distilling in the biography of Elijah he wrote while documenting the genealogy of the Craig family. [152]

Tracing the Origin of the Lore

The next time Elijah Craig's name appeared alongside distilling was in William Perrin's *History of Bourbon, Scott, Harrison, and Nicholas Counties, Kentucky* (1882). Perrin referenced *The History of Kentucky* (1874) by historians Lewis and Richard Collins, claiming they credited Elijah with making the first Bourbon whiskey at his fulling mill in Georgetown in 1789. Perrin added his own comment: "the blue grass region has kept up its reputation for good whisky and still makes the best in the world—if the word good may be, without violence, applied to the greatest known evil in existence."[153] It's obvious that Perrin was a teetotaler, as were the Collins brothers—as were most of the historians of that era. This temperance bias is one reason so little detailed information exists about the early days of Kentucky whiskey.

Having researched other distillers through Perrin's work, I've found it inaccurate in many places. It appears he leaned heavily on oral tradition and speculation. In the case of the Collins brothers, they don't exactly hand Elijah's connection to Bourbon over on a silver platter. It requires taking a sentence earlier in the chapter mentioning Elijah opening the first fulling mill in Kentucky and combining it with a later passage, "The First Bourbon Whisky was made in 1789, at Georgetown, at the fulling mill at the Royal spring." Both volumes are quite cavalier with their proclamations and show their lack of understanding in the origins of the name Bourbon in regards to whiskey. Unfortunately this would trip up the *Louisville Courier-Journal* in the 1930s, who repeated this piece of lore for a 20th-century audience.[154]

It wasn't until 1940 that documented evidence confirmed Elijah's role as a distiller. Willard Rouse Jillson's *Early Kentucky Distillers* (1940) references Elijah's name on a list of Scott County distillers who hadn't paid Alexander Hamilton's excise tax.[155] So, Elijah indeed had a still, but this tells us nothing about what he called his spirit. Thus, there is no clear evidence pointing to his status as "The Father of Bourbon"—it just remains a fun piece of lore.

The Real Father of Bourbon

So, where did the title "The Father of Bourbon" come from? Its origins are almost as elusive as the man it's often assigned to. The first known reference to Elijah as the father of bourbon occurred in an article about Georgetown College in the *Courier-Journal's* Sunday magazine in 1954.[156] However, like the early use of the term "master distiller" it seemed more off-the-cuff, than an official title. It wasn't until 1986 that Heaven Hill introduced the Elijah Craig brand as a 12-year-old, 94-proof Bourbon. Yet, neither the label nor advertising at the time used the term "The Father of Bourbon."

Then, in June 1989, Georgetown College professor George McGee honored the life of this local, almost forgotten figure with a play. Released on the 200th anniversary of Elijah's founding of his original school, *The Life and Times of Elijah Craig* portrayed the reverend's life from his early preaching days in Virginia through his impressive achievements on the Kentucky frontier. Within the play, it appears it was McGee that introduced the lore surrounding Elijah's supposed charring of barrels and his thriftiness, pointing to his research into family lore as the source. [157]The show was a hit and continued being performed through Kentucky's bicentennial celebrations in 1992.

Perhaps McGee deserves the credit for tying Elijah Craig to the title "The Father of Bourbon"[158] in the public consciousness. Heaven Hill eventually embraced this link, etching it into their bottles in 2016. On distillery tours across Kentucky, the stories vary: from the charring of new barrels to charring used barrels to remove the residue of its former contents. Whatever the story, the tie to Elijah was complete.

So, who is the real Father of Bourbon? If we're going for the earliest distiller in Kentucky, that is a near impossibility to determine, since distilling was a standard part of pioneer life. It's just as possible we should be looking for The Mother of Bourbon as the first distiller. And defining what Bourbon is creates another issue. The first distillers in Bourbon County like Jacob Spears didn't work with mash bills, they distilled what they had on hand. Then there is the official definition of Bourbon, which wasn't codified until the 20th century. Before that, the mash bill was likely corn, but not always. In the 1840s, something called Bourbon rye found its way to Charleston, South Carolina and Baltimore, Maryland.[159]

If we can't even pinpoint what Bourbon meant to 18th- and 19th-century distillers, how can we single out one person as its creator or the guiding hand behind its success? The temperance movement and poor early documentation leave us without a clear path to follow. In fact, the ancient Greeks may have left us more written records than Kentucky's early distillers. In the end, we may just have to accept that the Father of Bourbon is a mystery that will remain in the realm of whiskey lore.

Reality: False. Nothing complicated about it. He was a fascinating man, but the title has little historical evidence to support it.

Three Years and a Day

Myth: Whisky in Scotland must age three years and a day to be called Scotch

AI: False

To the Memphis media, it was just another Friday night news story: an argument between two friends playing cards at 4 AM had turned violent. The victim, 36-year-old Ira James Bowdery, was rushed to the hospital after 37-year-old Wilbert Rogers allegedly stabbed him in the heart. Rogers, charged with aggravated assault, was out on bond, awaiting trial. Bowdery, however, clung to life for over a year, slipping in and out of a coma after the attack on May 7, 1994. Then, on August 30, 1995, his obituary appeared in the *Memphis Commercial Appeal*. After a 15-month struggle, Bowdery had died of heart failure. The following day, Wilbert Rogers was charged with murder.[160]

A simple case of homicide, right? Not so fast. Rogers' attorneys had a surprising defense rooted in ancient English law, courtesy of a long-legged medieval king known as "Longshanks"—England's King Edward I.

The King's Forgotten Law

Despite King John's Magna Carta in 1215, and its limits on royal authority, a century later, kings still wielded tremendous influence over nobles and parliament.

Edward I, often called the "English Justinian," took an active role in codifying and expanding common law through a set of legal reforms known as the Statutes of Westminster. His reforms strengthened rules for property rights, inheritance, and local governance, but one particular rule would prove especially relevant to Rogers' defense: something known as the "year-and-a-day" rule.

The idea of the rule was to remove the ambiguity from murder cases after a year. With limited medical knowledge, it was believed that if a victim survived for over a year following an attack, the original injury couldn't be definitively blamed for the patient's demise. An unusual but intentional part of the rule was the added day, meant to account for calendar inconsistencies and to avoid technical loopholes. This timeframe for causation might have been fair in the medieval era, but it didn't account for the medical advances that followed over the next eight centuries.

Remarkably, the "year-and-a-day" rule made its way into American law and survived into the modern age. When early American courts established laws, they adopted principles from English common law that seemed practical, including this homicide rule. As states developed their legal frameworks, the "year-and-a-day" rule remained in effect as a standard for causation in murder cases. With the rise of medical and forensic advancements in the 20th century, however, many states began challenging and repealing this outdated statute.

Yet, at the dawn of the 21st century, a few states still kept it on the books—Tennessee being one of them. Though doctors agreed Bowdery had succumbed to his original wound after 15 months, Rogers' lawyers made a last-ditch effort to evade a second-degree murder charge, which carried a potential 33-year prison sentence, by invoking Tennessee's year-and-a-day rule.

When the court ruled against Rogers, his lawyers appealed to the Tennessee Supreme Court. Shocked by the rule's existence, the justices declared it outdated and abolished it. With second-degree murder charges imminent, and feeling the court had denied him due process under the Fourteenth Amendment, Rogers' attorneys pushed the case all the way to the U.S. Supreme Court. In a close 5–4 decision, the high court upheld Tennessee's ruling.

In her majority opinion, Justice Sandra Day O'Connor held that applying the change retroactively did not violate the Due Process Clause of the U.S. Constitution's Fourteenth Amendment. She noted the elimination of the "year and a day rule" by many jurisdictions, indicating a general agreement that the rule was outdated. Thus the change in ruling by the Tennessee Supreme Court was not "unexpected" or "indefensible" based on existing legal principles at the time of the crime.[161] Today, though, the "year-and-a-day" rule remains in a few state statutes, but if it is ever invoked, the precedence of the Supreme Court ruling of 2001 will render it moot.

Ancient Law Finds Its Way to Whisky

As for Britain, while Longshanks' common-law practice disappeared with The Law Reform Act 1996, this year and a day concept still gets some play—thanks to Scotland's distillery tour guides. According to some of them, to be called Scotch whisky, new make spirit must rest in a cask for no less than three years and a day.

When I first heard the "extra day" rule on a distillery tour, I became curious as to its origin. Each distillery seemed to have its own explanation, with the most popular reasons revolving around taxes and quality.

The tax argument suggests that revenue collectors added an extra day to prevent any "chicanery"—meaning they didn't want distillers dodging taxes for a day by invoking leap year or other timing excuses. But this never quite made sense to me. What difference would a 24-hour delay make to the national treasury?

The quality argument is usually more entertaining. It suggests that, while Irish whiskey must age for three years, Scots age theirs for three years and a day—supposedly making it superior. This is typically said with a wink, but I've heard some tour guides make very passionate cases. There are two problems with it, though.

First, the obvious issue: is there really a significant flavor impact by aging a whisky for 1,096 days instead of 1,095? The other issue: visit Ireland, and they'll tell you *they* age for three years and a day, while the Scots only age for three years. It's quite comical. Both sides are trying to one-up the other side with the same lore. Do they not think people travel over the Irish Sea?

Of course, the most reasonable explanation for tour guides telling this story is because they were trained to say it or heard someone else say it. That is the way with lore.

Not Hammered

So is the extra day myth or real? Unlike the mysteries of triple distillation or sour mash, we have a solid answer for this. Since the Immature Spirits Act of 1915, Scottish distillers have been required to age whisky for three years. The current law, under the Scotch Whisky Regulations of 2009, states that to be called Scotch whisky, the spirit must "mature for a period of not less than three years."[162] Sorry, Scotch fans—no extra day for you.

As for the Irish? Before you start feeling a sense of superiority, know that—like the Scots—Irish whiskey does not require the extra day either. Distillers in Northern Ireland are under British law, the same as the Scots. In the Republic of Ireland, the three-year minimum was set in the *1924 Excise Act* and briefly raised to five years in the mid 20th century before returning to three. Today, the *European Union's Technical File for Irish Whiskey* codifies the requirement, stating the spirit must age "for at least three years in wooden casks."[163]

So next time someone insists on that arbitrary extra day, you'll have the facts to hand. While the extra day once benefitted murder suspects, it doesn't hold much sway over whiskey or modern law. But when on a tour, rather than cutting the tour guide off to claim your advanced knowledge, listen to what they have to say and soak in the lore. No one likes a know-it-all on a tour. Maybe mention it to the guide afterwards or while enjoying your sample whiskies at the end of the tour. After all, myths and marketing are part of the game.

Reality: False. It is entertaining, but neither the Scots or Irish are getting away with murder.

First Female

Myth: The first female master or head distiller broke the glass ceiling in the 21st century.

AI: Complicated

"They're coming," came the low whispered voice from the front room of a two-room farmhouse. The calm, even tempered voice was that of 39-year old John Fleetwood Cumming—a Highland smuggler—who spotted two revenue men walking up the hill toward the house.

For his wife, 36-year-old Helen Cumming, this was nothing new and definitely not something to panic over. Ever since they had taken over the little house on Cardow farm, John's smuggling had remained a well-guarded secret. As too was hers—seeing that Helen was the source of much of John's smuggled whisky. It helped that the officers' movements ran like clockwork. Before making their rounds, they predictably stopped in to see the couple. Helen and John were quite hospitable and even offered to feed the officers before they made their appointed rounds, measuring stills and collecting tax payments from distillers along the River Spey. If the revenuers had an inkling of what the couple was doing, they didn't let on.

It was quite a devious plan actually. The illicit Highland distillers in the area numbered in the thousands and most of them took to the hills to stay hidden from the excise. But here was a couple, very warm and welcoming, without a still in sight, using a free lunch as the perfect ruse. If she was caught unawares, Helen would quickly dissemble the worm, kettle, and pot, then quickly yank the apparatus out the backdoor while John entertained the officers in the front room. Then she'd stoke the fires under her pot of stew, while praying that the revenuers wouldn't detect the telltale residual scent of wort or fresh spirits.

To help her neighbors avoid detection, when the excise men sat down to their meal Helen would excuse herself to prepare dessert, and would quickly run outside to raise a red flag above the house. When the Highlanders saw that flag waiving in the breeze, they knew the revenuers would soon be making their way through the area.

The scheme worked smoothly for a time. But one cold winter morning in 1816, the excise men arrived early. The officers noticed the smoky, sweet scent of peat and yeast in the air—one they knew well. Circling around the back of the farmhouse, they found buckets of malted grain and wort. They arrested John and took him to the sheriff's court. After paying a fine, he was released, and he and Helen soon resumed their clandestine business. Although John would be arrested twice more that year, some of the excise men had grown fond enough of Helen's cooking to eventually turn a blind eye to it.

The lore suggests that, eventually, John and Helen began collecting old equipment from their neighbors to hand over whenever the excise officers paid a visit. This way, the officers could return to their bosses in Edinburgh with evidence in hand, keeping everyone out of trouble. [164] Of course, this story falls apart when considering punishment usually included fines and arrests. It is a fun way to justify their continued distilling and smuggling, and as with most lore, there is probably some truth in it. But it is more left to the weakness of oral tradition.

When the Excise Act of 1823 lowered the cost of licensing a distillery, John and Helen decided to take advantage and lead their neighbors in going legit. Never again would John have to play lookout while Helen scrambled to disassemble her still.

Lost in Firsts

The story of John and Helen Cumming is not unusual in distilling history. From the monopoly system of King James I to tales of moonshining in the Appalachians, Highlands, and Irish hills, families have long found ways to evade excise officers, while making extra income through distilling. For some it may come as a surprise that the distiller in this story was Helen. While this reaction may stem from historic biases, it's often simply due to a lack of documentation about women's contributions.

Fortunately, recent years have seen a concerted effort to recognize groundbreaking female figures in the industry. However, these efforts sometimes bring forth historic assumptions that women had minimal involvement in distilling once it became a male-driven industry, keeping the research limited to the late 20th or 21st centuries. While the stories of women in the industry are few and far between, the idea women didn't have critical roles in the past is misguided.

This gap in historical knowledge recently sparked a social media debate over who could truly claim the title of "first female master distiller" in Kentucky. The argument centered on two women whose distilling careers began in the 21st century. For me, watching that discussion unfold was frustrating. After my research into the history of female distillery founders for a podcast episode with Lori Carcich of Country Smooth Whiskey, I found a good number of women involved with distilleries in the 19th century. Like with Tennessee whiskey being touted as "Bourbon that goes through an extra step," stopping people from investigating Tennessee's deep history, it seemed the fight for modern "female firsts" was keeping people from digging deeper into the past. My research into Lori's first female founder story showed me, there were a good number important females in the history of distilling.[165]

In the years since I created that episode, I've watched with admiration as women have risen to prominence in the modern whiskey industry. Today, there are numerous female founders, master distillers, master blenders, and C-suite executives driving the industry forward. Yet, beyond a volume or two, there still seems to be only the cursory glance toward women's historical impact in the industry. It's time to take a deep dive into the past and uncover the stories of these remarkable forgotten pioneers.

But before we dig in, the first thing we need to set aside is the title of "master distiller." As discussed in Chapter 3, this is a late 20th-century term. Limiting our search to official titles will exclude many significant figures. Instead, we'll look for the women who were responsible for distilling. Helen Cumming, for instance, could qualify, if we could prove definitively, beyond oral tradition,[166] that she was in fact the primary or only distiller at Cardow Farm.

Next, we should let go of finding a definitive "first." Just like trying to identify the Father of Bourbon or the first to use charcoal to mellow whiskey, we have to first admit that poor documentation—especially regarding women's roles in whiskey—stands in the way. As we'll see, women moved in and out of distilling roles over time due to societal shifts. Rather than seeking a definitive first, let's endeavor to embrace an overlooked chapter of whiskey history that has been hidden for far too long.

Women and Distilling

To set the stage for our quest it is good to take a snapshot of the ever changing roles of women in distilling history. Women have weaved in an out of the story of spirits since the days of ancient Mesopotamia. The earliest recorded association between women and distilling comes from the second century AD when a female alchemist named Maria Prophetissa (aka Maria the Jewess and Maria the Alchemist) was credited with creating one of the first distillation stills.

However, women's public roles faded during the Dark and Middle Ages. During those periods, St. Augustine of Hippo and Thomas Aquinas led the charge in casting women either in the image of Eve, representing original sin, or the Virgin Mary, embodying purity and motherhood—there was no in-between. Lower-class women found work as bakers, brewers, or barmaids, or working alongside their families on tenant farms. Meanwhile, women of the upper class inherited roles predefined by family wealth and their husband's status. A woman's autonomy usually came through what her husband passed to her in death or through a substantial dowry that she brought into the marriage.

In the 14th century, the Black Death swept across Europe and women initially took on a role as the caretakers and healers. As the family distiller, they likely prepared tonics to help ease their loved ones' suffering. However, with so many men lost to the plague, more women assumed control of households, giving them an unusual measure of autonomy. But this independence triggered a backlash. The image of Eve, associated with sin, took hold again, and women—especially those who owned land—were often accused of bringing on the plague through sorcery. Women distillers faced the danger of being labeled witches, especially if their aqua vitae caused any harm, real or perceived. This could explain the disassociation of women as distillers over the ensuing years.

During the Age of Enlightenment, women's roles were shaped by societal norms, laws, and cultural expectations, though they varied depending on class and location. Women were mostly seen as managers of the household. For the upper classes, this incorporated management of the servants, while in the lower classes, women were responsible for cooking, cleaning, raising children, and overseeing the daily operations of the home. Some worked alongside men in the fields and took part in preserving the food supply, and this brought the skill of distilling back to women. Yet their contributions remained largely unacknowledged. This was mostly due to coverture laws, where a woman's legal identity was absorbed into her husband's upon marriage. She could not own property, enter into contracts, or represent herself legally. This meant her husband was usually given credit for her achievements. In cases like Helen Cumming, coverture laws mean we'll likely never know the full extent of her role in the distilling process. Although John Cumming was arrested for illicit distilling, this doesn't necessarily mean he was the distiller; legally, he was responsible for her actions. There were a few widows in late 18th century Scotland inherited distilleries and held onto them with limited success—this showed cracks were developing in the old world norms.

In the 19th and 20th centuries, such laws gradually began to fade as women fought for their rights. New York's Married Women's Property Act of 1848 allowed married women to own property independent of their husbands. By the late 19th century, most U.S. states had followed suit, granting married women property rights and the ability to sign contracts. The United Kingdom followed with the Married Women's Property Act 1870, which allowed women to keep earnings they made after marriage; and in 1882, British women gained full legal control over their legal rights, property and earnings. Many European countries, however, wouldn't see such reforms until the 20th century.

Even as the laws evolved, societal attitudes lagged behind. The Victorian ideal of the dutiful wife still held sway, casting women more often as proponents of temperance and advocates against alcohol rather than as contributors within the distilling industry. This mindset likely discouraged many capable women from pursuing visible roles in the industry, let alone seeking recognition. Yet, despite these obstacles, a few remarkable women went against the grain and seized upon golden opportunities.

Taking the Reins

With limited documentation from 19th-century distilling, finding the names of lead distillers—let alone female ones—is challenging. The names we remember are typically those of the owners, not necessarily the distillers themselves. Among the earliest examples of female leadership in distilling, most known names are women who inherited the distillery from their husbands, then held onto the business and drove its success.

One of the great early examples is Helen Cumming's daughter-in-law, Elizabeth Robertson Cumming. Married to Helen and John's son Lewis in 1859, Elizabeth supported her husband as he gradually took over the family distillery. But when Lewis died in 1872, the humble little distillery's future was uncertain. At 95 years of age, and still an adept business woman, Helen, a long time widow herself, encouraged Elizabeth to take over the operation. With three children to support, managing a distillery may have seemed daunting,[167] but Helen saw something special in her.

Helen's instincts were correct. Within a decade, Elizabeth generated enough capital to sell off the old equipment while building a modern distillery. The new structure was a handsome stillhouse, with an increased capacity from 25,000 to 40,000 gallons a year. Whisky chronicler Alfred Barnard praised the new facility as "a handsome pile of buildings," noting that Elizabeth had created a distillery producing spirit "similar in character to that made at the old Distillery, which is of the thickest and richest description, and admirably adapted for blending purposes."[168]

Elizabeth eventually sold the distillery to John Walker & Sons, securing her son John a place on the company's board. The Cumming name remained influential in Johnnie Walker's leadership until the 1960s. Today, the renamed Cardhu brand, owned by London-based Diageo, still occupies the former Cardow farm. Cardhu whiskies honor Helen Cumming's legacy with an image of her raising a red flag on their packaging. She and her daughter-in-law Elizabeth may not have been labeled as "master distillers," but Elizabeth's impact on the early modern whisky industry is unquestioned.

Then there's the story of Catherine Spears Frye Carpenter. Born to German immigrant parents in Virginia in 1760, Catherine Spears married a man named John Frye while still in her teens. Catherine and John joined several other families in establishing Carpenter's Station along Carpenter's Creek in Lincoln County, not too far from modern day Danville, Kentucky. When the men were called off to fight in the War for Independence, it wasn't long before Catherine was greeted by the devastating news that John had been killed, while fighting with Daniel Boone at the Battle of Blue Licks. She remarried, but her second husband Adam passed away in 1806. After his death, tax records confirm that Catherine was running stills on her farm in 1815.[169] Furthermore, she left as part of her legacy a piece of paper showing recipes for both sweet and sour mash whiskey, indicating her production versatility.[170]

Could she be considered Kentucky's first women to solely own a distillery? It is possible, although this again leads us to minimize the role of all of the women who distilled in the state before her. How many women took the reins of their family farms after their husbands died and kept distilling to barter for the supplies they needed to survive? As has been clearly shown, distilling wasn't always an industry. Instead, rather than being a first, Catherine should be seen as an example of all the women whose names we don't know that came before her.

In Ireland, two historic distilleries were once owned by pioneering women. After inheriting the Locke Distillery from her husband in 1868, Mary Anne Theresa Locke built a spirits store onsite, consistently improved the equipment, and more than doubled the distillery's output in her 18 years of leadership. By 1875, her distillery was producing 78,000 gallons of whiskey annually.[171] Today, this distillery is known as Kilbeggan. Ellen Jane Corrigan inherited the Old Bushmills Distillery in the late 19th century and oversaw its further development into international markets.

In England, records of female distillers often arise from illicit activities. In East London's Stepney neighborhood, Hannah Reader and Mary Cale were arrested for running an illegal still and sentenced to three months in prison. The *London Morning Post* remarked that "in several cases of private stills lately discovered in this district, females have been the only persons found working them."[172]

Robertson County, Tennessee was home to two of the most successful female distillery owners in the country—Louisa Nelson and Josephine Brown. When her husband Charles passed away in 1893, Louisa took over Nelson's Green Brier Distillery, the largest in the state. Josie Brown, the daughter of Tennessee distilling legend Wiley Woodard, encouraged her husband Jordan Stokes Brown to open the Wartrace Distillery. When he passed away unexpectedly in 1890, she took control and rose to become one of the richest women in the state. When Tennessee closed the door on distilling in 1909, Louisa and Josie had the last two distilleries standing in legendary Robertson County. Josie went on to become a philanthropist, using her wealth to support her community. [173]

One of Kentucky's most fascinating female distillery owners was Mary Dowling of Lawrenceburg. Following her husband John's death in 1916, Mary inherited the Waterfill & Frazier Distillery. As World War I and Prohibition loomed, she faced losing everything to the temperance movement. But rather than let her family's legacy be erased, Mary moved the entire operation to Juárez, Mexico. There, she hired Joseph Beam, of the famous Beam family, as her distiller and produced Juárez Bourbon until her death in 1930.

She's the Boss

While there are few details about the distilling expertise of other female distillery owners, one forgotten woman from Tennessee has her life preserved in great detail as a "boss" distiller with a reputation for quality. Thanks to court records found by Tennessee whiskey historian Carole Roberts, this woman's story is one of the most complete of any female pre-Prohibition distiller.

Her name is Nancy Patterson and to say her story was unusual is an understatement. Born through an encounter between plantation owner James Puryear and an enslaved woman in 1830, Nancy was born into enslavement. When she was in her early 20s, an Irishman named Barney Patterson came to live on the plantation. Having lost his foot in a railroad accident, Nancy became his caretaker. The elderly James noticed the bond between the two and, not wanting his daughter sold off to another family if he died, he sold Nancy's rights and a plot of land to Barney. Barney used the land to establish a distillery, hiring a distiller to make brandy and whiskey in the early 1870s. Meanwhile, Nancy managed much of the farm work and took care of the household duties.

Things changed dramatically when Barney's distiller was caught stealing by a Federal storekeeper and sent to jail. In need of a replacement, Barney seemed out of options. But Nancy, who had quietly observed the distiller's techniques while managing her other responsibilities, told Barney she was ready to take on the role herself. From that day in 1879, she worked her craft, earning praise from her neighbors, and storekeepers and gaugers. Her boundless energy and talent with the stills earned her a reputation as the "Boss" distiller.

When Barney realized he wasn't going to live much longer, he amended his will to make sure Nancy would gain ownership. However, after his death, the will was contested by Barney's sister and niece. After a long court battle, at 65 years old, Nancy Patterson became the sole owner of the distillery and continued distilling into her late 80s.[174] The testimony of her friends and associates during that lawsuit is the only reason we know so much about this remarkable woman.

If You Dig Deep Enough

Hearing the story of Nancy inspired me to delve deeper into the archives to find who else we might be missing. It turns out Nancy had some company in the distilling world of the late 19th and early 20th centuries.

In an article titled "Female Occupations in the States" the *Glasgow* [Scotland] *Daily Mail* reported that there were eight female brewers and six female distillers in the United States in 1877.[175] In 1896, the *Kansas City Weekly Journal* noted nine female distillers across the states.[176] By 1899, Mrs. H. Henley of Tullahoma, Tennessee—not far from Nancy's distillery—was reported to have a 4,000-gallon-a-month distilling capacity.[177] Then, in 1903, the *Dayton Herald* ran a story titled "Will Man Become Obsolete?" which celebrated women's achievements in various fields, noting two women distillers and rectifiers operating in Chicago.[178] The article didn't specify if these women were owners or actual distillers, but it was clear more women than we've been aware of were establishing a foothold in the industry.

In an 1895 piece, *The Boston Globe* declared, "the new woman has broken out." It referenced two women from Jasper and Cherokee counties in Georgia appearing in the Internal Revenue books not as widows taking over from their husbands, but as independent founders of distilleries.[179] Another pioneering distiller, 22-year-old Hattie Shafer of Stokes County, North Carolina, applied for a license to distill peach brandy in her own name.[180] While their ultimate success with these endeavors is not documented, in 1910 a Kentucky distiller, Mrs. Lydia C. Rogers of Maysville, was noted upon her death as being "the only woman distiller in the states," and having left an estate worth $200,000 (about $6.6 million today).[181] A success by any measure.

However, achievement in the industry for women was expressed by contemporary journalists with a hint of surprise—less out of malice than due to societal conditioning. In 1893, a *Charlotte News* article demonstrated this vibe in an article about a revenuer going to meet Stanley County brandy distiller Eph Honeycutt. When it came to making brandy, Eph had one of the best reputations in the area. To the revenuer's surprise, when he arrived, a woman was hard at work running the operation. He asked where Honeycutt was.

"He's not here," she said. "[He] does not stay here."

The revenuer asked, "Well, who runs the still?"

"Why, I do of course," she said, telling him she made brandy ever as good as Eph.

"Well, who are you?" he asked with a puzzled look.

"I am his wife. I attend to things for him, because he has the farm and other matters to look after."

Then she went about her business distilling her latest batch of brandy. [182]

While women appeared occasionally in the world of legal distilling, it is illicit distilling where they seemed to have a stronger role—and in this case, age didn't matter. In Monmouth, Kansas, 69-year-old Mary Gradtke was apprehended after running off her fruit mash in front of two prohibition officers; then after showing off her equipment, offering them some liquid and her recipe.[183] Lizzie Nelson and Mary Gurganeous, both 75 years of age, were arrested in Wilmington, NC for making moonshine.[184] Omaha, Nebraska, was scandalized to learn that 22-year-old Elsie Rogers was producing 30 gallons of spirits a day from a three-boiler setup in her home.[185] Mrs. Jennie Berman of St. Paul, Minnesota, operated a 100-gallon still and was found with 50 gallons of moonshine on Topping Street. *The Atlanta Journal* reported in 1926 that several women in Lumpkin County, Georgia, had set aside knitting to distill up what they described as "something pure."

In the Age of the Master Distiller

So it's clear that women were active in distilling throughout the 19th and 20th centuries, though defining the extent of their roles can be challenging. Today, titles like "master distiller" and "master blender" are used to recognize those at the pinnacle of distillery leadership, overseeing production and quality. Surprisingly, though, these titles are new in regards to women, with the earliest appearance I can find coming as recently as 2014.

That's not to say there weren't trailblazers who could have claimed a similar title. In 2009, Cheryl Lins founded Delaware Phoenix Distillery as a one-woman operation in New York and began distilling absinthe and eventually whiskey. In 2011, Troy Ball started her Asheville, North Carolina, distillery, Troy & Sons, producing high-quality moonshine and initially labeling her platinum spirit as "moonshine whiskey." In 2012, Joan Verratti claimed the title of Pennsylvania's first licensed female distiller since Prohibition. And Marianne (Barnes) Eaves followed in 2015 by embracing the title "Kentucky's First Female Bourbon Master Distiller since Prohibition"[186] when she left Brown-Forman, to join the newly launched Castle & Key Distillery in Millville, Kentucky.

Is she really?

It appears she is the first woman in Kentucky to be given the title master distiller and since my research shows the term "master distiller" wasn't given to a woman until her—she might not need the "Kentucky" caveat. She could also consider dropping the superfluous "since Prohibition," since the title apparently wasn't applied to any distiller—male or female—before Prohibition.

The question is: beyond the title, how does it fit into history?

Let's take the case of Dolly Reed Wageman. Never heard of her? Neither had I, until I stumbled into an article written by Catharine Brewster of the *Women's News Service* titled "Real Women's Revolution Is Quiet, At-Home One." It tells the story of Wageman, a serial entrepreneur touting her new book *The 6-Week Make Yourself Over Plan*. Over an incredible career she was an author, magazine beauty editor, fashion director for a cosmetics company, and an advertising executive. [187]Where did she get her start? As a distillery operator for Seagram's in Louisville, Kentucky. What was her role? Was she, in effect, a "master distiller" before the term became commonplace? Unfortunately the article doesn't state when she worked there and I couldn't find any former Seagram's employees or records to confirm what her job entailed. Being well before the women's liberation movement—no one was looking for women breaking glass ceilings. It may be impossible to know what impact she had on the whiskey produced during that era, so we are left with a mystery.

What Dolly's story and those of so many of these women tell us is this: we need to be cautious about placing too much weight on "firsts." Comparing the achievements of today's master distillers to those of Nancy Patterson, Dolly Reed Wageman, or Lydia C. Rogers isn't just difficult—it's impossible. These women operated in an entirely different world, facing major barriers with little recognition or support. And what about modern era women like Bessie Williamson of Laphroaig, who in 1954 acquired ownership of the distillery and served as its distillery manager? Like some modern master distillers, she was less likely to have worked hands on with the stills and instead was more of an ambassador. How do you place her in the story?

Sadly, modern proclamations of "firsts" and the need to apply titles risks making us miss these older stories all together. It is time to do away with this impossible search for "firsts" and instead leave the door open to all of the great stories and achievements yet to be discovered.

Reality: Complicated. If we go by title, it is possible. But that doesn't begin to tell the story.

First Wheated Bourbon

Myth: W.L. Weller was the first wheated Bourbon

AI: True

A long time ago, in the shadow of the mighty Catskill Mountains, lived a man of humble and good-natured disposition whose world was stripped from him by the strangest of circumstances.

Loved by his friends and neighbors, he was a cherished member of his village. His wife, on the other hand, thought him indolent and lazy. She constantly nagged him about his lack of ambition and idleness. It is true the man liked to avoid work, preferred to spend his days wandering the village, helping neighbors with odd jobs, or sitting with his dog, Wolf, at the local tavern.

One day, he was chatting with the landlord of the inn, enjoying a smoke, when his wife stormed into the tavern. When she cursed his idleness in front of his close friends, it was the last straw. He picked up his gun, called his old dog Wolf to his side, and, with frustration heavy on his shoulders, left the village. The villagers watched as he and Wolf made their way into the hills and disappeared among the trees.

As he wandered deeper into the forest, lost in his thoughts, he was startled by a voice calling his name. Turning around, he saw a strange figure—a short, broad man with thick, bushy hair and a grizzled beard, carrying a stout keg on his shoulder. The stranger asked if he would help carry the keg over the mountain. Though he felt a pang of unease, he found himself compelled to assist. Together, they began their ascent, the path narrowing as they climbed. Eventually, they crested a ridge and, in the valley below, he saw several other figures engaged in a game of ninepins.

As they reached the bottom of the hill, the stranger poured the keg's contents into flagons. The players gathered, each picking up a drink, and tilted their flagons back, draining every drop. Then, wordlessly, they returned to their game with a fervor that seemed almost hypnotic.

The villager's curiosity grew. Noticing some of the strange liquor left in a flagon, he picked it up and lifted it to his lips. The liquid was cool and refreshing. It reminded him of the finest Holland genever. One drink turned into two, then three, and soon he felt his world spin, the liquid's potency clouding his mind.

In his drunken stupor, he made his way to a tree nearby, where he lay down and closed his eyes. Little did he know that when he awoke, the world he knew would be forever changed.[188]

A Trip Through Time

This is the story of Rip Van Winkle, a happy-go-lucky fellow whose love of unabashed laziness drove his wife mad and led him to a mysterious bottle. After an aggressive session of imbibing, he drifted off to a 20-year sleep, waking to find the British America he once knew transformed into the new United States of America.

Washington Irving's short story (1819) wasn't the first to deal with the concept of travel through time—in Samuel Madden's *Memoirs of the Twentieth Century* (1733), the author creates a commentary on the present by presenting letters sent back from the future. It wasn't until H.G. Wells' masterpiece *The Time Machine*

(1895) that the idea of a device enabling two-way travel was introduced. Since then, fans of the movies have been treated to several time travel tales.

One of the most memorable was the *Back to the Future* trilogy, where fictional character Marty McFly takes Doc Brown's silver Delorean back and forth through time to try to handle family problems. In the second movie, Biff, the antagonist, steals the Delorean and brings back a book of sports records from the future to win bets and amass a fortune.

As a whiskey fan, imagine having a whiskey time machine—where and when would you go? Would you head to 19th-century Dublin for a taste of John Jameson's pure malt whiskey? Or perhaps to Lindores Abbey in Scotland in 1494, to sample Friar John Cor's aqua vitae? Maybe you'd prefer a sip of George Washington's rye whisky or the chance to step into Johnson Distillery on Glenns Creek in 1855 to watch the old master James C. Crow distill up a batch of his legendary whiskey.

Perhaps you're like Biff, the antagonist, and you're just interested in grabbing a few bottles from the recent past, so you can profit big off of some highly valued whiskey. So, let's grab $1,000 bucks from the ATM, get the flux capacitor fired up and head to Louisville, Kentucky, in our Delorean time machine.

The mystery bottle we're after is none other than Pappy Van Winkle's Family Reserve Straight Bourbon Whiskey—a whiskey that, like Rip Van Winkle, spent 20 years in slumber. Today, a bottle retails for around $300, but due to the immense hype around the brand, it can fetch well over $3,000 on the secondary market. But what if I told you a savvy time traveler could get a bottle for a fraction of that price? Let's set the date for 1994. Prepare my friends, we're heading to the liquor store!

In Search of the Other Legendary Van Winkle

For those that have been asleep for the last 20 years or so, Pappy Van Winkle's Family Reserve is one of the most talked about and sought after Bourbon's on the market. But its origins were quite humble.

The bottle is named after the iconic and legendary owner of Louisville's Stitzel-Weller Distillery, Julian "Pappy" Van Winkle. The whiskey was conceived by Pappy's grandson Julian Van Winkle III, who took over the family's Old Rip Van Winkle brand when his father passed away in 1981. Having lost control over the Stitzel-Weller Distillery in 1972, Julian Van Winkle II decided to remain in the business, purchasing barrels of whiskey from his old distillery and bottling decanters and the Old Rip Van Winkle brand. When he died, his son Julian III carried on buying barrels from Stitzel-Weller, while acquiring warehouse space in Lawrenceburg, Kentucky on the site of the old Hoffman Distillery. It wasn't an easy time to be in the Bourbon industry. The Bourbon depression of the 1970s and 80s took its toll, but Julian carried on.

By the early 1990s, with single barrel and small batch Bourbons gaining traction, Julian saw an opportunity to create a bottle worthy of his grandfather's legacy. With a photo of a cigar-smoking Pappy on the label, he unveiled the 107-proof, 20-year-old Pappy Van Winkle's Family Reserve. Priced at an astonishingly modest $40 per bottle, it stood out for its use of wheat as a secondary grain instead of rye, giving it a softer, mellower profile that aged gracefully in oak over two decades.

Initially the Pappy brand was a local secret, becoming a favorite of Kentucky journalists, bartenders, restaurateurs, and a few connoisseurs who recognized its unique qualities. With this limited audience, a crafty time traveler might actually have a shot at finding a bottle of this fine spirit sitting alone quietly on a liquor store shelf.

Kentucky's little secret didn't last forever. In 1997, a bottle of "Pappy" reached the Beverage Testing Institute in Chicago. Scoring a record-breaking 99 out of 100 points, the 20-year Family Reserve was now big news. But surprisingly, bottles could still be found for around $35—with lore suggesting bottles were spotted collecting dust on the shelves. Undaunted, the Van Winkles released a 23-year-old wheated version and a 13-year-old rye. As the 20th century came to a close, the stars were aligning for the spirit as the Bourbon market began to recover.

But first, Julian had a problem to deal with. The Stitzel-Weller Distillery had ceased production in 1992 and was only working as a storage facility. If the brand was to continue, a new source of whiskey was needed. The recent acquisition of the historic Weller brand by Sazerac in 1999 created an opportunity for the Van Winkles. Since Weller Bourbon had a similar wheated formula, it made logical sense to follow the brand to the same facility—the Buffalo Trace Distillery in Frankfort.

Over time, Pappy's retail prices began to rise. By 2005, the 20-year retailed at $72, with a new 15-year bottling priced at $45. By 2013, as the Stitzel-Weller stock dwindled, a bottle of Pappy 20 retailed at $119.99, while the 23-year-old fetched $259.99. That same year, a grand theft of Pappy bottles from a warehouse at Buffalo Trace—known as "Pappygate"—only added to the brand's mystique (particularly after Netflix turned the event into a successful 2021 series). When I first encountered it in 2018, my local store was auctioning off its allocations starting at $800 per bottle. By now, if you can find a bottle of the 20-year Family Reserve, prepare to pay thousands of dollars per bottle.

That means, a well-timed time-machine trip might just pay for itself and more.

The Search for the Original Wheater

The more I learned about Pappy and the concept of long-aged wheated Bourbons, the more I began to wonder if there were other wheated Bourbons that might give me something close to the Pappy experience at a lower price. One night, sitting at the bar at Doc Crow's on Louisville's Whiskey Row, I decided to test this idea. Taking advantage of their half pours, I ordered a Weller 12-year for around $25. My palate wasn't particularly refined at the time, so the experience was mostly lost on me. But I remember it having an enjoyable flavor and scent.

A few months later, I was a guest on *The Bourbon Road* podcast, being interviewed by Jim Shannon and Mike "Big Chief" Hiatt. The discussion turned to stories I'd covered on *Whiskey Lore*. Mike wanted to know if I'd ever done an episode on Weller's claim of being the "Original Wheated Bourbon." I hadn't, but it piqued my curiosity.[189] Always suspicious of first claims, I should have dug right into it, but instead I let it drop.

It wasn't until I started researching the history of Bourbon County that the origins of wheated whiskey started to take shape in my mind.

One thing I can say with certainty is that wheat has long been a component of American whiskey. Even Noah Webster's dictionary defined American whisky as being made with wheat as one of its major ingredients. It's quite logical, really: farmers distilled a variety of grains to preserve profits from their yearly crops. Today we're accustomed to a Bourbon industry focused on mash bills, but back in the 18th and 19th centuries, distillers simply used what they had on hand. In early Bourbon County, wheat was a major crop, and the region became known not only for whiskey but also for flour, hemp, and livestock. With flour mills scattered across the county, there's little doubt that wheated whiskey from Bourbon County predates William Larue Weller's entry into the Bourbon industry in the mid-1800s.

But were distillers specifically marketing their spirit as "wheated"? Well, not on my initial searches. So, it did leave open the possibility that Weller was the first "advertised" wheated Bourbon. With my curiosity up again, I dug in a little deeper to learn more about William Larue Weller. I wanted to know when he started distilling wheated Bourbon and when he first began to advertise it.

The Story and Whiskey of William Larue Weller

The Weller family's story in America dates back to William's Prussian-born great-grandfather, Johannes. Arriving in Philadelphia in 1743 aboard the ship *Lydia* with his pregnant wife Catherine, Johannes set down roots in the Catoctin Mountains of Maryland. In 1776, he joined the First German Battalion, fighting as a private against the British in defense of his new homeland.[190] Johannes' son (William's grandfather), Daniel, followed in his father's footsteps, enlisting as soon as he was old enough to fight. Eventually, Daniel moved his family to Nelson County, Kentucky, where family lore says their distilling legacy began.[191] William's father, Captain Samuel Weller, reportedly took up the trade shortly after his discharge from the War of 1812.[192] Although records don't specify what they distilled, distillers from Maryland were known for using rye due to its higher market value over corn whiskey. Did Samuel distill wheat whiskey? It's possible, but there's no firm record to confirm it.

Into this lineage came William Larue Weller, born on July 26, 1825, in Larue County, Kentucky. In 1844, at 19, he gave up the farm life and moved to Louisville. Following a family tradition, when President Polk declared war on Mexico, William joined the Louisville Legion and headed south to fight. Upon his return, it might be thought he would follow his ancestors and immediately take up distilling. But times were changing: with the rise of steamboats and railroads, wholesale trade offered lucrative opportunities. Louisville, with its prime access to the Ohio River, became an ideal hub for William to enter the wholesale trade. On January 9, 1849, he became a whiskey merchant.[193]

Soon after, newspaper accounts of William L. Weller's exploits begin. Initially, his first advertised business was with a business partner, George Gonterman. In March 1852, they bought out the firm of Stewart & Owen on Sixth Street between Main and Market. As Weller & Gonterman they centered the business around rectified whiskey, as well as foreign and domestic liquors.[194] As mentioned before, rectified whiskey simply means they were fixing spirits they'd obtained from people who did the actual distilling. Because there was no excise or tax record at the time, it is impossible to know if they were just blending and filtering the whiskey or if they had a rectifying still on the premises. They soon expanded their trade to include items like Cognac, tobacco, and cigars. When the partnership dissolved,[195] William continued solo as W.L. Weller and shifted his focus toward solely rectifying whiskey.[196]

At the beginning of the 1860s, William invited his brother Charles David Weller into the business, rebranding as W.L. Weller & Brother.[197] This venture was short-lived, and by the end of the Civil War, another short-lived partnership, Weller & Buckner, fizzled out.[198] In 1870, William partnered with his son George Pence Weller under the name W.L. Weller & Son.

The decade started strong, with the firm announcing it was building a state-of-the-art column-still-based rectifying house that would rival the biggest rectifying plants in the country.[199] Soon, advertisements touted their redistilled Kentucky high wines, sparking a public feud between Louisville and Cincinnati. Considering their city the home of pure spirits, *The Cincinnati Commercial* referred to Kentucky rectified spirits as having come from "a second-rate house in a fifth-rate town." The *Louisville Courier* responded saying "though Cincinnati is a great market for a low grade of whisky, Louisville, now more than ever, controls the trade in the fine old Bourbon, old enough to have been made at a time when adulteration was less frequent and more easily detected."[200][201]

The Wellers ignored the barbs and built upon their business. Then disaster struck. On March 13, 1873 at 8 PM a jet of vapor escaped from the still and, after touching fire within a nearby lamp, the marriage led to an explosion. The loss was estimated at $55,000, with insurance only covering $37,500. In the inferno, 25,000 gallons of spirits were lost.[202] Grateful for the fast reaction of the fire department and the support of Louisville citizens, W.L. Weller & Son posted a thank you notice in the *Weekly Louisville Commercial*.[203] But if they thought that was the end of the misery, they were sadly mistaken. After moving and reestablishing the business at the corner of Brook and Main, another fire touched off in June 1875. Once again the machinery was lost at an estimated sum of $20,000.[204] It wasn't long before the company was fighting off creditors facing $48,646.52 in unpaid debts.[205] It would be three long and hard years before the firm re-established itself. To hold themselves over, they purchased spirits from R. Monarch & Co. at what would become the Glenmore Distillery in Daviess County.[206] As the business reestablished itself, William brought his second son John into the fold and business sailed on through the 1880s.

However, the closing decade of the 19th century wouldn't be so easy. A Peoria, Illinois based concern known as the Distillers & Cattle Feeders Trust (or simply the Whiskey Trust) was attempting to corner the market on spirits. In an attempt to rid themselves of quality distilling competition, they bought up distilleries across the Midwest only to shut them down. Being rectifiers and wholesalers, Kentucky companies like W.L. Weller & Sons and the Bernheim Brothers became their customers. But in 1891, William confessed that not only was the Whiskey Trust manipulating whiskey prices, they were also planning on building several distilleries in Kentucky to produce fast-aging whiskies to drown out their comp etition.[207] When the government finally went after the Whiskey Trust, they into receivership, but the damage was done. The market was soon flooded with cheap rectified whiskey.

Into this chaos came a fresh young salesman named Julian "Pappy" Van Winkle. The state of the industry and the Panic of 1893 that sent the country into a depression made his early years a trial by fire. Eventually, the Kentucky Distillers' Association pushed distillers to take a year or two off from production until older stocks were sold. Into this soft market came a reorganized Whiskey Trust, with its Kentucky Distillers & Warehouse Company branch jumping into the market in 1899. That spring, they gobbling up every Kentucky distillery they found any value in. For the Weller company, it could have been the end. Its founder, William Larue Weller passed away. Yet his sons George and John carried on, moving the business into the Bernheim Brothers old wholesale building on Whiskey Row in Louisville.

By 1907, the brothers decided to incorporate and took on a new investor Alex T. Farnsley. They were greeted again with disaster when in 1909 a massive fire completely destroyed their 133 West Main Street location.[208] Again W.L. Weller & Sons rose from the ashes. With Pappy and Alex taking more of the lead in the direction of the company, they decided to ditch the Whiskey Trust and in 1912 made a contract agreement with the Stitzel Brothers Distillery on Story Avenue.

Where Lore and Reality Cross

From everything I could see, in his lifetime, William Larue Weller never had any association with wheated Bourbon. Perhaps he sourced some from Monarch or one of his other suppliers, but if he did, he never promoted it. Then I came across something quite curious. In 1912, the first bottle of non-rectified whiskey with the Weller name appeared in an advertisement. Labeled Old W.L. Weller, it was an eight-year-old Bottled-in-Bond Bourbon, distilled in 1904.[209] The shocker was that it was touted as "the Highest Type KENTUCKY WHISKEY Ever Made 40% Rye."[210] And the brand continued to be marketed this way until 1915—the same year Pappy Van Winkle and Alex Farnsley bought out the Weller brothers. So this all but ends any chance of an association between the Weller family and promoting a wheated Bourbon.

So when did W.L. Weller finally become wheated? The seeds of an answer appeared when I picked up a copy of Sally Van Winkle-Campbell's book *But Always Fine Bourbon: Pappy Van Winkle and the Story of Old Fitzgerald* (1999). Sally is the granddaughter of Pappy Van Winkle and sister of Julian III. If you want to know more about Stitzel-Weller or Pappy Van Winkle, it is a delightful read. In one chapter, she goes through a description of the Stitzel-Weller distillery tours given by Norman Hayden (who sometimes had Pappy joining in) back in the late 1940s. It is here that she discloses origin of the wheat mash bill as being a creation of the Stitzel family. I was shocked I had never heard that before. The lore I came across suggests that Pappy chose wheat because that is what his employer W.L. Weller used. Turns out, it is the other way around. When Prohibition came to a close, W.L. Weller and the Stitzel Brothers Distillery, then under the control of Arthur Phillip Stitzel, merged. But apparently the Weller brand didn't immediately start using this recipe. The earliest post-Prohibition ad I could find for Old Weller listed it as a 5-year old straight rye.[211] Then when World War II caused distilleries to either stop distilling or shift to industrial alcohol production, Old W.L. Weller shifted into the blended market. But Pappy was never a fan of blending with grain neutral spirits, so Weller was blended with only straight whiskeys.[212] It wasn't until around 1950 that the brand shifted to 100% Kentucky straight Bourbon whiskey. But was this wheated? It is a good bet it was, since the ad states it was "made, mellowed, and bottled by Stitzel-Weller Distillery." Still, it didn't sell the mash bill, instead promoting itself as hand-made sour mash.[213] This remained the case until the Van Winkle family sold the distillery in 1972.

So when did the word wheated finally become associated with the W.L. Weller name? The earliest mention I can find is when Diageo, Inc (United Distillers) sold the brand to Sazerac in 1999, along with the historic Old Charter brand. The press release mentions W.L. Weller along with Rebel Yell and Old Fitzgerald as one of "only a handful of 'wheated' Bourbons."[214] The first time the words "Kentucky's Original Wheated Bourbon" appears in an ad isn't until 2011.

Why did it take so long for them to finally reveal to the public that the whiskey was wheated? You might ask the same of Maker's Mark. Throughout the 20th century, both brands leaned heavily into the hand-made sour mash angle. The truth is, in the middle of a Bourbon depression, brands were more into selling people on concepts that were comfortable with and that drew their eye. What did you think the first time you heard the term "wheated Bourbon?" Being an unusual term, it takes some explaining. Today, Bourbon is popular and fans are always looking for the something cool or unique. Back then, it was only the die-hards that really cared.

So of current brands, it is possible W.L. Weller is the oldest to *advertise* itself as a wheated Bourbon. It doesn't make it the first or the original. Like many of our other pieces of lore, there are just too many undocumented historical possibilities for us to have any chance to nail one down. It definitely wasn't William Larue Weller's rectified whiskey.

Still, none of that prevents me from hunting down a Weller 12-Year Old as a lower cost substitute for Pappy, although it is almost as hard to find. Plus, even though it uses a wheated recipe like Pappy, that doesn't take into account the barrels used, the barrels picked for sale, the length of aging, the specific warehouse at Buffalo Trace (each with a different personality), and the location of the cask within said warehouse. I'll just have to enjoy it for what it is.

By the way, if you ever do stumble upon a time machine, don't miss out on other historical Bourbon bargains from before the whiskey boom of the past 15 years. If you make a stop in 2001, the first year Weller 12-year hit the market, you could find it for as little as $15.99. Not bad, even if it doesn't tout itself on the label as being wheated.

Reality: False. It may be the first to advertise itself that way, but it is far from the first made.

Moonshine Blindness

Myth: During Prohibition people went blind from drinking moonshine made by inexperienced distillers

AI: True

Late on a Friday night, two businessmen, weary from a tough business meeting, were making their way back to New York when they decided to stop for the night in Springfield, Massachusetts. As they approached their hotel, a man in a gray trench coat appeared just outside the entrance.

"Hey, you wanna buy some liquor?" he said in a hushed voice.

With National Prohibition in full force, finding a belt of booze in unfamiliar territory was no easy feat. Buying from streetwise bootleggers always carried a risk, but after a long road trip, the promise of a quick snootful was too tempting to pass up. Money slipped into the dealer's hand, and a quart of brown liquor slid into one of the men's travel bags.

Once in their room, they found two glasses, inspected the brown, nondescript bottle, and slowly eased out the cork to avoid the telltale pop. Passing the bottle back and forth, each took slugs until they started to feel a little wobbly.

Then, suddenly, everything went black.

"Hey, can you see?" one man asked, panic creeping into his voice.

"Not a thing," the other replied.

"Oh no, this must be some bad hooch. Have we gone blind?"

One of the men fumbled to where he thought the phone was. "I dunno, but maybe we should call for a doctor, just in case."

Grabbing the candlestick phone, he pulled the receiver off the hook and lifted it to his ear, immediately connecting to the switchboard.

"What can I do for you?" asked the front-desk clerk.

"I'm ashamed to say, my friend and I just had a bottle of hooch and we think it's tainted and we've gone blind! Could you send up a doctor?"

A slight chuckle came through the receiver. "Actually, go ahead and polish off that bottle. By the time you're done, hopefully, the electrician will have the lights back on. We blew a fuse!"[215]

That Nasty First Cut

In an era when newspapers were firmly divided between pro-Prohibition "drys" and anti-Prohibition "wets," this was one of the few humorous articles about the subject, offering some levity amid the tension. After a 90-year struggle, Prohibitionists had won the day, leaving Americans to navigate a new world of either avoiding or creatively acquiring alcohol. One consequence of pushing alcohol production underground was the rise of unregulated spirits from a variety of questionable sources.

On distillery tours, when discussing the process of taking spirits off the still, guides often emphasize the dangers of people going blind from tainted hooch, typically blaming the methanol found in the early parts of the distillation run, known as the heads. The story goes that if left in the spirit by an inexperienced or unscrupulous distiller, the methanol it contains could lead to methanol poisoning, potentially causing blindness.

Curious to learn more, I spoke with distillers in the U.S., Scotland, and Ireland. I knew there were people in the Prohibition era who had malicious intent, but I couldn't shake the feeling that inexperienced distillers might be getting unfairly grouped with the bad actors. My question was simple: could someone really go blind just from not knowing they needed to remove the heads in a distillation run?

While legal cautions steer most distillers away from discussing methanol risks too casually, The answers were surprisingly mixed. Of course, for legal reasons, it's not good to tout leaving any poisonous substance in a spirit run. But some felt the dangers from inexperience might be overstated, while others argued it could indeed be a serious hazard. Not convinced either way, I decided to do my own sleuthing to see if there was a clearer answer.

The Alcohol You Don't Want

Any investigation into an unfamiliar subject starts with getting a baseline. The first thing to know is where this methanol comes from in the process.

Surprisingly, it first appears during fermentation as pectins in the cell walls of grains and fruits break down. In grains such as barley, corn, wheat, and rye, these methanol levels remain in trace amounts, while fruits like apples and peaches yield higher amounts. Once the resulting wash or mash makes it to the still, the amount of methanol increases. Since it evaporates at a lower temperature than ethanol, it is released within the first few moments of the distillation process. These foreshots are removed along with the rest of the heads as a standard distilling practice. However, although the initial run of methanol is removed, some remains blended in with the "hearts" as it is impossible to remove 100%. However, these trace amounts are considered safe for consumption.

But what if you didn't cut out the foreshots, heads, and tails from your run? How much methanol remains? Unfortunately, I couldn't find a concrete answer. Logically, though, a spirit made this way would taste highly unpleasant. The heads have a strong acetone or turpentine smell, and the tails bring in harsh, off-putting flavors, making a nasty concoction.

Still, in times of desperation, people have tried drinking anything—Milwaukee, for instance, once had an epidemic during Prohibition where people were drinking "wood alcohol," which can contain nearly 100% methanol.

Proof or Propaganda?

There was obviously bad liquor circulating in the 1920s. Nebraska Prohibition Director James H. Hadley rang the warning bells in the early days saying, "We must stop this traffic, for it is killing and blinding the patrons of the bootleggers all over the state."[216] The reports slowly increased until, by 1925, the *Buffalo News* was warning "all who indulge in illicitly-made liquor, moonshine or bootleg, risk death, blindness, and insanity."[217]

Was the problem in Buffalo really that severe? It is hard to say. American newspapers have always shown bias, often divided along party lines, since the country's founding. The rise of the Temperance movement introduced a new divide, creating an overlap where publications also took sides as 'wet' or 'dry. In the decades before Prohibition, wet newspapers painted themselves as defending American freedoms from overbearing do-gooder Prohibition advocates, and stoked men's fears by suggesting it was all a guise for women's suffrage. The dry newspapers told stories of families being destroyed by the evils of alcohol and how it ruined society. Once Prohibition became the law of the land, the wets gained the upper hand and were well trained in rhetoric based on fear. Because of this, as a researcher, it is hard to determine just how bad the situation was.

While the actual number of "moonshine blindness" cases during Prohibition is unclear, I couldn't find a single report that pointed specifically to inexperienced or negligent distillers as the source of blindness. Then I thought, how many reports of "moonshine blindness" were reported in the days before Prohibition? It turns out there was only one in 1891, but its warning was about the dangers of staring at the moon for too long.[218]

Testing Theories with AI

Just for fun, I decided to consult AI for its take on methanol safety. Although AI responses are only as trustworthy as the sources they're trained on, it's still a useful tool to gauge where to focus further research. I do keep in mind, though, that early versions of AI once advised people that eating rocks was healthy—a mistake that could, of course, destroy both your health and your teeth! Still, I was curious to see how it would respond.

I started by asking about the methanol levels deemed safe by American and European government agencies. AI indicated that safe levels generally fall below 0.1% of the total alcohol content. Then I asked how much is present in a total uncut spirit run. For spirits distilled from fruit, methanol could make up approximately 0.1% to 0.5% of the total distillate volume—or higher with apples or grapes, which are highly toxic. In grain-based spirits, however, methanol concentrations are typically much lower—often well below 0.1%, sometimes as low as 0.02–0.04% of the total distillate volume.

When I asked how much methanol could cause blindness, it didn't provide a percentage but rather stated that "as little as two teaspoons could cause blindness, and six teaspoons could be fatal."[219]

It is definitely not something to fool with and I understand why no one wants to be a lab rat in this experiment.

Piecing It All Together

My attempt to exonerate inexperienced distillers wasn't going too well. Both AI and distillers provided insights, but potential answers only turned cloudy. Since Prohibition-era newspapers were more interested in persuasion rather than investigative journalism, we'll never know how many cases of "moonshine blindness" were actually due to inexperienced distillers.

The majority of cases could likely be traced to bad actors. One of the most blatant tricks was selling pure wood alcohol to desperate people. Others were more covert, adding just a little wood alcohol or denatured alcohol into moonshine to give it a kick. Some other dangerous additives included sterno, chemical dyes, formaldehyde, chloroform, and even creosote (a wood preservative).

Of course, 'moonshine blindness" wasn't always due to added poisons. Many moonshiners used lead-containing materials, like car radiators or poorly soldered pipes, for distillation. Lead leaching into alcohol could cause blindness, organ failure, and death. Additionally, toxic substances like ethylene glycol (antifreeze) were present in radiators or other equipment if not thoroughly cleaned.

The people who should be off the hook are the long-standing moonshining families who had distilled for generations before Prohibition. It's no surprise there wasn't a widespread issue of "moonshine blindness" reported in the days before bootleggers began transporting liquor nationwide. Back then, moonshine was sold locally, often to friends and neighbors, and traditions dictated carefully removing the unpleasant heads and tails. The real problems began when these spirits were acquired by bootleggers who would dilute or adulterate the product to increase profits, knowing they'd likely never see their customers again.

During Prohibition, a new wave of opportunistic moonshiners started distilling solely for profit, often with little experience and even less regard for safety. Some, alerted to revenuers approaching, might have hurriedly collected the heads and just a portion of the hearts before shutting down—then sold this uncut product anyway. Unfortunately, actions like these hurt the reputation of all moonshiners—family and opportunists alike— casting doubt even on those who followed traditional, careful methods.

While we can take inexperienced grain-based distillers not taking cuts off the hook as a *primary reason* for "moonshine blindness," it is inconclusive as to whether their moonshine contributed in any way to the issue. With their naturally higher methanol levels, apple, peach, and grape brandy distillers are another matter.

Unfortunately for the thousands who were poisoned, they likely crossed paths with the devious work of the unscrupulous distiller or bootlegger.

Hopefully, our friends in Springfield didn't cross paths with one of these dark, deadly merchants in their travels. If they did, let's hope that a lucky escape taught them to avoid repeating the mistake.

Reality: Inconclusive. Yet, inexperienced distillers get a little too much blame with little to no newsworthy proof.

SINGLE MALT > BLENDED

MYTH: SINGLE MALT WHISKY IS SUPERIOR TO BLENDED WHISKY

AI: Subjective

As the hammer fell, news of the sale reverberated across the whisky industry: A single bottle of Scotch whisky had just sold for a record-breaking $2,714,250 at Sotheby's Auction House in London. This record-breaking bottle was the Macallan Adami 1926, a single malt that had aged 60 years in a sherry cask before spending 37 more years in a bottle. Only 40 bottles were ever produced from this cask, and this one was especially unique, adorned with a label by the Italian painter Valerio Adami. However, it wasn't the first bottle sold from the lot. Just four years earlier, another bottle from the same cask went for $1.5 million.

But what if this had been a blended Scotch instead of a single malt? Would it have commanded such a sum? Take one of the most prestigious blends: The John Walker Masters' Edition. This blend of rare 50-year-old and older single malts and grain whiskies, some from long-closed distilleries, was packaged in an elegant black crystal Baccarat decanter and an exquisite wood case crafted by N.E.J. Stevenson, Cabinet Makers by Appointment to Her Majesty Queen Elizabeth II. Yet its retail price was only $25,000.

With these eye-popping numbers and the disparity between them, it's easy to assume that because single malts are achieving record-breaking prices, they must be superior to a blend. But does this price differential alone prove superiority?

The Opinion of the Crowd

The first thing to understand about whisky is that its beauty lies in the senses of the beholder; nosing and tasting are subjective experiences. Not everyone loves peated Scotch, but does that make it inferior to unpeated Scotch? Hardly.

This subjectivity makes whisky highly susceptible to trends. When you think of trends, consider shag carpeting. In the 1970s its plush feel made people feel it was superior. You can still find various forms of shag carpeting today, but do we consider it superior? And what vinyl records? In the 1970s they were considered far superior to 8-track tapes. By the 1990s compact discs' clean sound without pops or scratches almost put an end to records. Today, there is a resurgence in the popularity of vinyl with people claiming it delivers a superior sound. But digital music dominates sales. If digital music is so popular, how is it inferior to a vinyl record?

Whiskey is the same. Single malt fell out of favor in the 1860s, after the British parliament opened up the blending of single malts with grain neutral spirits. Blending became an artform and the public embraced it. It took well over a century before single malts started making inroads in terms of market sales. And today, blends still control over 90% of the whisky market. If blends were and still are so popular, how could they be inferior to single malt?

It was the question taken up by the Royal Commission on Whiskey and Other Potable Spirits in the UK in 1909 when determining whether "silent spirit" was worthy of being called whiskey. After extensive deliberation, the commission concluded that blends and grain spirits that retained the character of grain could be considered whiskey. They pointed to the superior sales of blends over single malt and Irish pot still whiskey at the time.[220] It wasn't an admission that blends were better than undoctored spirits—just that sales trends showed they were the superior choice for consumers at the time.

The Quality Question

Some argue the superiority of single malt because it is made entirely from malted barley at a single distillery, it provides a unadulterated sense of the distillery's character. But single malt didn't always have the best reputation for quality. Before the Excise Act of 1823, it was hard to throw a pebble and not hit an illicit Highland still. These small-scale distillers made everything from blend-worthy spirits to something akin to paint stripper. It wasn't until blending houses came along in the 1830s that they began vatting (or blending) different Highland malts in an effort to refine the flavor. Technically not single malts, because they didn't come from a single distillery, these were the forerunners to grain-spirit and malt-spirit blends. Once the law changed in 1863, the Walkers, Dewars, and Bells did their best to transition to the new spirits while marketing these new blends as tamer than drinking vatted malts. It was the harshness of the unadulterated stuff that drove customers of that era to the gentler flavors of blends.

Today, those gentler flavors are often dismissed by single malt drinkers who crave a full-bodied spirit that expresses the art of the distiller, the essence of the grain, and the influence of the cask. It has led to an era of small batch, single cask, and barrel strength whiskies. A fine single malt in the hands of an experienced distiller with an incredible palate is a fine thing to behold.

But does that automatically make a single malt better? What if a distiller grows a certain arrogance around their skills, or is in it for the money not the flavor, or what if they take shortcuts or are too beholden to accountants? While there are plenty of single malts with fancy prices and great placement on the shelves, there are plenty of rough single malts. Either the distiller took the wrong cut points in the heads, hearts, and tails. Or maybe they chose the wrong cask to age in. Or maybe they let it sit in the cask so long, so it became off-putting with astringent flavors that only that distiller appreciates.

These factors make it clear that the term single malt does not automatically imply superiority.

The Art of the Blend

One aspect often overlooked in the 21st century is the art of the blender. Unlike single malt distillers, who are at the mercy of what they have in storage, a skilled blender can draw from multiple sources, creating a unique and crafted flavor profile. Compass Box is a prime example of a blending house that creates exceptional whiskies from a variety of distilleries.

Another misconception is that blended whiskies are automatically of lower quality because they're "diluted" with grain spirits. However, not all blends are the same. One of my personal favorites is Shackleton—a blended malt whisky, much like the vatted malts of pre-1863. The only difference between a blended malt and single malt is that the malt whiskies came from different distilleries. So is it really inferior to a single malt?

And as for the price argument, keep in mind that a million-dollar bottle is an auction price, where figures can skyrocket. Who knows what that bottle of Johnnie Walker might fetch 37 years from now at auction—especially if there is another trend toward the appreciation of blends. And don't bet that won't happen. Compass Box and Barrell are doing a great job of converting the masses to premium style blends.

As for your own opinions, before sticking your foot in your mouth touting what the "so-called" experts say, do some blind tastings with blends versus single malts. Go beyond the bottom-shelf blends and try to elevate your experience. After all, you are the best judge of what ranks in quality on your own palate—not some shelf tag, hyped historic bottle, or distant whisky critic. Even if everyone else hates it and you find pleasure in it—that is all that is necessary to be considered a superior whisky.

Reality: Subjective. Trends and personal taste mean all bets are off. What do you think?

Six Medicinal Licenses

Myth: During Prohibition, six Kentucky distilleries were granted medicinal licenses to sell and produce whiskey

AI: True

To Prohibitionist ex-Governor Gifford Pinchot, the lack of law enforcement was an outrage. "The Coolidge administration talks in favor of drys," he told a reporter in August 1928, "but acts in favor of the wets."[221]

Much of his frustration was aimed at his fellow Pennsylvanian, Secretary of the Treasury Andrew Mellon. A businessman and financier turned politician, Mellon's business-friendly monetary policies ushered in the Roaring 20s with lower taxes and less regulation. But it wasn't Mellon's economic strategies that frustrated Pinchot. Instead, it was Mellon's past as a whiskey man—Mellon had once owned the historic Overholt Distillery in Broad Ford, Pennsylvania, and yet was in charge of the very department enforcing Prohibition.

"When appointed as Secretary of the Treasury," Pinchot pointed out, "Mellon was, if not *the* largest, one of the largest makers of whisky in America. Because of his personal views and business interests, he was just the wrong man to enforce the law. The results proved it."[222]

After eight and a half years under Mellon's leadership, the Bureau of Prohibition was still plagued by issues that had existed from the start: insufficient funding, an undermanned law enforcement team, corruption within the department, and inadequate training. The result was a thriving underground economy driven by moonshiners, rum runners, bootleggers, and speakeasies—all entangled with the bloodsoaked hands of organized crime.

In the heat of a presidential race, both Republican candidate Herbert Hoover and his opponent, New York Governor Al Smith, criticized the Coolidge administration's halfhearted support of Prohibition. To sway the dry vote in Hoover's favor, Pinchot hoped to imply that Mellon's past in the whiskey business was an embarrassment to the administration—making it look like the secretary was on the way out.

This wasn't Mellon's first brush with controversy over the distillery. When President-elect Warren G. Harding originally tapped Mellon for the Secretary of the Treasury post in 1921, alarm bells went off in the halls of Congress. Mellon, who had bought into the distillery in the 1880s, was the sole owner after inheriting his business partner Henry C. Frick's portion in 1919. Frick was the grandson of Abraham Overholt. But it wasn't just the plant's distilling capabilities that worried politicians; it was the 1.5 million gallons of whiskey stored in its bonded warehouses. Pennsylvania Senator Boies Penrose, a moderate Republican, tried to calm his progressive colleagues by suggesting that Mellon's distillery ownership would soon be nullified, "because of the known desire of the next administration to transfer the duty of enforcing the prohibition law from the commissioner of internal revenue to the department of justice."[223]

This reassurance and the Republican majority were enough to secure Mellon's appointment, but the distillery kept him in the crosshairs whenever the subject of lax enforcement frustrated the drys. It didn't help that his boss, Harding, was a known playboy and imbiber of liquor. Coolidge's belief that enforcement was more of a state and local issue only increased the pressure on Mellon, who tried to de-emphasize his interest in the bonded whisky under his control. Still, the distillery was his baby and he really didn't want to give it up. To quiet his critics, namely prohibition leader William H. Anderson, he turned its control over to the Union Trust Company of Pittsburgh before taking office. Then in 1925, Union Trust sold the distillery to the New York grocery firm Parks & Tilford, closing out any connection to Mellon.[224]

Still, no matter how he tried, he couldn't distance himself from his long-term relationship with whisky. When the President-elect Hoover put Mellon's name up in 1929 for another term as Treasury Secretary, he was attacked again as if he still owned the distillery. Still, with the economy thriving, few wanted to upset the status quo, and Mellon held onto his post.

Mellon might have thought his troubles were finally behind him, but later that year he found himself embroiled in a new whiskey controversy—this time over issuing permits for medicinal whiskey distillation. And here, Secretary Mellon planted the seeds of what would become one of the most persistently held bits of lore surrounding Kentucky Bourbon and Prohibition.

The Search for Whiskey Licenses

Head to Kentucky, tour some distilleries, and you're likely to hear a persistent bit of lore surrounding six medicinal distilling licenses granted to Kentucky distilleries during Prohibition. Several modern-day distilleries are named including Four Roses (Frankfort Distillery), Old Forester (Brown-Forman), A. Ph. Stitzel (Stitzel-Weller), and Jim Beam (American Medicinal Spirits/National Distillers). But when these licenses were issued and what they were for is less clear. When I'd ask, some would say they distilled throughout Prohibition, others would say they were warehouse licenses for selling old stocks that later turned into distilling licenses, and others said the licenses didn't come about until warehouses started going dry at the end of the 1920s.

With my usual skepticism, I started piecing together the various myths and theories, aiming to get a complete picture of Prohibition: when licenses were granted, who they covered, what they covered, and under what specific circumstances. Predictably, the answers were far more complicated than a quick sound bite on a tour.

To make sense of it all, like a symphony, we need to break American Prohibition up into four separate movements.

First Movement: World War I Prohibition

The events that led to government-controlled medicinal whiskey began in 1917 with the passage of the Lever Food and Fuel Control Act. With the U.S. recently entering World War I, Congress sought measures to conserve grain for the war effort. Distillers and millers, eager to show their patriotism, supported the act, believing their sacrifice would help soldiers overseas. Section 15 of the act, set to take effect on September 8, 1917, effectively banned the distillation of spirits across the nation for the war's duration.[225] In the three months leading up to the ban, distillers scrambled to fill barrels as fast as they could to ensure they'd have enough profit to survive. But as the ban approached, many felt this was simply a gateway to National Prohibition and that those precious drops coming out of the still on September 7 would be the end of their craft and family heritage. A few distilleries stayed open to produce industrial alcohol for the war effort, including eight in Kentucky, three in Maryland, and an unspecified number in Pennsylvania, but production of fruit and grain spirits for consumption were off-limits. [226]

Second Movement: The 18th, Volstead, and Willis-Campbell

The second movement arrived with the passage and ratification of the 18th Amendment, marking the start of National Prohibition on January 17, 1920. With a ban on the horizon, distilleries rushed to sell off stock. Rochester Distilling Company, owners of the O.F.C./George T. Stagg Distillery, put its operations up for auction but found no buyers. Newspapers announced, "Whiskey Brands

Not Worth Bidding For."[227] That same week, Kentucky Distilleries & Warehouse Company, part of the Whiskey Trust, auctioned off 19 Kentucky distilleries, along with their equipment and trademarks, once valued at millions. They sold for a mere $205,000, with unsold distilleries falling into receivership.[228]

To put a legal framework around the amendment, Congress passed the Volstead Act, which aimed to eliminate the production, sale, and distribution of alcoholic beverages. However, because the act inherited some language from the Lever Act, it left a loophole: States could theoretically reopen distilleries for medicinal whiskey production, circumventing the federal law.

Ironically, in Pennsylvania, the Brooks Law, the same high license legislation that had given rise to the speakeasy, opened the door for distilling. On July 21, 1919, Pennsylvania state legislators allowed licensing, and by December, the Large Distilling Company in Pittsburgh legally fired up its stills, marking the only instance I could find of American medicinal whiskey being distilling during this period.[229]

The federal government soon acted to close the loophole with the Willis-Campbell Act of 1921. In a bill promoted as ending medicinal beer, it also revoked states' authority to grant distilling permits. Most significantly, it included a provision banning distillation of new spirits until existing medicinal stocks reached a level deemed "sufficiently low" by the Prohibition Commissioner. It further restricted prescriptions to a quarter pint (12 ounces) per patient every ten days and tightened regulations on licensing for doctors and pharmacists. It had the desired effect, as demand for medicinal whiskey took a nosedive.[230]

Meanwhile, numerous distilleries were permitted to apply for licenses to sell the whiskey aging in their bonded warehouses. But this was far from limited to six Kentucky distilleries; in fact, hundreds of distilleries nationwide were permitted to sell their stocks to pharmacies and medical establishments, which could then dispense it with a doctor's prescription. Predictably, profit-seeking individuals exploited this system. Permit books, pre-printed with government signatures, were frequently stolen, forged, or copied, enabling large amounts of whiskey to be moved illegally from warehouses.

Third Movement: Warehouse Consolidation

With too many vulnerable warehouses to patrol and books to track, the federal government decided it was time to centralize supply. The Concentration Act of 1922[231][232] authorized the government to transfer approximately 30 million gallons of whiskey from over 300 bonded warehouses into just a handful of states.[233] However, taking the whiskey away from those who made it wasn't going to be easy. Frustrated with what they saw as government overreach, warehouse owners challenged the constitutionality of what amounted to a confiscation of private property. The battle ended up in the Supreme Court, but ultimately they upheld the lower courts' decisions. By 1924, the number of bonded warehouses had been reduced to around 137.[234] By 1925 it was reported the number was down to 28, with just under half in Kentucky—that is not quite six and that is not a Kentucky exclusive.[235] So where did this mythical number come from?

Fourth Movement: Invoking Section 23

Enter the fourth movement of the National Prohibition symphony—and the return of our Prohibition scapegoat, Andrew Mellon.

In early 1926, not long after Mellon saw his beloved Overholt Distillery sold to New Yorkers, concerns grew over America's dwindling supply of medicinal whiskey stored in concentration warehouses. Government mandates required whiskey to age for four years to qualify as medicinal, and estimates indicated only a five-year supply remained. Drys in Congress were expected to resist any attempt to restart distilleries for producing consumable spirits—including medicinal whiskey. Mellon's assistant, General Lincoln C. Andrews, who had recently urged Congress to permanently transfer whiskey storage away from private individuals, initially seemed like an opponent of renewed distillation.[236] But, to the Secretary's surprise, Andrews took the side of the distillers. In November, he formally requested that Congress allow 3,000,000 gallons of medicinal whiskey to be produced annually.[237] As anticipated, the drys in Congress stood firm against the idea. The next move came from Representative Willis C. Hawley of Oregon, who proposed the Medicinal Spirits Act of 1927. This act would provide medicinal distilling permits for the production of either Bourbon or rye whiskey. The permits would last 10 years, were renewable, and would go to existing plants. The bill also required the further consolidation of whiskey down to "not more than six warehouses."[238] Is this where the magic six Kentucky distilleries enter the picture? No—the bill didn't pass. And if that is frustrating to you, it was to General Andrews and Secretary Mellon also.

At their wits end, the two men decided to use the only power at their disposal—a get out of jail free card in the Willis-Campbell Act.

Section 23, paragraph 3, section 2 stated:

> *"No spirituous liquor shall be imported into the United States, nor shall any permit be granted, authorizing the manufacture of any spirituous liquor, save alcohol, until the amount of such liquor now in distilleries or other bonded warehouse shall have been reduced to quantity that in the opinion of the commissioner will, with the liquor that may thereafter be manufactured and imported, be sufficient to supply the current need thereafter for all non-beverage uses."*[239]

Basically Congress had already given the Prohibition Commissioner the power to decide, as long as whiskey stocks were low.

Ready to go to war for the drys, Wayne B. Wheeler, head of the Anti-Saloon League and a fervent advocate for Prohibition, quickly filed a protest with Dr. James M. Doran, the newly appointed Prohibition Commissioner, to halt the move.[240] Then to Wheeler's great relief, August figures were revised, showing

20 to 30 million gallons of whiskey in bonded warehouses, not 10 million. At an annual consumption rate of 2 million gallons, restarting distilleries could be delayed for several more years.[241]

The issue dropped until early summer 1929, when Prohibition Commissioner Doran announced that government stocks were down to 9,549,017 gallons. With supplies critically low, he finally exercised his authority to issue permits for medicinal whiskey production, aiming to produce 2,000,000 gallons in 1930, with a target of 70% Bourbon and 30% rye.[242] By then, Prohibition forces had lost their influential leader—Wayne B. Wheeler passed away in September 1927—leaving Doran free to push forward with his plan.

Who Fired Up Their Stills?

In July 1929, five Kentucky distilleries announced their intention and readiness to resume whiskey production, including Sunnybrooke, R.E. Wathen, and Stitzel in Louisville; O.F.C. (George T. Stagg) in Frankfort; and Glenmore[243] in Owensboro. Within a week, Commissioner Doran confirmed his issuance of permits to five or six distilleries, though he stopped short of specifying which ones.[244] As rumors circulated, newspapers watched distillery activities to deduce who would win the licenses.

By November, as word started circulating over which distilleries seemed primed to start distilling, concerns arose about how much production was allocated to a single company. Roughly 40% of all allocated whiskey—and 60% of Bourbon production—looked to be directed to one entity: the American Medicinal Spirits Company (AMS). Besides having a bead on the bulk of distilling permits, AMS controlled some of the largest government-consolidated warehouses. Price fixing was a major concern.[245] To soothe any concerns, rather than handling out five or six licenses at once, they would be issued at a much slower pace.

On November 22, 1929, the first spirits to make their way through a still since 1921 came from R.E. Wathan's old Bernheim Distillery (AMS)—the initial run was destined for the “Old McBrayer” label.[246] Two days later, at 9 AM on Saturday, December 7, under the guidance of Julian "Pappy" Van Winkle," Stitzel-Weller became the second Kentucky distillery to fire up their stills.[247] Beyond producing for their own brands, they also took on contract distilling for Frankfort Distillery, producers of Four Roses. The last of the initial five activated licenses went to Glenmore in Owensboro, producing for their own labels and contract distilling for James E. Pepper of Lexington.

By January 1930, Commissioner Doran announced that there were 24 concentration warehouses where medicinal stocks were stored and six distilleries with licenses to make whiskey. Perhaps this is where the six distillery number comes from. However, he states that there are only three in Kentucky, so he apparently wasn’t counting contracted work through Frankfort and Pepper’s permits. The other three licenses were issued to rye distilleries, including Large and Schenley in Pittsburgh and Overholt in Broad Ford, Pennsylvania.[248] The initial eight licenses expanded to nine with the addition of the O.F.C. Distillery in Frankfort, KY on April 1.

By mid-1930, concerns of monopoly resurfaced. In May 1930, Commissioner Doran admitted that AMS controlled 45% of the country’s existing supply and that permits might have to be adjusted for 1931. It didn’t help that in August, the Large Distillery Company was sold to AMS’ Overholt. When the addition of the Lee Redmon Distillery in Louisville and the American Medicinal Spirits Co at Baltimore, MD. exacerbated the situation, Overholt Distillery went on hiatus for a year. Meanwhile, the O.F.C./George Stagg would go offline on March 30, 1932 thanks to a fire. While the numbers of active medicinal licenses continued to shift, the only thing that remained consistent was the total amount of whiskey distilled each year—just 2,000,000 gallons.

Proving that old habits die hard, when the Overholt Distillery announced its renewal of distilling in 1933, fingers were once again wagging in Secretary Mellon’s direction. Cries of foul play and favoritism were brought up in Congress. The charge by the dry politicians was that the whiskey man was conniving his way into making fat profits off a generous government contract. Mellon and his family had to defend themselves, first reminding the politicians they had sold ownership in the distillery some eight years earlier and that the report that Overholt was on the schedule for a permit in 1933 was false. The unnecessary squabble was a fitting end to Prohibition's troubled history.

By August 1933, the country's patience had worn thin, and the repeal of the 18th Amendment appeared inevitable. With the end in sight, permits were offered to any distillery that had retained its equipment since the September 1917 shutdown, signaling the end of America's so-called "noble experiment."

Sadly, upon retirement from his government service, Andrew Mellon didn't get to reunite with his beloved Overholt Distillery. The distillery became part of National Distillers and eventually moved to Kentucky. Mellon passed away in January 1937.

Reality: False. The plan was for Kentucky and Pennsylvania to share the licenses evenly, but plans went awry.

The Oldest Distillery

Myth: Bushmills is the oldest licensed distillery in the world

AI: True

Paint a picture in your mind of an Ireland long before the castles and stone walls developed after the arrival of Roman and Catholic culture. These rolling green hills and misty valleys was the homeland of the Gaels—Celtic warriors, farmers, and storytellers who lived deeply connected to the rhythms of the land. Due to their lack of monarchy, later cultures referred to them as uncivilized, but in reality, the Gaels had a sophisticated web of rules under a system called Brehon Law. These laws emphasized fairness and balance, resolving disputes with wisdom rather than brute force. Powerful clans held sway, each bound by kinship and tradition, their influence stretching across territories marked by stone circles and sacred groves. It was a world where music, poetry, and oral history intertwined with daily life, and where the natural world was the heartbeat of their culture.

Into this world came an unlikely missionary. A teenager named Patrick, who was kidnapped from his English home by Irish raiders and sold into enslavement. Forced to tend sheep for six years on the island, he eventually made a daring escape back to England. Despite his ordeal, St. Patrick chose to return to Ireland with a bold mission: to convert the pagans to Christianity. However, rather than seeking to eradicate their pagan traditions, he incorporated Celtic symbols and rituals into Christian practices. This fusion gave the Irish a unique form of Catholicism, deeply intertwined with the land and its ancient customs.

But by the early 17th century, this harmony was unraveling thanks to constant pressure from the English crown. The forces of English expansion, Protestant Reformation, and political centralization were closing in, threatening to dismantle the Gaels' way of life.

The year 1607 was a major turning point in the history of Irish culture.

Just four years earlier, following the death of Queen Elizabeth I, King James I—formerly James VI of Scotland—ascended to the throne, uniting the crowns of England and Scotland and ushering in the Stuart reign. Seeking to tighten his grip over Ireland, James began confiscating lands from Gaelic Irish lords and Irish Catholics who resisted the rise of Protestant rule. In their place, he offered lands to both Scottish and English Protestants with the hope of bringing more loyal tenants to the Emerald Isle.

As their lands were seized, the Irish lords, led by Hugh O'Neill, decided to fight back. Finding Spain sympathetic, the Gaelic lords formed an alliance with Spain, hoping to reconquer their lands. But the anticipated Spanish support never materialized, and the lords fled in 1607, in what became known as The Flight of the Earls.

With the loss of his main rivals, the king went about creating a hierarchy of laws, installing leaders, imposing taxes, and centralizing economic control. He established a monopoly system on the island, where certain individuals or companies were given exclusive rights to produce or trade specific goods—many being the essentials of life, including salt, grain, fish, timber, and alcohol. Only a handful of patent holders were assigned, and the territories they covered were vast.

In a stinging blow to the Irish Gaels, Hugh O'Neill's great rival, Lord Deputy Arthur Chichester, was put in charge of assigning monopoly rights. The first patent was given to Charles Waterhouse of Munster. But the real dagger to the heart came in 1608 when O'Neill's former lands were handed over to Chichester's trusted deputy, Sir Thomas Phillipps, in Ulster.

Today, the story behind this 1608 patent is a distant memory, but the date endures, celebrated as the birth of what is claimed to be not only Ireland's oldest distillery but the oldest distillery in the world—Old Bushmills. At first glance, the claim seems legitimized by the official-sounding license granted in that year. However, as usual, I'm here to take a closer look and see whether this is truth or lore.

The Monopoly of Sir Thomas Phillipps

Let's start with what the license actually covered. While often described as a license to distill, it was much more comprehensive. This wasn't just a permit for one operation—it was a sweeping monopoly. Anyone in the region who wanted to distill, sell, or distribute spirits had to answer to Sir Thomas Phillipps. And we're not talking about a small plot of land. Phillipps controlled a vast expanse of Irish coastline that included an area known as the Rowte, and lands in County Coleraine.

The patent was granted on April 20, 1608 and one of its major features was allowing Phillipps control over production of aquavitae. Past laws had prohibited production of aquavitae in Ireland—except for nobles and freemen with prior authorization. Yet illicit distilling continued, despite threats of imprisonment and fines. This led to grain shortages and economic chaos. Part of what the king was pushing was for monopoly holders like Phillipps to reign in the chaos and control the distillers and their output.

Seeing the land of Limavaddy and Castledawson in County Coleraine as the most fruitful along the Rowte, he set up residence to manage his domain.[249]

So what of the land in County Antrim within the current footprint of Old Bushmills? Any chance there was distilling in this area is entirely speculative, but even if someone did fire up a still, it would have had no connection to the modern distillery. In those days the village was originally known as Portchaman. The name Bushmills evolved, thanks to the area's relationship to the River Bush and the grain mill established there some years later.[250]

Another big issue in the connection between this permit and the future distillery was the fact this monopoly wasn't permanent. Like most monopolies of its time, it had an expiration date. And when Oliver Cromwell overthrew the monarchy during the English Civil War (1642–1651), he abolished royal monopolies altogether, viewing them as symbols of royal privilege. In their place, he introduced the first excise tax on distillation in 1653. When the monarchy was restored under Charles II in 1660, the old monopoly system wasn't revived. Instead, Cromwell's excise system remained, allowing anyone to apply for a license to distill.

So, even if Bushmills could trace its name back to 1608, the idea that a continuous license existed through the upheavals of the 17th century simply doesn't hold up. The romantic notion of an unbroken lineage from 1608 to today is more marketing myth than historical fact.

The History of Bushmills

The true origin story of the Old Bushmills Distillery is thought to begin in 1784. Like many distilleries of its era, there are whispers of smugglers and illicit distilling occurring on the land long before it was officially licensed. But, as with most illegal activities, these stories lack documentation. History tells of a man named Hugh Anderson[251] who tradition suggests built his distillery in 1784.[252]

What's fascinating is that, if you visit the Old Bushmills Distillery today, their historic bottles prominently display the 1784 date—not 1608. So, when and why did the switch occur? And who made it?

Some speculate that the change was the work of Diageo's marketing department after the company acquired the Old Bushmills Distillery in 2005 from Pernod

Ricard, who also owned Irish Distillers (Jameson, Powers, Redbreast, etc). But my inner skeptic needed proof. To get to the bottom of it, I delved into old newspapers, searching from the early 1800s to the modern era. I wanted to see if there was consistency in the date given in the past and any clue as to events that might have caused the shift to the 1608 date. I also wanted to get a sense of how Bushmills marketed themselves for two and a half centuries.

What is wonderful about deep dives into true history is that you get more than you bargained for. I went looking to disprove one myth and found myself discovering other false narratives about the brand.

One of my earliest finds came from a May 1828 advertisement in the *Belfast News-Letter*. Today we know Bushmills for its milder flavored single malt and blended Irish whiskeys. But in this advertisement, a Belfast wholesaler named William Carson revealed that he was in possession of a good amount of peat-flavored pure malt whiskey from the Bushmills Distillery.[253] While I knew peated malt wasn't exclusive to the Scots, I'd heard that peat was fading from coastal regions by the early 19th century, due to easy access to shipments of coal for steam production. However, Bushmills' connection to peat seemed to only linger into the 1830s. In 1831, Bushmills was celebrated for its superior quality and distinctive "Ennishowen flavour."[254] This reference ties it to the Inishowen Peninsula, which, just 16 years earlier, had been the battleground where Aeneas Coffey and the revenuers clashed with the Poitín Republic.

By 1833, Bushmills whiskey had crossed the Atlantic and was being sold in Philadelphia by David Ranken of 73 Chestnut Street as "old Irish malt."[255] This prompted another discovery: in the 18th and 19th centuries, rather than calling a spirit "single malt" or "whiskey," it was often termed "malt spirit." But what type of malt spirit was Bushmills making? Was it Irish-style pot still whiskey (a mix of malted and unmalted barley with other grains), or was it pure malt whiskey (100% malted barley, like today's single malts)? Whatever they were making, it was greatly prized, according to the *London Times*. In 1849, an advertisement claimed "the unprecedented demand for, and acknowledged superiority of this whisky has already induced a near and unprincipled imitation of the name." What's curious about this newspaper article is that they give the distillery founding date as 1792 instead of 1784.[256]

In 1891, the Dublin *Freeman's Journal* gave the most compelling evidence yet of what was being made at Bushmills. They proclaimed it "famous all over the world as one of the finest and most superior pot-still whiskies ever manufactured in Ireland." This was followed by a statement that Bushmills rose to a higher-class product than Belfast distillers and that they hadn't succumbed to using the patent still. The article further aligned Bushmills with the "great Dublin distilleries," that achieved worldwide fame. This desire to separate themselves from Belfast distillers may explain why Bushmills was the only known distillery in Ulster spelling whiskey with the "e," like most of the rest of Ireland[257]

So were they making the Irish pot-still style with unmalted barley? Before our Chapter 11 deep dive into what Dublin distilleries were making in the 1880s, that might have been an obvious conclusion—especially when a 1896 article references Bushmills' "superior pot-still" spirit. But showing how vagueness of language and speculation on myths leads to more myths, the article dispels this notion, clearly stating "malt alone has been the material used," at Bushmills for the last 113 years. It later suggests that "we are not aware of the existence of any other distillery in Ireland [where] the only material used ... is exclusively malt."[258] It clarifies the 1828 reference to pure malt and matches with what the distillery runs through its stills today. Alfred Barnard concurred in his 1887 account, describing the malting process and the two pot stills used that produce 100,000 gallons of spirits a year. One interesting note from the whisky traveler is his mention that Old Bushmills was the oldest distillery, noting the date when smuggling began in 1743. No doubt the "oldest" label was well worn about the premises for decades.

The first signs of a break in the malt whiskey tradition occurred in 1935, when the familiar tall square bottles underwent a subtle change. For years, the words "pure malt" were positioned on the sketch of the pot still on the label. However, in this year, the pot still lost this claim and the words "A Blend" were introduced below the pot still.[259] At the time, blending dominated the market, so it was a savvy business move. However, when Quality Importers, Inc. took over distribution their marketing muddied the waters by claiming the whiskey was "produced under the same formula for 150 years."[260] Over the next couple of decades, Bushmills focused its advertising on distancing itself from smoky Scotches, pushing a mild whiskey theme.

As I dug through newspapers in the mid-20th century, another myth bit the dust. It has been suggested that in the 1960s, Irish whiskey had been gone from the American market for so long that few people remembered it. It's also been suggested that Jameson's reintroduction to the market in 1970 was the first time Irish whiskey was bottled by an Irish distillery—since bonding houses were historically used to bottle spirits they secured from distilleries. But I found no evidence showing that Bushmills ever relied on bonding houses for bottling. And, up to the 1920s, it was clearly stated in advertisements that their pure malt whiskey was "distilled and bottled at Bushmills."[261] After that and into the 1970s, advertisements were a little more vague, simply stating the whiskey came from the "World's Oldest Distillery."

Who Came Up With 1608?

That claim of being the "World's Oldest" must have created some pressure on Bushmills' marketers as their neighbors in Scotland began claiming distillery origin dates back into the 1700s. This brings us back to our original question—when did they change the date of origin from 1784 to 1608 and who made the change?

The first mention of the 1608 date I could find was in Palm Springs, California—but not in relation to marketing. It appeared in a caption under a photo of the Old Bushmills Distillery. Its suggested the pictured pond provided water for the distillation of whiskey "long before the distillery was licensed in 1608."[262] Yet during that time bottles still showed blended whisky from a distillery with a 1784 date.

Then, two events occurred in 1972 that appear to have had a bearing on the future of that "oldest distillery" claim. First, Old Bushmills was sold to Joseph E. Seagrams (New York), part of a Canadian owned company that stood as the world's largest distilling company. For years, Seagrams had tried to gain a foothold in the Irish whiskey market by acquiring shares in Irish Distillers Ltd. (IDL—owners of Jameson, Powers, and other iconic brands), but their advances were repeatedly rebuffed. It seems that IDL was more interested in acquiring Bushmills to complete the consolidation of the Irish whiskey industry—but Bushmills turned them down. So, Seagrams did a sidestep maneuver: they purchased Bushmills outright, then sold 25% back to IDL in exchange for 15% ownership in the company. Suddenly, Bushmills was part of the IDL's portfolio.

With a complete consolidation of the Irish whiskey industry, there was a hope Seagrams would be the right partner that could get them into stores across the globe. But things didn't work out like they planned. Production lagged behind demand, and Seagrams scaled back Bushmills' advertising. Compounding the challenges, the Troubles in Northern Ireland further complicated matters.

Then, in November 1974, a controversy over Bushmills' labeling arose in the United States. Brown-Forman, then the U.S. distributor for Bushmills, faced legal challenges spearheaded by Irish-American activist Thomas F. Mahoney. Mahoney argued that labeling Bushmills as a "Product of Ireland" was deceptive, given Northern Ireland's status as part of Great Britain. Chicago's Department of Consumer Sales agreed, giving Bushmills 30 days to remove "Product of Ireland" from their labels.[263] Brown-Forman and Seagrams defended the label and ultimately prevailed. It was around this time that Bushmills returned to advertising that the whiskey was bottled only by the distillery and for the first time placed on the label "original grant to distill 1608."

So in the end, it was a combination of Seagrams and the IDL that ultimately changed the origin date of the distillery in 1975. While the exact reasons behind the shift remain unclear, it's evident that the 1608 claim was a product of modern branding, not historical accuracy—and Diageo had nothing to do with it.

So which distillery is the "world's oldest?" Well, you know me and "firsts," if there is one thing I want you to walk away from this book knowing, it is that "firsts" in whiskey are nearly impossible to prove.

But as I close out volume one of this Whiskey Lore book series, I will give you a few distillery options that could be in the running. The first thing to note is Bushmills not only has challengers for the oldest claim in the world, but also in Ireland. Opened as the Brusna Distillery, supposedly in 1757, the current Kilbeggan Distillery seems to hold the record. However, if Alfred Barnard's claim of smugglers at the Old Bushmills location is valid and we decided to include smugglers and not licenses, that opens up a good number of Scottish distilleries to the claim of the world's oldest. And with that, we'll definitely never know since smugglers and moonshiners obviously didn't keep records. The Bols Distillery in Amsterdam (who produces genever) touts origins back to 1575, although not in the same location. One of the strong contenders may be Frapin in Cognac, which traces its roots to 1270 and its distilling history to the 16th century. However, their current facilities date only to the 19th century, leaving room for debate.

The magic of all of this lore is it gives us the perfect subjects to discuss over a dram.

Reality: False. They aren't the oldest licensed. As to whether their smuggling date is correct, well, that opens another can of worms.

BONUS CHAPTER

Excerpt from "The Lost History of Tennessee Whiskey"

From the Author:

Now that you have seen how whiskey history has so easily fallen prey to lore, I want to give you a taste of history through a story you have likely never heard before. 250 years ago a settler brought his family west beyond the Appalachian Mountains. Up until this time, Americans were not allowed to settle this country, thanks to a proclamation by King George III. Long before Daniel Boone paved the Wilderness Road in Kentucky, this Marylander brought distilling to what would become the Tennessee hills. For those that think America's whiskey tradition first moved from Pennsylvania to Kentucky due to the Whiskey Rebellion, you are in for a surprise.

In the spirit of opening your mind to a deeper understanding of American whiskey, I want to share with you one of the chapters from my book *The Lost History of Tennessee Whiskey*. It's a book that uncovers not only the origins of Tennessee whiskey, but also American whiskey history. It's a story Bourbon-centric whiskey writers have missed. I give it to you as a demonstration that we are only scratching the surface of American whiskey history. If you decide to pursue the book further, you will find plenty of Whiskey Lore style stories and lore debunking waiting to be explored. May it be a book that quenches your thirst for whisky stories until the release of *Whiskey Lore: Volume Two*.

I hope you enjoy.

Cheers and slàinte mhath!
Drew Hannush

Chapter Two: The Early Distillers

In the search for the origins of Tennessee whisky, few would think to look in Ben Franklin's *Pennsylvania Gazette*. But page six of the June 28, 1770 edition holds a clue to the inception point of Tennessee distilling.

In the last column was an advertisement that read, "To be SOLD by the SUBSCRIBER, living in Frederick county, Maryland, the following tracts of LAND..."[264]

Some have made the claim that the author is Tennessee's first distiller. His name: Evan Shelby, Jr.

The Enterprising Welshman

Born in Tregaron, Wales in 1720, Evan Shelby, Jr. was the second son of Evan and Catherine Davis Shelby. Encouraged by the opportunities offered by the New World, the Shelbys packed up everything they owned and moved to America. They began their new lives in Lancaster County, Pennsylvania, but eventually settled in Frederick County, Maryland.

Evan Jr. was in his early teens when the family purchased their Maryland farm. He spent his first few years helping his father on the farm and improving his hunting skills on his own. At 25, he married Letitia Cox, the daughter of a nearby plantation owner.

Evan, who would eventually attain the rank of Brigadier General in the American Army, started his military career far from the glory of battle, working as a road builder in the British Army. His leadership abilities impressed his superiors, and he was soon at the head of a group of rangers. When soldiers first met him, he looked the part of a scrapper. Short and muscle bound, his love and tolerance for spirits had him drinking other men under the table. But he never let it keep him from peak performance on a mission, and it never stole his ambition. His sharp focus endeared him to his superiors, as did his competence, and his ability to inspire his men. He rose to the rank of captain during the French and Indian War and commanded an advanced scouting team at the battle of Fort Duquesne near modern-day Pittsburgh.

After the war, Evan tried his hand at several occupations. He acquired lands, tended to his farm, raised and sold cattle, and opened a mercantile. But his first love was the fur trade, so he found two partners and jumped in with both feet. His company developed relationships with trading posts around the Great Lakes. But the timing was poor. Chief Pontiac of the Ottawa tribe was waging war on settlers throughout the area. With danger all around and no one to trade with, their business quickly dried up. His partners lost everything and moved to Canada to avoid paying their debts. Evan was left to sell his lands to keep himself out of debtor's prison. If not for the land grants he received for his military service, he might have lost it all. With the loss of his primary income, he took a post as justice of the peace and began to rebuild his life.

By the late 1760s, he grew tired of the struggles in Maryland and was eager to find a new home in the south, initially purchasing a few hundred acres in Rowan County, North Carolina. Then when he learned of the treaties of Fort Stanwix and Hard Labour, his interest shifted. The land west of the Appalachian Mountains had long been prized for the promise it held. Without hesitation, he placed an ad in the *Pennsylvania Gazette*, and took off with his wife Leddie for southwest Virginia.

Watauga and Holston

The Shelbys weren't the first Europeans to settle in the Cherokee Overhill region. The earliest settler, as the legend goes, was a Virginian named William Bean. A friend of Daniel Boone's, he joined the longhunter on some of his scouting expeditions through the Watauga River Valley. By the end of the 1760s, he built a cabin and moved his family to the banks of Boone's Creek.

Boone would introduce another early settler, Wake County resident James Robertson, to the region. While traveling to Kentucky Country with Boone, Robertson became enamored with the Watauga River Valley. He purchased a piece of land, planted corn, and went back east to fetch his wife Charlotte. James Robertson became an important early settler, with his ability to speak the Cherokee language, his leadership skills, and his pioneering spirit.

What Robertson didn't do, however, was distill his corn into whisky. This is because he and his wife were pious teetotallers. It is possible they distilled alcohol for their own medicinal use, but not for sale or trade.

Another more adventurous settler moved far west of the Watauga settlement. John Carter, a bold Tidewater Virginian, saw the benefits of opening up a trading post along the Holston River. He encouraged his business partner, William Parker, to get in on the scheme and set up shop on the west bank of the Holston in 1770, near modern day Rogersville, Tennessee. The Holston was a well-traveled river connecting eastern markets with the endless hunting grounds of the south and west. River traffic, vigorous trade with the Cherokee, and new settlers to the area made the trading post a success. Soon it expanded into a well stocked mercantile. But a move this deep into tribal lands was risky, and a friendly local tribesman warned Carter that an attack on his store might be imminent. Ignoring the warning, his business was ransacked. Instead of rebuilding, Carter left the business to his partner and moved east to the Watauga settlement.

The Mercantile at Shelby Station

John Carter wasn't the only one to see value in the Holston River. In December 1770, Evan Shelby, his wife Leddie, and part of his family drove cattle from Maryland to Southwest Virginia, using the river as a guide. Evan was so impressed with the area he began looking for property. But then, bad news came from Maryland. Leddie's father, David Cox, had died. Evan took his wife back north and the couple spent the next year settling the family's affairs in Maryland.

But Evan never forgot Southwest Virginia. His plan was to establish a large mercantile to supply both settlers and travelers heading into Kentucky country. He convinced both his extended family and his good friend Isaac Baker to move south.

He chose a large plot of land known as Sapling Grove. Located to the east of the Cumberland Gap along the North Carolina-Virginia border, it perfectly fit Evan's plans. He paid a fellow military man, Captain Anthony Bledsoe, to erect a store there. Evan went back to Maryland to complete the sale of his land holdings and put in orders for goods from suppliers back east to stock his new store. Then he and Isaac Baker officially purchased Sapling Grove in November 1773.[265] His friend took the northern half, while Evan took the southern half, including the building for his store and access to a creek.

The move to Sapling Grove was an inspired one. It wasn't long before Evan's store became a magnet for settlers in the Watauga River Valley and the newly populated Nolichucky River Valley. James Robertson, William Bean, and even John Carter and his son Landon were frequent shoppers. The first stop for newcomers like Virginian Valentine Sevier and his son John was Evan Shelby's store. It was part welcome center, gathering spot, and news outpost, as well as a store for supplies. Eventually a stockade surrounded the mercantile store, making it an area of protection as well. Known as Fort Shelby, it became a staging point for military battles and trips into Kentucky country, just as Evan had hoped. It became a favorite stop for longhunters and land surveyors like Daniel Boone and Richard Henderson.

The store's popularity was due, in great measure, to its plentiful supply of the essentials of life. There were sacks of salt, sugar by bulk or in loaves, and bags of tea (they were still British citizens, after all). Chocolate, consumed as a beverage, was sold, and spices were also stocked, though they were beyond the budget of most settlers. There were perishable items like salted pork and beef brought from Evan's farm and eggs supplied by local farmers looking for store credit. Items like vegetables and fruits were rarely in stock because of spoilage and as most settlers foraged or had gardens of their own.

But there was more than just food on the shelves. Settlers could find shoes, homespun, socks, clothing, and sewing supplies like needles and thread, scissors and buttons. Cooking pots, knives, forks, spoons, cups and dishes were all available, too. From time to time fancy dresses or hats might arrive from Philadelphia, London or Paris. There were also lifesaving tools--flintlocks and gunpowder to protect against intruders and for hunting needs. Shoes and saddles were available for horses to make sure transportation was reliable

As for alcohol, Evan stocked plenty of it. But rather than whisky, his primary spirit was rum. In fact, one of the first invoices from Evan's store at Shelby Station was a purchase of two quarts of rum by none other than Daniel Boone himself.[266] He also became a supplier to the Continental Army, providing spirits for the soldier's daily rations.

Where's the Whisky?

There are several factors that cause the mind to drift to whisky as the preferred spirit choice of settlers west of the Alleghenies.

The first is the belief the Scots-Irish (who were known as Scotch-Irish until the end of the 19th century) are the reason there is distilling in Tennessee. However, there are more English and Welsh names associated with Tennessee's early distilling than there are Scots-Irish.

Next is the myth that Tennessee distillers came to the area to escape taxation after the Whiskey Rebellion. In reality, Evan Shelby was selling locally distilled spirits over two decades before the Whiskey Rebellion.

The third factor is Kentucky's dominance over the story of American spirits. With the Bourbon style of whiskey referred to as "America's Spirit," it's easy to forget that early Americans actually preferred rum.

The other way a Bourbon-first attitude messes with the mind is through its late arrival as a spirit. The earliest Kentucky distillers on record started after the Revolutionary War. Evan sold his spirits before the Boston Tea Party, an event that led to the Revolution. When rum became scarce during the war, George Washington began including rye whisky in the soldiers' rations. This move was a real turning point for American tastes, earning whisky a patriotic vibe.

Another reason whisky wasn't a featured part of the store's inventory comes down to the frontier barter system. Life for these settlers wasn't easy, and actual cash was scarce. In order to get supplies from the local store, like food, salt, and other necessities, they would trade items like eggs, tobacco, pelts, or distilled spirits. In the 1770s, rum's popularity made it more valuable in trade.

But this raises another question. Where did these inland pioneers get the sugar and molasses needed for distilling rum?

This question assumes that all rum is a product of West Indies molasses and sugarcane. In New England, before the war, a lot of it was. And while Evan Shelby could secure stocks of these types of goods, they were too expensive for most of the Overhill distillers. So instead of island rum, distillers made continental rum from local sources.

The most widely available source to Overhill distillers was the sugar maple tree. Sugar maples are an excellent source of wood sugars; eight gallons of sap make a pound of sugar. You could distill the syrup or you could make the sugar first and then distill that. While it didn't bring the profits island rum did, continental rum was still more valuable than corn whisky.

The First

For a shining example of how hard it is to find firsts in whisky history, look no further than Evan Shelby, Jr. While his life on the frontier is one of the most well documented, thanks to the preservation of the Shelby Family Papers at the Library of Congress, there are still many reasons to question his standing as Tennessee's first distiller.

Scholars have long used 1770 as the date of his arrival to the area. It's a case that should be strengthened by his decision to move to the region with the treaties that broke the Royal Proclamation Line in 1768. However, when he and his family made their first trek to the area in December 1770, it was likely some miles north of Sapling Grove, closer to the Holston River. The earliest he arrived at Sapling Grove was sometime in 1772, giving other distillers the opportunity to get the jump on his first claim.

Then there is the question of what defines the first distiller. Does this mean the first person to fire up a still, the first person to barter spirits, or the first person to sell their spirits for profit? With Evan Williams, historians suggest he is Kentucky's first "commercial" distiller. They specify "commercial" because it would be impossible to confirm the first person who fired up a still. After all, distilling was a chore like slopping hogs or tilling a field.

Another issue is the realigning and establishing of borders. A 1783 distillery in Louisville would have been in Virginia, not Kentucky. Kentucky didn't exist as a state until 1792. And the same problem exists for Evan Shelby. Tennessee didn't become a state until July 1796, two years after his death. Then there is the additional problem of an area known as Squabble State. Until 1779, Evan believed he lived in Virginia, not North Carolina (the future Tennessee). In fact, he fought as a colonel in the Virginia militia. This only changed when Governor Thomas Jefferson had the border of Virginia and North Carolina resurveyed to stop the squabbling. The new survey split Sapling Grove in half, with Evan's southern property lying in North Carolina and Isaac Baker's northern half in Virginia.

Having a popular mercantile like Shelby Station is another reason some historians consider him the first. Many future grocers rectified spirits. But if Shelby Station is considered on this point, John Carter's store on the Holston predates Shelby by three years. John Carter's son Landon, who was a pre-teen in those days, eventually became a distiller. Is it possible that he learned the craft from his father? Is John Carter the real first distiller? If the inventory taken from his will is any indication, he probably wasn't. Not a single piece of distilling equipment is mentioned.

Then there is the question: how do we know if Evan Shelby ever distilled? Yes, he had a mercantile, a gristmill, and a large farm with cattle. Everything points to distilling. Yet, the first reference to distilling is an order for whisky in 1780. The document shows a transaction with a distiller named Peirce Wall. It states that Evan agreed to provide rye meal and malt to Peirce. In return, the distiller was allowed to keep a fifth of the rye whisky he made while returning the rest to Evan as part of the transaction.[267] That doesn't make Evan sound like a distiller. It makes him sound like a good businessman who contracted others to distill. Yet his son Isaac went on to own a distillery in Kentucky. So was Isaac the distiller at Sapling Grove? Or perhaps it was a hired hand, or an enslaved person.

We may never know. And it's just as well. Whether Evan Shelby was the first or wasn't doesn't really matter. The records of his store and his life at Sapling Grove give us a glimpse into frontier life we rarely get. Those records give us a sense of whisky's true importance on the frontier, a focus on more than just corn whisky in early Tennessee distilling, and proof that whisky came to the area long before the Whiskey Rebellion. And that is enough to make him special in the history of Tennessee distilling and Tennessee whiskey.

Further Reading

Whiskey Lore will return with more volumes in this series

If you enjoyed this book, **please consider leaving a review on Amazon, Good Reads** or your favorite bookseller's website.

Also check out the complete historical work:

The Lost History of Tennessee Whiskey (2023)

Take a journey through 250 years of Tennessee whiskey history, tracing the roots of America's whiskey industry. Decades before Jack Daniel, Evan Shelby was selling spirits to legendary pioneers like Daniel Boone. Explore Tennessee's tangled relationship with Prohibition, uncover the origins of the charcoal filtering process, and learn how a dramatic shootout in the streets of Nashville pushed the state to go dry long before National Prohibition. Told in Drew Hannush's signature Whiskey Lore storytelling style, this book lays the foundation for a deeper understanding of American whiskey history. Available in paperback and audiobook through your favorite online bookseller.

Drew Hannush's Travel Books:

Whiskey Lore's Travel Guide to Experiencing Irish Whiskey (2022)

Whiskey Lore's Travel Guide to Experiencing Kentucky Bourbon (2020)

Whiskey Lore's Distillery Travel Resources

Find over 600 distilleries at: whiskey-lore.com/travel

Hear the stories of craft distilleries on the Whiskey Lore Podcast:

whiskey-lore.com/flights

Acknowledgements

Where to begin?

First and foremost, I need to send out a huge thank you to everyone who has listened to and enjoyed the Whiskey Lore: Stories podcast. Your reviews, feedback, encouragement, and excitement whenever I released a new story and busted an old myth kept me motivated and made me determined to hunt down the truth. It was your encouragement that helped me realize, there is a place in this world for both the lore and the truth behind it.

To my Patreon family, thank you for your unwavering support. We've become friends over the years and its been wonderful getting to know you. Your financial support has helped me justify what I'm doing. Here is a shoutout to each of you: Mike Hanson, Fernando Rivera, Todd Ritter, Matthew King, Brian Scott, Jim Reichel, Nick Streeter, Mike Kirkpatrick, Alexandra Sklansky Clough, David Lavine, Jason Espinoza, Chris Dykstra, fellow traveler Jennifer Henshaw, Jasper Leenarts, and past patrons who have helped build this foundation of whiskey education.

I also have to send a big thank you out to my pal Pete, who wasn't really a big whiskey fan but decided to listen to my interview with Owen Martin (then of Stranahans) on a road trip. He told me afterwards I needed to write a book. Well, the original book concept he had for me, morphed into this idea. I'd long wanted to turn my podcast into books and he lit a fire under me. He has had a few ideas after that, so you might be seeing more than just multiple volumes of a Whiskey Lore series.

Thank you also to all the distillers, blenders, founders, tour guides, and whiskey historians who helped inspire this journey. Sharing stories helped drive my curiosity--especially at Jack Daniel's, George Dickel, and all around Ireland including Peter Mulryan at Blackwater for sitting and chatting Irish whiskey history with me. Thanks to Leslie McBride for inspiring my Scottish whisky travel. Cheers to my friends Mark, Jarrod, and Jason for the whisky tastings that kicked this all off. To the team at Grain & Barrel (Chicken Cock) including Kyle Harder, Maggie Vickrey, Tyler Rothenberg, Will Woodington, Ashley Smith, Matti Anttila, and Aaron Brost for getting me inspired to dig deeper and James A. Miller for creating such a mystery around yourself. Nelson Eddy of Jack Daniels and Fawn Weaver of the Nearest Green Foundation and Uncle Nearest. Nancy O'Malley for the ride around old Bourbon County and amazing detailed historical documents, and Becca Lawyer at the Bourbon County Citizen (formerly the Western Citizen). Special thanks to Lauchie MacLean of Glenora for the emails back and forth. I wish I was a whisky fan when I was up in your beautiful Cape Breton, I would have stopped in. But I will be back! And to Brian Haara and Mark Gillespie for the help on keeping me straight on the Makers Mark story. Thanks to Phil Prichard for our conversation--Tennessee craft distillers owe you a lot. Also, thanks to Alan Bishop, Ari Sussman, and Laura Fields for the discussions and keeping whiskey history alive through your work. And to Dr. Don Livermore for reviewing the book and then cluing me in on more of the misconceptions around Canadian whisky--I think we could talk for days on end and I'd never grow tired. The Great White North and its whisky history are things I need to know more about. Also, thanks to Jim Winton for the photographic evidence of those McLaren bottles in your collection.

A strange but wonderful thank you to OpenAI's ChatGPT. Honestly, when I started working with it, I argued with it, yelled at it in ALL CAPS, and gave up on it multiple times. But soon we learned each other's requirements and it has actually been a great help, especially with things like formatting, having it jog my memory on details, determining if there are modern misconceptions, and giving me suggestions like an editor, before I sent the manuscript to the editor.

You were also a massive time saver in drafting footnotes and the bibliography and consolidating my thoughts.

Other sources that were of great help were Find-a-Grave, FamilySearch.org, and Ancestry.com. These help me firm up dates and in the case of James Crow, a beat on his travels before Kentucky. Newspapers.com has also been a wonderful resource for finding prices, hunting down people and distillers of the past, and bumping into stories and situations I've never heard before. WebMD and the Mayo Clinic site were also helpful when trying to verify some hangover cures. And a big thanks to Joel Whitburn for writing all those great Billboard chart books. I spent most of my youth looking through them and they still benefit me when I am challenged to some old school music trivia.

Thanks to all of my friends and family who put up with me disappearing for months into my research and writing. Also a big thanks to all of my social media followers--those who are there for the history and those that support a world of craft distillers. Today's craft distillers are the source of today's incredible flavors and tomorrow's lore.

To all of these and anyone I missed, thank you for being a part of this journey.

Cheers and slàinte mhath.
Drew Hannush

Bibliography

Barnard, Alfred. *The Whisky Distilleries of the United Kingdom*. Reprint edition. Aaron Barker Publishing, July 24, 2013.

Bowmar, Daniel Mayes. "Old Jim Crow's Little Still-House." *The Courier-Journal* (Louisville, KY), September 5, 1897, 23.

Braunberg, Andrew. *Fires, Floods, Explosions, and Bloodshed: A History of Texas Whiskey.*

Carpenter, Virginia T. *The Carpenters of Carpenter's Station.* Manuscript, 1976. Accessed November 27, 2024. https://freepages.rootsweb.com/~carpenter/genealogy/manuscript.html.

Carson, Gerald. *The Social History of Bourbon*. Lexington, KY: University Press of Kentucky, 1963.

Coffey, Æneas. *Observations on the Rev. Edward Chichester's Pamphlet, Entitled Oppressions and Cruelties of Irish Revenue Officers.* London: Printed by W. Clowes, Northumberland-Court, Strand, 1818. Accessed November 21, 2024. http://opac.oireachtas.ie/Data/Library3/Library3/DCT051005.pdf.

Dewar, Tommy. *A Ramble Round the Globe*. London: Chatto & Windus, 1894.

Ferriss, Timothy. *The 4-Hour Workweek: Escape 9–5, Live Anywhere, and Join the New Rich*. New York: Crown Publishers, 2007.

"Glenora Distillery History." *Glenora Inn & Distillery.* Accessed November 21, 2024. https://www.glenoradistillery.com/history.

Green, Ben. *Jack Daniel's Legacy*. Nashville, TN: Rich Printing Company, 1967.

Greenwood, Malcolm. *A Ramble Round the Globe Revisited: In the Footsteps of Tommy Dewar*. Edinburgh: Angels' Share, 1999.

Hill, George. *An Historical Account of the Plantation in Ulster at the Commencement of the Seventeenth Century.* Belfast: McCaw, Stevenson & Orr, 1877.

Minnick, Fred. *Whiskey Women: The Untold Story of How Women Saved Bourbon, Scotch, and Irish Whiskey*. Lincoln: Potomac Books, 2013.

Mulryan, Peter. *The Whiskies of Ireland*. London: O'Brien Press, 2002.

O'Connor, Fionnán. *A Glass Apart: Irish Single Pot Still Whiskey*. London: The Lilliput Press, 2015.

Railey, William E. *History of Woodford County.* Frankfort, KY: Roberts Printing Company, 1928.

Rightor, Henry, ed. *Standard History of New Orleans, Louisiana.* Chicago: Lewis Publishing Company, 1900. Accessed November 21, 2024. https://www.google.com/books/edition/Standard_History_of_New_Orleans_Louisian/Q60UAAAAYAAJ.

Roberts, Carole. *A Dozen Tennessee Distilleries and "Old Sport": Pre-Prohibition Distillery Profiles of Bedford County Region.*

Scudder, Horace E. *Noah Webster.* Boston: Houghton, Mifflin and Company, 1882. Accessed November 21, 2024. https://www.google.com/books/edition/Noah_Webster/VzcFAAAAYAAJ.

Spitta, Philipp. *Johann Sebastian Bach: His Work and Influence on the Music of Germany, 1685–1750.* Translated by Clara Bell and J.A. Fuller-Maitland. Vol. 1–3. London: Novello & Co., 1889.

Stafford-Wilson, Arlene. "John McLaren Whiskey – Perth, Ontario." *Arlene Stafford-Wilson: Celebrating the Past in Lanark County, Tay Valley Township, and the Rideau Corridor* (blog). Accessed November 21, 2024. https://arlenestaffordwilson.wordpress.com/tag/john-mclaren-whiskey-perth-ontario/.

St. Patrick. *The Life and Writings of St. Patrick.* Edited by Charles H. H. Wright. London: Religious Tract Society, 1905.

Van Winkle-Campbell, Sally. *But Always Fine Bourbon: Pappy Van Winkle and the Story of Old Fitzgerald*, Kindle ed. (Louisville, KY: Limestone Lane Press, 1999).

Veach, Michael. *Kentucky Bourbon Whiskey: An American Heritage*. Lexington: University Press of Kentucky, 2013.

Whittaker, E.T. *A History of the Theories of Aether and Electricity*. London: Longmans, Green, and Co., 1910. Accessed November 27, 2024. https://archive.org/details/historyoftheorie00whitrich/page/n5/mode/2up.

Young, Al. *Four Roses: The Return of a Whiskey Legend*. Louisville, KY: Butler Books, 2010.

Zoeller, Chester. *Bourbon in Kentucky: A History of Distilleries in Kentucky*. 2nd ed. Louisville, KY: Butler Books, 2010.

ENDNOTES

1. "Pure Old Bourbon," *The Louisville Daily Courier* (Louisville, Kentucky), July 19, 1858, 2.

2. S.Res. 294 (110th): A resolution designating September 2007 as "National Bourbon Heritage Month." GovTrack.us. Accessed November 21, 2024. https://www.govtrack.us/congress/bills/110/sres294/text.

3. U.S. Congress. *A Concurrent Resolution Recognizing Bourbon Whiskey as a Distinctive Product of the United States.* S. Con. Res. 19, 88th Congress (1964). https://www.govinfo.gov/content/pkg/STATUTE-78/pdf/STATUTE-78-Pg1208-2.pdf.

4. "Labrot & Graham Discover the Difference." *Lexington Herald-Leader*, August 27, 2000, p. 87.

5. "In the Business World." *The Miami Herald*, May 12, 1972, p. 57.

6. "This Sunday." *Atlanta Journal & Constitution Magazine*, January 6, 1980, p. 158. Note: The article uses the phrase "America's native distilled spirit" rather than "America's native spirit."

7. "Tomorrow." *New York Daily News*, December 22, 1981, p. 148.

8. "Visit Jim Beam's American Outpost." Advertisement. *The Louisville Courier-Journal*, September 12, 1993, p. 58.

9. S.Res. 294 (110th): A resolution designating September 2007 as "National Bourbon Heritage Month." GovTrack.us. Accessed November 21, 2024. https://www.govtrack.us/congress/bills/110/sres294/text.

10. "McLaren's Malt Whiskey" Advertisement, *The Perth Courier*, December 26, 1873, 3. Note: Thanks to Arlene Stafford-Wilson for her blog in helping me discover this story: http://arlenestaffordwilson.wordpress.com/

11. Robert Lorne Richardson. "The Camerons of Bruce." *The Winnipeg Tribune* (Winnipeg, MB), January 14, 1908, p. 8.

12. Jim Winton (Perth, Ontario). Photo from his collection.

13. Bate & Co. "In Scotch Whiskey." Advertisement. *Ottawa Daily Citizen*, October 11, 1897, p. 1.

14. Jim Winton (Perth, Ontario). Photo from his collection.

15. "Spinal Paralysis: Death of J.A. McLaren, Well-Known Perth Distiller." *The Daily Whig* (Kingston, ON), December 19, 1901, p. 6.

16. "The McLaren Will." *The Ottawa Citizen* (Ottawa, ON), November 17, 1903, p. 5.

17. "McLaren's Scotch Whisky." Advertisement. *The Hamilton Spectator* (Hamilton, ON), July 23, 1912, p. 20.

18. "Find 50 Quarts Scotch Whisky." *Spokane Chronicle* (Spokane, WA), April 6, 1921, p. 1.

19. "Protection for Whisky." *Evening Telegraph* (Dundee, Scotland), June 7, 1933, p. 4.

20. United Kingdom. *Finance Act, 1933, No. 24: Amendment as to Permits and Certificates Accompanying Spirits.* 23 & 24 Geo. 5 c. 19. Accessed November 21, 2024. https://www.legislation.gov.uk/ukpga/Geo5/23-24/19/enacted.

21. Jon Filson. "The Battle of the Glens." *The Toronto Star* (Toronto, ON), August 11, 2004, p. 46.

22. United Kingdom. *Scotch Whisky Act 1988.* c. 22. Accessed November 21, 2024. https://www.legislation.gov.uk/ukpga/1988/22/enacted.

23. United Kingdom. *The Scotch Whisky Regulations 2009.* No. 2890, Regulation 10. Accessed November 21, 2024. https://www.legislation.gov.uk/uksi/2009/2890/regulation/10.

24. *The Scotch Whisky Association v. The Virginia Distillery Company, LLC.* Case No. 1:19-cv-01264, U.S. District Court for the District of Delaware, 2019. Accessed November 21, 2024. https://www.pacermonitor.com/public/case/28978039/The_Scotch_Whisky_Association_v_The_Virginia_Distillery_Company%2C_LLC.

25. "Green River Whiskey." Advertisement. *The Savannah Morning News* (Savannah, GA), November 22, 1904, p. 2.

26. "Old Still Creek." Advertisement. *Daily Arkansas Gazette* (Little Rock, AR), December 21, 1913, p. 15.

27. "Randolph Rose of Chattanooga, Tennessee." Advertisement. *The Atlanta Constitution* (Atlanta, GA), May 5, 1912, p. 6.

28. "Taylor & Williams Distilleries." Advertisement. *The Courier-Journal* (Louisville, KY), January 1, 1937, p. 27.

29. "Jim Beam." Advertisement. *Fort Worth Star-Telegram* (Fort Worth, TX), March 11, 1960, p. 20. Note: Carl Beam is listed as Master Distiller in the advertisement, while Frederick "Booker" Noe II held the same position at the Boston, Kentucky, facility.

30. Daniel Mayes Bowmar. "Old Jim Crow's Little Still-house." The Courier-Journal (Louisville, KY), September 5, 1897, p. 23.

31. "Scotland Births and Baptisms, 1564–1950." Database. *FamilySearch*. Accessed February 12, 2020. https://familysearch.org/ark:/61903/1:1:XTT5-Z5C.

32. *The Pharmacist and Chemist.* Vol. 1. New York: William Wood & Co., 1870, 390. Accessed November 21, 2024. https://www.google.com/books/edition/The_Pharmacist_and_Chemist/VlyFy6zJQpUC.

33. William E. Railey. History of Woodford County. Frankfort, KY: Roberts Printing Company, 1928, 112.

34. "A List of Letters." *Kentucky Gazette* (Lexington, KY), July 27, 1820, p. 1.

35. *Records and Briefs of the United States Supreme Court.* Vol. 45. New York: Law Publishers of New York, 1922, 126, 669. Accessed November 21, 2024. https://www.google.com/books/edition/Records_and_Briefs_of_the_United_States/JxvBAhE6lrgC.

36. "Anderson & Stevenson." Advertisement. *The Commonwealth* (Frankfort, KY), February 10, 1836, p. 4.

37. "Wm. F. Gourtnay." Advertisement. *Vicksburg Weekly Sentinel* (Vicksburg, MS), January 6, 1846, p. 4. Note: Listed as "Crow's Whiskey."

38. *Records and Briefs of the United States Supreme Court.* Vol. 45. New York: Law Publishers of New York, 1922, 192. Accessed November 21, 2024. https://www.google.com/books/edition/Records_and_Briefs_of_the_United_States/JxvBAhE6lrgC.

39. *Records and Briefs of the United States Supreme Court.* Vol. 45. New York: Law Publishers of New York, 1922, 697. Accessed November 21, 2024. https://www.google.com/books/edition/Records_and_Briefs_of_the_United_States/JxvBAhE6lrgC.

40. *Records and Briefs of the United States Supreme Court.* Vol. 45. New York: Law Publishers of New York, 1922, 736. Accessed November 21, 2024. https://www.google.com/books/edition/Records_and_Briefs_of_the_United_States/JxvBAhE6lrgC.

41. *The Pharmacist and Chemist.* Vol. 1. New York: William Wood & Co., 1870, 390. Accessed November 21, 2024. https://www.google.com/books/edition/The_Pharmacist_and_Chemist/VlyFy6zJQpUC.

42. *Records and Briefs of the United States Supreme Court.* Vol. 45. New York: Law Publishers of New York, 1922, 175–176. Accessed November 21, 2024. https://www.google.com/books/edition/Records_and_Briefs_of_the_United_States/JxvBAhE6lrgC.

43. "Thompson & Co." Advertisement. *The Courier-Journal* (Louisville, KY), August 17, 1870, p. 1.

44. *Records and Briefs of the United States Supreme Court.* Vol. 45. New York: Law Publishers of New York, 1922, 739. Accessed November 21, 2024. https://www.google.com/books/edition/Records_and_Briefs_of_the_United_States/JxvBAhE6lrgC.

45. *Records and Briefs of the United States Supreme Court.* Vol. 45. New York: Law Publishers of New York, 1922, 205. Accessed November 21, 2024. https://www.google.com/books/edition/Records_and_Briefs_of_the_United_States/JxvBAhE6lrgC.

46. *Records and Briefs of the United States Supreme Court.* Vol. 45. New York: Law Publishers of New York, 1922, 176–177. Accessed November 21, 2024. https://www.google.com/books/edition/Records_and_Briefs_of_the_United_States/JxvBAhE6lrgC.

47. *Records and Briefs of the United States Supreme Court.* Vol. 45. New York: Law Publishers of New York, 1922, 734. Accessed November 21, 2024. https://www.google.com/books/edition/Records_and_Briefs_of_the_United_States/JxvBAhE6lrgC.

48. Ambrose Cooper, *The Complete Distiller* (London: Printed for P. Vaillant and R. Griffiths, 1757), 90–96. Accessed November 22, 2024. https://books.google.com/books/about/The_complete_distiller.html?id=rfAHAAAAQAAJ.

49. Harrison Hall. *Hall's Distiller.* Philadelphia: John Bioren, 1813, 171. Accessed November 21, 2024. https://www.google.com/books/edition/Hall_s_Distiller/DflAAQAAMAAJ. Hall suggests that Allison used the process as far back as 1786.

50. "John Quincy Adams Diary," Massachusetts Historical Society, December 27, 1804, accessed October 30, 2023, https://www.masshist.org/publications/jqadiaries/index.php/document/jqadiaries-v27-1804-12-27-p112

51. "Robertson County, Tennessee and Its Capital." *The Courier-Journal* (Louisville, KY), April 19, 1896, p. 26.

52. "E.R. Betterton & Co." Advertisement. *The Chattanooga News* (Chattanooga, TN), November 21, 1905, p. 10.

53. "Jack Daniel's." Advertisement. *Springfield Leader and Press* (Springfield, MO), October 24, 1952, p. 5.

54. "Jack Daniel's." Advertisement. *Albuquerque Journal* (Albuquerque, NM), February 13, 1954, p. 14.

55. "Jack Daniel's." Advertisement. *The Chattanooga News* (Chattanooga, TN), December 12, 1908, p. 16.

56. *Records and Briefs of the United States Supreme Court.* Vol. 45. New York: Law Publishers of New York, 1922, 232-233. Accessed November 21, 2024. https://www.google.com/books/edition/Records_and_Briefs_of_the_United_States/JxvBAhE6lrgC.

57. "Tennessee Whiskey Law." PDF file. Accessed November 21, 2024. http://static.squarespace.com/static/5101b837e4b0202016c6b5c9/t/52363a84e4b0855d9f5aca50/1379285636684/Tennesee%20Whiskey%20Law.pdf.

58. "Massachusetts." Syndicated article from *The New Yorker. The Enterprise and Vermonter* (Brattleboro, VT), October 17, 1838, p. 2.

59. "Spirited Republic: Alcohol in American History." *Prologue Magazine*, Winter 2014. National Archives. Accessed November 21, 2024. https://www.archives.gov/files/publications/prologue/2014/winter/spirited.pdf.

60. George Faber Clark. *History of the Temperance Reform in Massachusetts, 1813–1883.* Boston: William E. Smythe, 1888, 8–12. Accessed November 21, 2024. https://www.google.com/books/edition/History_of_the_Temperance_Reform_in_Mass/yRcPAQAAMAAJ.

61. *Investigation into the Fifteen Gallon Law of Massachusetts.* Boston: Samuel N. Dickinson, 1838, 5. Accessed November 21, 2024. https://www.google.com/books/edition/Investigation_Into_the_Fifteen_Gallon_La/t1xZAAAAcAAJ.

62. "The Fifteen Gallon Law in Massachusetts." *The St. Johnsbury Caledonian* (St. Johnsbury, VT), October 16, 1838, p. 2.

63. "Massachusetts." Syndicated article from *The New Yorker. The Enterprise and Vermonter* (Brattleboro, VT), October 17, 1838, p. 2.

64. "Striped Pig." *The Baltimore Sun* (Baltimore, MD), September 21, 1838, p. 4.

65. "Massachusetts Fifteen Gallon Law." *Madisonian* (Washington, DC), October 17, 1838, p. 3.

66. "Women on the Warpath." *The Monett Eagle* (Monett, MO), January 23, 1880, p. 6.

67. "House of Representatives." *Republican Banner* (Nashville, TN), October 15, 1841, p. 3.

68. "They Fared Badly." *The Pittsburgh Post* (Pittsburgh, PA), September 30, 1888, p. 1.

69. "Anti-Speak-Easy Society." *The Canonsburg Weekly Notes* (Canonsburg, PA), December 28, 1888, p. 1.

70. "The Speak Easies." *Pittsburg Dispatch* (Pittsburgh, PA), June 30, 1889, p. 16. And yes, this was the correct spelling of this newspaper. Traditionally spelled Pittsburgh, there was an attempt to normalize the name into "-burg" but by the early 20th century citizens lobbied against it.

71. "Testing the High License Law." *The Scranton Republican* (Scranton, PA), September 28, 1887, p. 2.

72. "The Speak-Easy Evil." *Pittsburg Dispatch* (Pittsburg, PA), November 4, 1889, p. 3.

73. "The Illegal Speak-Easies." *The New York Times* (New York, NY), July 6, 1891, p. 2.

74. "Mrs. Hester." *Pittsburg Dispatch* (Pittsburgh, PA), April 7, 1889, p. 3.

75. "McKeesport Matters." *The Pittsburgh Press* (Pittsburgh, PA), March 29, 1888, p. 6.

76. "The Illegal Speak-Easies." *The New York Times* (New York, NY), July 6, 1891, p. 2.

77. "Illicit Vending of Spirits." *Sydney Monitor and Commercial Advertiser* (Sydney, NSW), October 3, 1829, p. 4.

78. John Badcock. *A Dictionary of the Turf, the Ring, the Chase, the Pit, or Bon-ton, and the Varieties of Life, Forming the Completest and Most Authentic Lexicon Balatronicum Hitherto Offered to the Notice of the Sporting World.* London: Printed for the Author, 1823, 163. Accessed November 21, 2024. https://www.google.com/books/edition/Slang/URdKAAAAMAAJ.

79. "Death from Fighting." *Stockport Advertiser* (Stockport, England), December 7, 1827, p. 3.

80. "The Pittsburg Times Says." *The Canonsburg Weekly Notes* (Canonsburg, PA), December 21, 1888, p.2.

81. George Waller. "Excise Office Dublin." Advertisement. *Londonderry Journal* (Derry, Ireland), November 20, 1810.

82. "Distilleries." Advertisement. *The Times* (London, England), March 10, 1823, p. 3.

83. "Scotch and Irish Distilleries." *The Waterford Mirror* (Waterford, Ireland), June 23, 1823, p. 4.

84. "Remonstrance of the Irish Distillers." *The Waterford Mirror* (Waterford, Ireland), June 23, 1823, p. 4.

85. "Mr. Coffey." *The Kilkenny Moderator*, republished in *The Waterford Mirror* (Waterford, Ireland), December 27, 1823, p. 4.

86. E. J. Rothery. "Aeneas Coffey (1780–1852)." *Annals of Science* 24, no. 1 (1968): 61. Accessed November 21, 2024. https://www.tandfonline.com/doi/pdf/10.1080/00033796800200041. The patent was officially granted on March 5, 1831.

87. E. J. Rothery. "Aeneas Coffey (1780–1852)." *Annals of Science* 24, no. 1 (1968): 61. Accessed November 21, 2024. https://www.tandfonline.com/doi/pdf/10.1080/00033796800200041.

88. "A Letter from Donegal." *The Bury and Norwich Post* (Bury St. Edmunds, England), November 16, 1842, p. 4.

89. "Coffey's Still." *The Courier Mail* (Brisbane, Australia), October 6, 1862, p. 2.

90. Sydney Buxton. *Finance and Politics: An Historical Study, 1783–1885.* Vol. 1. London: John Murray, 1888, 195.

91. *An Act to Reduce into One Act and to Amend the Excise Regulations Relating to the Distilling, Rectifying, and Dealing in Spirits, 23 & 24 Vict. c. 114.* In *A Collection of the Public General Statutes Passed in the Twenty-Third and Twenty-Fourth Years of the Reign of Her Majesty Queen Victoria,* 897. London: Eyre and Spottiswoode, 1860. Accessed November 21, 2024. https://www.google.com/books/edition/A_Collection_of_the_Public_General_Statu/cGFFAAAAcAAJ.

92. *Customs and Inland Revenue Act, 26 & 27 Vict. c. 22.* In *Compendious Abstract of Public General Acts Passed in the Twenty-Sixth and Twenty-Seventh Years of the Reign of Her Majesty Queen Victoria,* 2. London: Eyre and Spottiswoode, 1863. Accessed November 21, 2024. https://www.google.com/books/edition/Compendious_Abstract_of_Public_General_A/KssuAAAAIAAJ.

93. "Deaths." *The Standard* (London, England), November 30, 1852, p. 4.

94. "Imperial Parliament: The Blending of Whisky." *Glasgow Herald* (Glasgow, Scotland), April 5, 1876, p. 5.

95. "Imperial Parliament: The Blending of Whisky." *Glasgow Herald* (Glasgow, Scotland), April 5, 1876, p. 4.

96. *Truths About Whisky.* United Kingdom: Sutton, Sharpe and Company, 1879. Accessed November 21, 2024. https://www.google.com/books/edition/Truths_about_Whisky/KixFAAAAYAAJ.

97. "Whisky." *The Wells Journal* (Wells, England), January 21, 1904, p. 3.

98. E. J. Rothery. "Aeneas Coffey (1780–1852)." *Annals of Science* 24, no. 1 (1968): 65. Accessed November 21, 2024. https://www.tandfonline.com/doi/pdf/10.1080/00033796800200041. The patent was officially granted on March 5, 1831.

99. "Somerset Importers, Ltd." Advertisement. *The Republican* (Springfield, MA), December 7, 1933, p. 7. While owned by Joseph P. Kennedy, his government tasks made him a hands-off owner.

100. Drew Hannush. "New Orleans Drinks Historian Elizabeth Pearce." *Whiskey Lore Podcast*, episode 5, at 30:00. Accessed November 21, 2024. https://www.whiskey-lore.com/interviews/elizabeth-pearce-of-drink-learn-podcast.

101. Michael R. Veach. Kentucky Bourbon Whiskey: An American Heritage. Lexington: University Press of Kentucky, 2013, chap. 2. Accessed November 21, 2024. https://www.google.com/books/edition/Kentucky_Bourbon_Whiskey.

102. Michael R. Veach. "Where Bourbon Really Got Its Name and More Tips on America's Native Spirit." *Smithsonian Magazine*, January 22, 2013. Accessed November 21, 2024. https://www.smithsonianmag.com/arts-culture/where-bourbon-really-got-its-name-and-more-tips-on-americas-native-spirit-145879/.

103. Drew Hannush. "New Orleans Drinks Historian Elizabeth Pearce." *Whiskey Lore Podcast*, episode 5, at 30:00. Accessed November 21, 2024. https://www.whiskey-lore.com/interviews/elizabeth-pearce-of-drink-learn-podcast.

104. Josiah Stoddard Johnston. *Memorial History of Louisville from Its First Settlement to the Year 1896.* Chicago: American Biographical Publishing Company, 1896, 244. Accessed November 21, 2024. https://www.google.com/books/edition/Memorial_History_of_Louisville_from_Its/l60yAQAAMAAJ.

105. Henry Rightor, ed. *Standard History of New Orleans, Louisiana.* Chicago: Lewis Publishing Company, 1900, 546-548. Accessed November 21, 2024. https://www.google.com/books/edition/Standard_History_of_New_Orleans_Louisian/Q60UAAAAYAAJ.

106. Henry B. Russell. *An Illustrated History of Our War With Spain.* Hartford, CT: A.D. Worthington & Co., Publishers, 1898, 94–96. Accessed November 21, 2024. https://www.google.com/books/edition/An_Illustrated_History_of_Our_War_with_S/ANlCAAAAIAAJ.

107. "The Franklin Repository Weekly." *The Franklin Repository Weekly* (Chambersburg, PA), May 4, 1803, p. 3.

108. "W.M. Brown." Advertisement. *Louisiana State Gazette* (New Orleans, LA), June 11, 1811, p. 2.

109. "Smiths & Morrison." Advertisement. *Louisiana State Gazette* (New Orleans, LA), June 17, 1811, p. 3.

110. "Wm F. Osborn." Advertisement. *Louisiana State Gazette* (New Orleans, LA), February 15, 1820, p. 1.

111. "H. McKinnell & Co." Advertisement. *The Times-Picayune* (New Orleans, LA), April 12, 1842, p. 2.

112. "Fetter & Lonsdale." Advertisement. *The Times-Picayune* (New Orleans, LA), November 15, 1842, p. 3.

113. "J.W. Trembly." Advertisement. *The Natchez Weekly Democrat* (Natchez, MS), January 23, 1826, p. 7. Note: "For Sale 50 barrels Old Bourbon County Whiskey."

114. "Hartman & Schmidt." Advertisement. *Louisiana State Gazette* (New Orleans, LA), January 11, 1821, p. 2.

115. "J.W. Trembly." Advertisement. *The Natchez Weekly Democrat* (Natchez, MS), January 23, 1826, p. 7.

116. "Noah Webster's Dictionary." Originally published in *Boston Daily Advertiser*; republished in *The Vermont Journal* (Windsor, VT), December 27, 1828, p. 1.

117. Drew Hannush. "The Mysteries and History of Canadian Whisky with Author Davin de Kergommeaux." *Whiskey Lore Podcast*, episode 88. Accessed November 21, 2024. https://www.whiskey-lore.com/interviews/ep-88-the-mysteries-and-history-of-canadian-whisky-with-author-davin-de-kergommeaux.

118. Canada. *Food and Drug Regulations, C.R.C., c. 870, Section B.02.020.* Accessed November 21, 2024. https://laws-lois.justice.gc.ca/eng/regulations/C.R.C.,_c._870/section-B.02.020.html.

119. Drew Hannush. "J.P. Wiser's Whisky Doc: Deconstructing and Constructing Canadian Whisky." *Whiskey Lore Podcast,* episode 104. Accessed November 21, 2024. https://www.whiskey-lore.com/interviews/ep-104-j-p-wisers-whisky-doc-deconstructing-and-constructing-canadian-whisky.

120. Alfred Barnard. *The Whisky Distilleries of the United Kingdom.* Reprint edition. Aaron Barker Publishing, July 24, 2013.

121. Drew Hannush. "The Life and Times of an Irish Whiskey Legend: John Teeling of Great Northern Distillery." *Whiskey Lore Podcast*, episode 70. Accessed November 21, 2024. https://www.whiskey-lore.com/interviews/ep-70-the-life-and-times-of-a-irish-whiskey-legend-john-teeling-of-great-northern-distillery.

122. Alfred Barnard. The Whisky Distilleries of the United Kingdom. Reprint edition. Aaron Barker Publishing, July 24, 201

123. "How to Cure 'Em." *The Missouri Republican* (St. Louis, MO), September 1, 1872, p. 6.

124. John Marshall. *The Life of George Washington*. Vol. V. Philadelphia: C.P. Wayne, 1807, pp. 22-25.

125. Pliny the Elder. *The Natural History of Pliny*, translated by John Bostock and Henry T. Riley. London: Henry G. Bohn, 1855, Book XXVIII, Chapter 18, p. 299.

126. John Heywood. *The Proverbs and Epigrams of John Heywood.* London: A. J. Valpy, 1874, 37. Accessed November 21, 2024. https://www.google.com/books/edition/The_Proverbs_and_Epigrams_of_John_Heywoo/DG5SAAAAcAAJ.

127. "Hair of the Dog Good for the Bite." *The Baltimore Sun* (Baltimore, MD), July 24, 1858, p. 1.

128. "Samuels Family Legacy," *The Samuels House*, accessed November 27, 2024, https://www.thesamuelshouse.com/samuels-family-legacy

129. "Notice of Dissolution," *The Kentucky Standard*, June 28, 1923, 7.

130. "Samuels' Distillery Makes 1st Run, Is Third Distillery in Nelson County to Open," *The Kentucky Standard*, May 3, 1934, 1.

131. *Records and Briefs of the United States Supreme Court.* Vol. 45. New York: Law Publishers of New York, 1922, 179. Accessed November 21, 2024. https://www.google.com/books/edition/Records_and_Briefs_of_the_United_States/JxvBAhE6lrgC.

132. Chuck Cowdery, "Is Jack Daniel's Bourbon? The Definitive Answer," *Chuck Cowdery's Blog*, January 19, 2018, accessed November 27, 2024, http://chuckcowdery.blogspot.com/2018/01/is-jack-daniels-bourbon-definitive.html. Note: The letter is in graphic form within the blog.

133. "'It's Not Bourbon. It's Jack.'" *Jack Daniel's Official Website*. Accessed November 21, 2024. https://www.jackdaniels.com/en-us/vault/its-not-bourbon-its-jack.

134. *Internal Revenue Record and Customs Journal*, vol. 29, no. 26 (June 28, 1873): 410, accessed November 27, 2024, https://babel.hathitrust.org/cgi/pt?id=umn.31951002033581i&view=1up&seq=434.

135. Samuel Johnson, *A Dictionary of the English Language*, 4th ed., vol. 2 (London: W. Strahan, 1773), 511, accessed November 27, 2024, https://archive.org/details/bim_eighteenth-century_a-dictionary-of-the-engl_johnson-samuel_1773_2/page/n511/mode/2up. Note: spelled with an "e"

136. Noah Webster, *An American Dictionary of the English Language*, vol. 2 (New York: S. Converse, 1828), 922, accessed November 27, 2024, https://archive.org/details/americandictiona02websrich/page/n921/mode/2up. Note: Noah goes as far as to say the spirit is made from barley in the north of England while it is made from wheat, rye, or maiz in the United States.

137. Blackwater Distillery, "Irish Whisky," accessed December 1, 2024, https://blackwaterdistillery.ie/irish-whisky/.

138. *Truths about Whisky* (Dublin: James Duffy and Sons, 1878), accessed November 27, 2024, https://www.google.com/books/edition/Truths_about_Whisky/KixEAAAAYAAJ.

139. "The Royal Commission on Whiskey and Potable Spirits," *The Hospital: A Journal of the Medical Sciences and Hospital Administration*, series no. 50, vol. II, no. 1122, vol. XLIII (February 29, 1908), accessed November 27, 2024, https://pdfs.semanticscholar.org/36f4/ca0ffb0bd25fbebe38520b497adfce5f6b85.pdf.

140. James Taylor. *Virginia Baptist Ministers.* New York: Sheldon & Company, 1859, 85–89.

141. J. H. Spencer. *A History of Kentucky Baptists.* Vol. 1. Cincinnati: J. R. Baumes, 1885, 87–89.

142. Charles Fenton James. *A Documentary History of the Struggle for Religious Liberty in Virginia.* Lynchburg, VA: J. P. Bell Company, 1898.

143. "To James Madison from George Mason, 2 June 1778." *Founders Online*, National Archives. Accessed November 21, 2024. https://founders.archives.gov/documents/Madison/01-01-02-0057#JSMN-01-01-02-0057-fn-0007.

144. James Madison, "Notes on the Virginia Ratifying Convention," June 6–25, 1788, in *The Papers of James Madison*, vol. 9, ed. William T. Hutchinson et al. (Chicago: University of Chicago Press, 1975), accessed November 27, 2024, https://founders.archives.gov/documents/Madison/01-09-02-0034.

145. "Education," *The Kentucky Gazette*, January 5, 1788, 1.

146. *Lewis Sanders Genealogy Notebook*, manuscript, n.d., 41, accessed November 27, 2024, https://archive.org/details/lewis-sanders-genealogy-notebook/page/n41/mode/2up.

147. Perrin, William Henry, ed. *History of Bourbon, Scott, Harrison, and Nicholas Counties, Kentucky.* Chicago: O.L. Baskin & Co., 188, 1882.

148. Samuel McHarry, *The Practical Distiller* (Harrisburg: Printed by John Wyeth, 1809), Section VII, accessed November 27, 2024, https://www.gutenberg.org/files/21252/21252-h/21252-h.htm#Page_102.

149. Michael R. Veach, "Early Distilling Papers at The Filson," *The Filson News*, vol. 5, no. 3 (2005), from the Corlis-Respess Family Papers, accessed November 27, 2024, https://www.filsonhistorical.org/archive/news_v5n3_distilling.html.

150. "By Lewis Sanders," *The Argus of Western America*, September 19, 1827, 2.

151. "Our History." *Elijah Craig Official Website.* Accessed November 21, 2024. https://elijahcraig.com/our-history.

152. *Lewis Sanders Genealogy Notebook*, manuscript, n.d., 41, accessed November 27, 2024, https://archive.org/details/lewis-sanders-genealogy-notebook/page/n41/mode/2up.

153. William Henry Perrin. *History of Bourbon, Scott, Harrison and Nicholas Counties, Kentucky.* Edited by Robert Peter. Chicago: O. L. Baskin & Co., 1882, 164. Accessed November 21, 2024. https://archive.org/details/cu31924081311676/page/164/mode/2up?q=%22bourbon+whisky%22.

154. "Buffalo Springs Whisky Plant Gets U.S. Permit, Starts Rebuilding Work," *The Courier-Journal*, February 13, 1934, 12A.

155. Willard Rouse Jillson. *Early Kentucky Distillers, 1783–1800.* Louisville, KY: The Standard Printing Co., Inc., 1940, 46.

156. Joe Creason, "School of Hard Knocks," *The Courier-Journal Magazine*, May 2, 1954, 54.

157. Byron Crawford, "A Charring Note," *The Courier-Journal*, June 21, 1989, B1, B3.

158. "History Comes Alive in Craig," *Advance Yeoman* (La Center, Kentucky), September 2, 1992, 1. Note: Mentions Craig as being credited with this title.

159. Elder, Gelston & Co., Advertisement, *The Baltimore Sun*, June 19, 1845, 3. Note: Listed as "Old Bourbon Rye Whiskey"

160. *Rogers v. Tennessee*, 532 U.S. 451 (2001).

161. *Rogers v. Tennessee*, 532 U.S. 451 (2001).

162. *The Scotch Whisky Regulations 2009*, S.I. 2009/2890, Regulation 3, accessed November 27, 2024, https://www.legislation.gov.uk/uksi/2009/2890/regulation/3.

163. "Irish Whiskey / Uisce Beatha Eireannach / Irish Whisky: Technical File." Department of Agriculture, Food and the Marine, Ireland. Accessed November 21, 2024. https://www.marketaccess.agriculture.gov.ie/media/marketaccess/content/IrishWhiskeyUisceBeathaEireannachIrishWhisky030519.pdf.

164. Note: There are several versions of this story and it relies heavily on oral tradition. This is an attempt to capture the spirit of the story in my own words.

165. Drew Hannush, "Underestimated (featuring Lori Carcich of Country Smooth Whiskey)," *Whiskey Lore,* August 17, 2020, accessed November 27, 2024, https://www.whiskey-lore.com/episodes/season-three/underestimated-featuring-lori-carcich-of-country-smooth-whiskey.

166. There are several sources with versions of this story. Many suggest she played a part in distilling including: https://whiskipedia.com/distilleries/cardhu/https://www.alcoholprofessor.com/blog-posts/blog/2014/04/08/speysides-cardhu-the-extraordinary-story-of-the-women-behind-the-whisky and https://thewhiskeywash.com/whiskey-styles/scotch-whiskey/women-scotch-whisky-helen-cummings/ Accessed December 22, 2024.

167. "Elizabeth Cumming," *Find a Grave,* accessed November 27, 2024, https://www.findagrave.com/memorial/214528811/elizabeth_cumming.

168. Alfred Barnard, *The Whisky Distilleries of the United Kingdom* (London: Harper's Weekly Gazette, 1887).

169. *Carpenter Genealogy*, accessed November 27, 2024, https://freepages.rootsweb.com/~carpenter/genealogy/.

170. *Recipes for Distilling by Sweet and Sour Mash*, May 18, 1818, Manuscript Collection, Kentucky Historical Society, accessed November 27, 2024, https://kyhistory.com/digital/collection/MS/id/364/rec/2https://kyhistory.com/digital/collection/MS/id/365/rec/2.

171. Shaun Boylan, "Locke, John," *Dictionary of Irish Biography*, accessed November 27, 2024, https://www.dib.ie/biography/locke-john-a4863.

172. "Female Distillers," *The Morning Post* (London), January 1, 1842, 7.

173. Drew Hannush, *The Lost History of Tennessee Whiskey* (Greenville, SC: Travel Fuels Life, 2023), 247–251.

174. "D.G. McCarthy, wife Mollie, et al versus Nancy Patterson, MT 1171." Tennessee State Library and Archives.

175. "Female Occupations in the States," *Glasgow Daily Mail* (Glasgow), December 27, 1877, 2.

176. *Kansas City Weekly Journal* (Kansas City), February 13, 1896, 4.

177. "Female Distiller," *Omaha Daily Bee* (Omaha), December 17, 1899, 35.

178. "Will Man Become Obsolete?" *The Dayton Herald* (Dayton), April 11, 1903, 4.

179. "Women Make Brandy," *The Boston Globe* (Boston), August 16, 1895, 8.

180. "A Woman Distiller," *The Chatham Record* (Chatham), July 18, 1895, 2.

181. "Only Woman Distiller," *Nashville Banner* (Nashville), May 1, 1911, 3.

182. "A Woman Distiller," *The Goldsboro Headlight* (Goldsboro), October 26, 1893, 1. Originally published in *The Charlotte News.*

183. "Woman Distiller Found," *Statesman Journal* (Salem, Oregon), November 7, 1925, 1.

184. "Female Distillers Given Extra 'Days,'" Associated Press, *The Montgomery Advertiser* (Montgomery), July 14, 1920, 2.

185. "Alleged Woman Distiller Held by Omaha Police," *The Lincoln Star* (Lincoln), January 25, 1921, 5.

186. "Biography." *Marianne Eaves Official Website.* Accessed November 21, 2024. https://www.mariann eeaves.com/me-bio.

187. Catharine Brewster, "Real Women's Revolution Is Quiet, At-Home One," *The Daily Times-News* (Burlington, North Carolina), July 31, 1970, 8. Written for the Women's News Service.

188. Washington Irving. *The Sketch Book of Geoffrey Crayon, Gent.* New York: C.S. Van Winkle, 1820, 55–72. Accessed November 21, 2024. https://www.google.com/books/edition/The_Sketch_Book _of_Geoffrey_Crayon_Gent/eSggAAAAMAAJ.

189. *The Bourbon Road*, Episode 112, "Gotta Love Some Whiskey Lore," podcast, accessed November 27, 2024, https://thebourbonroad.com/podcast/.

190. "Johannes 'John' Weller," *FamilySearch*, accessed November 27, 2024, https://ancestors.familysearc h.org/en/LDKC-RD9/johannes-%E2%80%9Cjohn%E2%80%9D-weller-1716-1792.

191. "Daniel P. Weller," *FamilySearch*, accessed November 27, 2024, https://ancestors.familysearch.org/e n/9VSZ-NJ5/daniel-p.-weller-1762-1807.

192. "Captain Samuel Weller," *FamilySearch*, accessed November 27, 2024, https://ancestors.familysearc h.org/en/L71H-1Q5/captain-samuel-weller-1787-1854.

193. "W.L. Weller Dead," *The LaRue County Herald News* (Hodgenville, Kentucky), March 30, 1899, 1.

194. Weller & Gonterman, Advertisement, *The Courier-Journal* (Louisville, Kentucky), July 6, 1852, 1.

195. Weller & Gonterman, Advertisement, *The Pick and Plow* (Louisville, Kentucky), November 12, 1853, 3.

196. W.L. Weller, Advertisement, *The Courier-Journal* (Louisville, Kentucky), September 24, 1856, 1.

197. "Copartnership Notice," *The Courier-Journal* (Louisville, Kentucky), January 6, 1860, 2.

198. "Copartnership," *The Courier-Journal* (Louisville, Kentucky), January 6, 1864, 3. Note: W.L. Weller and Jas. P. Buckner

199. "Another Louisville Enterprise," *The Courier-Journal* (Louisville, Kentucky), August 24, 1871, 4.

200. *The Courier-Journal* (Louisville, Kentucky), March 6, 1872, 3.

201. "Old Bourbon," *The Courier-Journal* (Louisville, Kentucky), March 8, 1872, 4.

202. *The Standard and Times* (Philadelphia, Pennsylvania), March 19, 1873, 4.

203. "A Card to the Public from W.L. Weller & Son," *Weekly Louisville Commercial* (Louisville, Kentucky), March 26, 1873, 4.

204. *The News Democrat* (Carrollton, Kentucky), June 12, 1875, 2.

205. "Big Bankruptcies," *The Courier-Journal* (Louisville, Kentucky), February 9, 1878, 4.

206. "Lost," *The Courier-Journal* (Louisville, Kentucky), December 1, 1881, 3.

207. "Whisky Trust," *The Courier-Journal* (Louisville, Kentucky), December 10, 1892, 6.

208. "Brief State News," *The News-Herald* (Hillsboro, Ohio), September 2, 1909, 1.

209. "Old W.L. Weller Bourbon," *Bowling Green Messenger* (Bowling Green, Kentucky), May 30, 1912, 7. Note: The artist rendering shows a tax stamp with "Bottled 1912" and "Made Spring 1904."

210. Harry Tabb, Advertisement, *Ledger-Star* (Norfolk, Virginia), November 26, 1912, 14.

211. "Kelley's State Liquor Dispensary," Advertisement, *Lexington Herald-Leader* (Lexington, Kentucky), May 11, 1934, 12.

212. "Eig's Liquor," Advertisement, *The Washington Daily News* (Washington, D.C.), February 18, 1943, 20.

213. "Old W.L. Weller Brand," Advertisement, *Green Bay Press-Gazette* (Green Bay, Wisconsin), October 11, 1950, 40.

214. "Sazerac Company, Inc., Completes Purchase of W.L. Weller and Charter Bourbon Brands from Diageo, Inc.," *PR Newswire*, April 28, 1999.

215. *The Morning Union* (Springfield, Massachusetts), May 25, 1924, 4. Note: A creative retelling of a creative anecdote.

216. "'Moonshine' Causing Blindness in State," *Evening World-Herald* (Omaha, Nebraska), December 16, 1920, 7.

217. "Fronczak Warns of Deadly Moonshine," *The Buffalo News* (Buffalo, New York), March 16, 1925, 3.

218. "Blinded by the Moonlight," *Evening Star* (Washington, D.C.), June 26, 1891, 3.

219. ChatGPT, response to a queries by Drew Hannush, October 10, 2024.

220. "The Royal Commission on Whiskey and Potable Spirits," *The Hospital: A Journal of the Medical Sciences and Hospital Administration*, series no. 50, vol. II, no. 1122, vol. XLIII (February 29, 1908), accessed November 27, 2024, https://pdfs.semanticscholar.org/36f4/ca0ffb0bd25fbebe38520b497adfce5f6b85.pdf.

221. *The Warrick Enquirer* (Boonville, Indiana), August 10, 1928, 2.

222. "Mellon a Whiskey Man," *The Warrick Enquirer* (Boonville, Indiana), August 10, 1928, 2.

223. "Mellon Favored as Chief of Treasury," *The Minneapolis Journal* (Minneapolis, Minnesota), February 14, 1921, 10.

224. "Big Distillery and Rum Gets $15,000,000," Associated Press, *The Waco Times-Herald* (Waco, Texas), May 26, 1925, 1.

225. *Lever Food and Fuel Control Act*, *United States Statutes at Large*, vol. 40, 65th Cong., 1st sess., chap. 53 (1917), accessed November 27, 2024, https://en.wikisource.org/wiki/United_States_Statutes_at_Large/Volume_40/65th_Congress/1st_Session/Chapter_53.

226. "Whisky Making in the State Ends," *The Courier-Journal* (Louisville, Kentucky), September 9, 1917, 7.

227. "Whisky Brands Not Worth Bidding For," *Democrat and Chronicle* (Rochester, New York), November 27, 1918, 18.

228. "KY Distilleries Bring $205,000: Paris Distillery Also Sold," *The Kentuckian-Citizen* (Paris, Kentucky), November 23, 1918, 3.

229. "First State License to Make Whiskey," *The Daily Republican* (Rushville, Indiana), December 5, 1919, 1.

230. *United States Statutes at Large*, vol. 42, chap. 134 (1921), 222.

231. "The Creation of Concentration Warehouses and Their Impact on the American Whiskey Trade," *Dram Devotees*, accessed November 27, 2024, https://www.dramdevotees.com/the-creation-of-concentration-warehouses-and-their-impact-on-the-american-whiskey-trade/. Note: This is an excellent blog post that dives deep into the act and its effects.

232. "Handles Whiskey Just About as He Pleases," *The Whittier News* (Whittier, California), September 18, 1923, 6. Note: Went into effect on February 17, 1922.

233. "Treasury Makes Ready to Order Whisky Distilled," *Kansas City Journal* (Kansas City, Missouri), August 27, 1929, 12. Originally published in *The New York Times.*

234. "Three Years of Prohibition Law Enforcement," *Springfield Weekly Republican* (Springfield, Massachusetts), June 19, 1924, 2.

235. "Law Enforcement Results," *News Record* (Rutherfordton, North Carolina), January 23, 1925, 3.

236. "May Refuse Rum Permits," Universal Services, *Press of Atlantic City* (Atlantic City, New Jersey), August 3, 1926, 2.

237. "Andrews to Ask Solons for Distilling Permits," United Press, *Evening Courier* (Camden, New Jersey), November 15, 1926, 1.

238. New Bill Reported on Medicinal Liquor," Associated Press, *The Boston Globe* (Boston, Massachusetts), February 15, 1927, 22.

239. "The Early Years of Prohibition: The Volstead Act and the Bandaid Legislation That Followed," *Dram Devotees,* accessed November 27, 2024, https://www.dramdevotees.com/the-early-years-of-prohibition-the-volstead-act-and-the-bandaid-legislation-that-followed/. Note: Another excellent deep dive into this era.

240. "The Contest over Medicinal Whiskey," *Danville Register and Bee* (Danville, Virginia), May 29, 1927, 6.

241. "Treasury Not to Make More Medicinal Whisky for Several Years Yet," *The Bee* (Danville, Virginia), August 9, 1927, 8.

242. "Must Start Making New Whiskey Supply," Associated Press *The Boston Globe* (Boston, Massachusetts), July 22, 1929, 3.

243. "Five Distilleries Ready," Associated Press, *The Cincinnati Enquirer* (Cincinnati, Ohio), July 17, 1929, 12.

244. "Commissioner Doran Reports on Stocks on Hand and Plan of Operation," Associated Press, *The Spokesman-Review* (Spokane, Washington), July 22, 1929, 9.

245. "Monopoly Is Seen at Early Date in Liquor Supply," *The Owensboro Messenger* (Owensboro, Kentucky), November 20, 1929, 1.

246. "Legal Whisky Making Is Resumed in State," Associated Press, *The Mayfield Messenger* (Mayfield, Kentucky), November 25, 1929, 3.

247. "40 Barrels of Rum Made Here," *The Courier-Journal* (Louisville, Kentucky), December 8, 1929, 56.

248. "Three Permits to Distill Rye Whisky," *The Evening Sun* (Baltimore, Maryland), January 10, 1930, 12.

249. George Hill, *An Historical Account of the Plantation in Ulster at the Commencement of the Seventeenth Century, 1608–1620* (Belfast: McCaw, Stevenson & Orr, 1877), 393–394, accessed November 27, 2024, https://archive.org/details/historicalaccoun00hill_0/page/394/mode/2up.

250. George Francis Savage-Armstrong, *The Ancient and Noble Family of the Savages of the Ards: With Sketches of English and American Branches of the House of Savage* (London: Marcus Ward & Co., 1888), 127, accessed November 27, 2024, https://www.google.com/books/edition/The_Ancient_and_Noble_Family_of_the_Sava/MU5RKM6ekl4C.

251. *A Topographical Dictionary of Ireland*, ed. Samuel Lewis, vol. 1 (London: S. Lewis & Co., 1837), 201, accessed November 27, 2024, https://books.google.com/books?id=P3IRAAAAYAAJ.

252. "The Old Bushmills Distillery Co. Limited," *The Freeman's Journal and National Press* (Dublin, Ireland), August 20, 1896, 2. Note: Another source put the date at 1797 although this is an isolated mention: "The Old Bushmills Whiskey," *The Times* (London, England), May 7, 1849, 13.

253. William Carson, Advertisement, *Belfast News-Letter* (Belfast, Ireland), May 27, 1828, 3.

254. "Bushmills Distillery," Advertisement, *Belfast News-Letter* (Belfast, Ireland), September 20, 1831, 3. Note: This was placed by James McKibbin, the distiller at Bushmills who took over after Hugh Anderson. It also featured the note – Wanted—A PRACTICAL DISTILLER.

255. "David Ranken," Advertisement, *The Philadelphia Inquirer* (Philadelphia, Pennsylvania), January 12, 1833, 3.

256. "The Old Bushmills Whiskey," *The Times* (London, England), May 7, 1849, 13

257. "The Old Bushmills Distillery Company Limited," *Freeman's Journal and Daily Commercial Advertiser* (Dublin, Ireland), November 5, 1891, 8.

258. "The Old Bushmills Distillery Co. Limited," *The Freeman's Journal and National Press* (Dublin, Ireland), August 20, 1896, 2.

259. Alex D. Shaw & Co., Advertisement, *Daily News* (New York, NY), December 4, 1935, 567.

260. "Quality Importers," Advertisement, *The Plain Dealer* (Cleveland, Ohio), December 21, 1954, 4.

261. "Old Bushmills," Advertisement, *Free Press Evening Bulletin* (Providence, Rhode Island), March 2, 1927, 12.

262. "St. Patrick's Toast," Photo Caption, *The Desert Sun* (Palm Springs, California), March 15, 1971, 14.

263. "Irishman Naturally Refuses Whiskey Not from the Old Sod," United Press International, *Progress Bulletin* (Pomona, California), July 31, 1974, 21.

264. "To Be Sold by the Subscriber," Newspapers.com. *Pennsylvania Gazette*, June 28, 1770, 6. All but a handful of newspaper references in this book are courtesy of searches on Newspapers.com by Ancestry.

265. Robert H. Land. "The Shelby Family Papers." *Quarterly Journal of Current Acquisitions* 11, no. 3 (1954): 143. http://www.jstor.org/stable/29780743.

266. "Evan Shelby, Pictured as a Man, Fighter, Strategist," *Bristol Herald Courier*, June 13, 1925, 24.

267. Evan Shelby, "Agreement Between Evan Shelby and Pierce Wall to Manufacture Rye Whiskey SC263_FF1_001," Kentucky Historical Society Digital Collection, February 19, 1780, accessed October 28, 2023, https://www.kyhistory.com/digital/collection/MS/id/25849/rec/3.

www.ingramcontent.com/pod-product-compliance
Lightning Source LLC
Chambersburg PA
CBHW072150070526
44585CB00015B/1070

9781734865196